The Software Test Engineer's Handbook

Graham Bath's experience in testing spans over 25 years and has covered a wide array of domains and technologies. As a test manager, he has been responsible for the testing of mission-critical systems in spaceflight, telecommunications, and police incident-control. Graham has designed tests to the highest levels of rigor within real-time aerospace systems such as the Tornado and Eurofighter military aircraft.

As a principal consultant for the T-Systems Test Factory he has mastered the Quality Improvement Programs of several major companies, primarily in the financial and government sectors. In his current position, Graham is responsible for the company's training program and for introducing innovative testing solutions to Test Factory's large staff of testing professionals.

Graham is co-author of the new ISTQB Advanced Level Certified Tester syllabus. He is a long-standing member of the German Testing Board and chairman of their Working Party on the advanced syllabus.

Judy McKay has spent the last 20 years working in the high tech industry with particular focus on software quality assurance. She has managed departments encompassing all aspects of the software lifecycle including requirements design and analysis, software development, database design, software quality assurance, software testing, technical support, professional services, configuration management, technical publications, and software licensing. Her career has spanned across commercial software companies, aerospace, foreign-owned R&D, networking and various Internet companies.

In addition to working a "real job", Judy teaches and provides consulting services. Her courses cover the spectrum of software quality assurance, including creating and maintaining a world class quality assurance team, designing and implementing quality assurance and effective testing, and creating and implementing useful test documentation and metrics. Judy is co-author of the new ISTQB Advanced Level Certified Tester syllabus and is a member of the Technical Advisory Board of the American Testing Board. She has authored *Managing the Test People*, a book filled with advice and anecdotes for new as well as experienced software test managers and leads.

Graham Bath • *Judy McKay*

The Software Test Engineer's Handbook

A Study Guide for the ISTQB Test Analyst and
Technical Test Analyst Advanced Level Certificates

rockynook

Graham Bath, graham.bath@t-systems.com
Judy McKay, judyamckay@earthlink.net

Editor: Jimi DeRouen
Copyeditor: Judy Flynn
Layout and Type: Gerry Ichikawa, The TypeStudio
Cover Design: Helmut Kraus,, www.exclam.de
Printed in the USA

ISBN 978-1-933952-24-6

1st Edition
© 2008 by Graham Bath and Judy McKay
16 15 14 13 12 11 10 09 08   1 2 3 4 5

Rocky Nook Inc.
26 West Mission Street Ste 3
Santa Barbara, CA 93101
www.rockynook.com

Library of Congress Cataloging-in-Publication Data

McKay, Judy, 1959-
  The software test engineer's handbook : a study guide for the ISTQB test analyst and technical
test analyst advanced level certificates / Judy McKay, Graham Bath.
      p. cm.
  ISBN 978-1-933952-24-6 (alk. paper)
  1. Computer software--Testing. 2. Electronic data processing personnel--Certification. I. Bath,
Graham, 1954- II. International Software Testing Qualifications Board. III. Title.
  QA76.76.T48M45 2008
  005.1'4--dc22
                        2008018383

Distributed by O'Reilly Media
1005 Gravenstein Highway North
Sebastopol, CA 95472

This book is printed on acid-free paper.

Preface

This book will probably fill a gap between the software testing books on your shelf. We're sure you'll agree that there are lots of good books around covering fundamental testing techniques, but there are relatively few which provide a well-balanced coverage of both functional and technical testing.

This book brings both functional and technical aspects of testing into a coherent whole which should benefit not only test analysts but also test managers. Test analysts and managers don't live in a sheltered world; they need to be able to communicate effectively with many other people, including their fellow testers. To do that properly they need to understand both the functional (domain) and technical aspects of testing, including the testing techniques required.

This book fully considers the testing of all quality attributes covered in ISO 9126, including performance, reliability, security, functionality, usability, maintenability and portability. The steps in the standard test process defined by the International Software Testing Qualifications Board (ISTQB) are considered for each quality attribute to give a rounded, well-balanced coverage of these quality attributes.

The content of the book is based on the "Certified Tester" Advanced level syllabus [ISTQB-CTAL] issued by the ISTQB in 2007. We cover everything you will need to know to successfully sit the examinations for advanced test analyst and advanced technical test analyst. For those of you planning to sit one or both of those exams, the book provides a solid base for preparation and clearly indicates which sections apply to which specific examination. All examinable information is indicated.

Full coverage of the ISTQB syllabus 2007 for test analysts and technical test analysts

Even though the content is primarily aligned to the ISTQB Advanced level syllabus, we have taken efforts to ensure that any professional tester can gain benefit from reading the book. We have therefore supplemented the content with additional information and real-world examples and experiences.

Acknowledgements

Our thanks go to our fellow members of the international core team of authors with whom we spent many hours producing the ISTQB Advanced Level Certified Tester Syllabus:

Rex Black, Sigrid Eldh, Bernard Homès, Jayapradeep Jiothis, Paul Jorgensen, Vipul Kocher, Thomas Mueller, Klaus Olsen, Randy Rice, Jürgen Richter, Eric Riou Du Cosquer, Mike Smith, Geoff Thompson, Erik Van Veenendaal.

I (Graham) would especially like to acknowledge:

- Prof. Dr. Andreas Spillner, my colleague at the German Testing Board, for motivating me to write the book.
- My colleagues at T-Systems, Test Factory, for their helpfulness and professionalism.
- My family (Elke, Christopher, Jennifer) for their understanding and patience.

I (Judy) would especially like to acknowledge:

- My family for their help and patience

- Rex Black for opening doors and presenting opportunities as well as professional growth and guidance
- The good folks at Cedar Glen Inn who let me spend my extended lunchtimes writing this book in their restaurant
- Gary Garman for showing me that even when you're impossibly over-committed on projects, there's always room for one more!

Table of Contents

1 Introduction

It was a dark and stormy project... No wait, that's the beginning of another book, although it does accurately describe some test projects that seem to be perpetually in a crisis with management in the dark—but we'll save that for later.

This book is designed to serve two purposes. First and foremost, it is a useful book full of techniques and practices that will make you, the advanced tester, successful in the real world. Second, it covers everything you need to know to successfully complete the exam for the ISTQB Advanced Level Test Analyst certification and the ISTQB Advanced Level Technical Test Analyst certification. In this first chapter, we explain the objectives we set out to achieve and the basic layout of the chapters. After that we explore some fundamental questions: what does the word advanced mean in the context of tester certification and what is the role of the test analyst and technical test analyst?

One note of clarification: The term test engineer is in the title of this book. Test engineer, in most but not all countries, is the title given to the senior, most technically adept tester. In deference to areas where this term might have a different meaning, ISTQB decided to use the terms test analyst (less technically inclined and more business oriented) and technical test analyst (more technically inclined, probably with a strong development background as well as a strong testing background). We have adopted the use of test analyst and technical test analyst throughout this book to keep the terminology consistent with the ISTQB.

1.1 Requirements for This Book

We established some fairly tough requirements for this book. Before we launch into the actual content of domain and technical testing itself, we'd like to give you a brief overview of those requirements. This will help you understand the general approach we have taken.

As the authors, we require that the book be both readable and complete.

1.1.1 Completeness

This book is based on the ISTQB Advanced syllabus (2007) and covers everything you will need to know to successfully sit the examinations for test analyst and technical test analyst. You can also use the information in this book to become a very good, very employable test analyst.

1.1.2 Readability

The book's not just about covering the Advanced syllabus

When writing a book based on a predefined syllabus, it's easy to fall back into a style that focuses on syllabus coverage alone. Of course, syllabus coverage is essential, but too often this results in a rather dry, definition-oriented style with all kinds of fancy fonts and symbols to indicate specific parts of the syllabus. We don't want this. We want you to have a book that gives you syllabus coverage and is readable.

We intend to make this book readable by adopting a standardized approach to each chapter:

- Technical content
  After a brief introduction, we present with the actual technical content of the chapter. The learning objectives in the ISTQB advanced syllabus don't focus on just learning and repeating: they are meant to help you apply what you have learned and provide reasoned arguments for your choices. To that end, we go beyond the information provided in the syllabus and add more descriptive material to give you a more well rounded level of knowledge.

We use a realistic, complex, real-world example application

- Let's be practical
  Most chapters include a section called "Let's Be Practical" to help you further understand and assimilate the information provided. It's also a chance to get away from the textbook style that unfortunately prevails with syllabus-oriented books, so this section should appeal to those of you who are not necessarily focused on the ISTQB syllabus alone.
  We will refer to our example application "Marathon" for this section (see chapter 2 below for a description). This realistic example is based on a real-world system and accompanies us throughout the book to give us a consistent view of the many testing issues covered.

- Learning check

  At the end of each chapter we give you a summary of what can be learned from the content provided. The ISTQB terms that were covered in the chapter are listed in this section. The definitions of these terms are found in [ISTQB Glossary] and in the mini-glossary in appendix A. Terms noted with an asterisk (*) in front are not specifically called out in the ISTQB Glossary, but they are commonly used industry terms and are included in our mini-glossary. And, speaking of industry terms, you will find we use the terms "bug" and "defect" interchangeably. Again, being practitioners in the industry, we tend toward the more commonly used terms.

  We have also included a list of specific learning objectives. These are primarily based on the learning objectives provided in the ISTQB Advanced Level syllabus and will be of particular use for those of you studying for the certification exam. Where appropriate, we have added our own learning objectives to those taken from the syllabus.

- Experience reports and lessons learned

  We, the authors, have gained a wealth of experience in our testing careers, and we'd also like to share some of these experiences with you. As often occurs in life, things don't always go "according to the book"; these experiences may therefore help us realize that being a certified tester doesn't always guarantee success, mainly because reality doesn't politely conform to theory! Look for these grey-shaded blocks throughout the book.

  Who is talking? For each chapter, there is a principal author. The following table shows who wrote each chapter so you can figure out who "I" is when we relate experiences, lessons learned, and things we'd rather forget.

- Exercises

  The exercises are there to help develop your ability to apply the theory. You will not, of course, find these exercises in the ISTQB examination (that would be too easy!).

Table 1–1

Who wrote what?

Ch.	Title	Author: Judy	Author: Graham
1	Introduction	X	X
2	Example Application Marathon		X
3	Management Issues		
3.1	Types of Systems		X
3.2	Test Process	X	
4	Specification-Based Testing Techniques	X	
5	Structure-Based Testing Techniques		X
6	Defect-Based Testing Techniques	X	
7	Experience-Based Testing Techniques	X	
8	Analysis Techniques		X
9	Testing Software Characteristics		X
10	Functional Testing	X	
11	Usability and Accessibility Testing	X	
12	Efficiency Testing		X
13	Security Testing		X
14	Reliability Testing		X
15	Maintainability Testing		X
16	Portability Testing		X
17	Reviews	X	
18	Tools Concepts	X	
19	Incident Management	X	
20	Communication Skills	X	

1.2   What Does "Advanced" Mean?

Saying that you are an "advanced" anything can be like waving a red rag in front of a bull. A typical reaction might be, "OK, wise guy; let's see if you can solve this one." Faced with this kind of challenge, the testing professional should be able to explain what it means to be an advanced tester. Here are a few quick replies for you to have ready, just in case:

- Advanced testers have chosen a career path in testing, having already successfully become an ISTQB certified tester at the foundation level.
- They have demonstrated both theoretical and practical testing skills to an internationally recognized high standard.
- They have gained experience in testing projects.
- They can fulfill the role of test manager, test analyst, or technical test analyst in a project.
- They recognize that we never stop learning and improving.
- They have (therefore) more chances of being employed.

Just one other (occasionally controversial) point on the issue of certification: being certified at an advanced level doesn't actually guarantee anything. There are plenty of good testers about who are not certified. However, having certification does demonstrate that you have achieved a high standard of testing professionalism and that you are likely to speak a "common testing language" with others in the testing world. In a global IT industry where many testing projects are spread over several countries, this is a big plus.

Testing professionals benefit from speaking a common testing language

By the way, we are Certified Testers at the Advanced Level in all three roles (and proud of it). The major organizations we work with have embedded the certified tester schemes into their career development plans and consider this to have been highly successful as a staff motivator and in achieving satisfaction for their customers.

In addition to the certification aspect of this book, it is also packed full of good, useful information that an advanced tester will find valuable. So, regardless of whether you think certification is right for you, we think you will benefit from learning and applying the information provided.

1.3　What Is a "Test Analyst"?

Defining a role at the international level is not easy. Often countries, even different companies within the same country, have different names for a role or have a slightly different understanding of what a person with a particular role should do. There is no one reason for this—it's usually just the way things developed.

At the Foundation level, the ISTQB improved the situation somewhat by introducing the roles of test manager (which can also be referred to as test leader) and tester.

The test analyst adds
specialty to the tester role

At the Advanced level, the ISTQB continued this standardization trend by establishing the role of test analyst. Essentially, the test analyst should be able to do all of the tasks of the tester defined in the ISTQB Foundation syllabus. However, the test analyst adds specialty to the tester role, and it's this specialty that we address in this section.

What would be expected of a test analyst? At the highest level, an employer would want to see the following fundamental abilities when hiring a test analyst:

- The ability to support the test manager in creating appropriate testing strategies
- The ability to structure the testing tasks required to implement the test strategy
- The ability to perform analysis on a system in sufficient detail to permit the identification of appropriate test conditions
- The ability to apply appropriate techniques to achieve the defined testing goals
- The ability to prepare and execute all necessary testing activities
- The ability to judge when testing criteria have been fulfilled
- The ability to report on progress in a concise and thorough manner
- The ability to support evaluations and reviews with evidence from testing
- The ability to implement the tools appropriate to performing the testing tasks

In general, the test analyst has a good understanding of the test manager's role and an appreciation of the fundamental principles of test management. This includes the ability to understand requirements and appreciate different forms of risk.

Two specific types of test
analyst are defined

The test analyst position is further defined into two roles according to the Advanced syllabus and industry practices. Two specific types of test analyst are defined. Both roles share the generic abilities outlined earlier but apply them in different testing contexts. In broad terms, the technical test analyst serves more of a techical function, whereas the domain test analyst has a more business-oriented approach.

The technical test analyst:

- Focuses on technical software characteristics such as reliability and efficiency.

- Applies structure-based testing techniques, such as decision testing, in addition to certain specification-based testing techniques like equivalence partitioning.
- Performs static and dynamic analysis.
- Applies review techniques on code and technical documents, such as architectural designs.
- Is able to implement test automation effectively.
- Can apply tools for efficiency testing, such as performance, and for analysis.

The domain test analyst:

- Focuses on functional, domain-specific software characteristics such as functionality and usability.
- Applies a wide range of specification-based testing techniques (more so than the technical test analyst).
- Applies review techniques on domain-specific documents, such as requirements and use cases.

The ISTQB Advanced syllabus shortens the name "domain test analyst" to plain "test analyst". To ensure consistency with the syllabus, we will also adopt this naming convention.

We refer to the "domain test analyst" simply as "test analyst"

Throughout the book we will be clear on which sections apply to which role when we explain the learning objectives. This is especially important to those of you who wish to take a training course and/or sit for the certification exam, since these are provided according to role (i.e., test analyst and technical test analyst).

2 Marathon, the Example Application

Testing concepts are usually easier to understand when applied to a realistic project. We have created a fictitious application that we will use to illustrate the various techniques and types of testing covered in this book. The application, called Marathon, is typical of many systems we find today in that both functional and non-functional testing will be required.

As you would expect from a book pitched at the ISTQB Advanced level, the example application is sufficiently complicated to provide realistic test scenarios; however, the effort you put in to understanding the Marathon system will be rewarded later by a more thorough appreciation of specific testing issues in the context of a realistic application.

At various stages in this book, we will expand on the general description of Marathon provided in this chapter (this simulates the scope creep we all experience!) so that particular points can be covered in more detail.

That said, don't expect the design of the Marathon system to be absolutely watertight in all respects (the authors are, after all, testing experts, not system architects). Should you find holes or inconsistencies in the design, well done; you're thinking like an advanced tester already!

2.1 Overview of Marathon

Essentially, the system allows organizers of major marathon events (e.g., Boston, London) to set up and organize the races efficiently using modern-day technology.

Take a look at figure 2-1 below. What do you see? You probably noticed our durable marathon runner. You probably also noticed that the Marathon system is actually made up of a number of independent hardware and software components that work together to make the complete

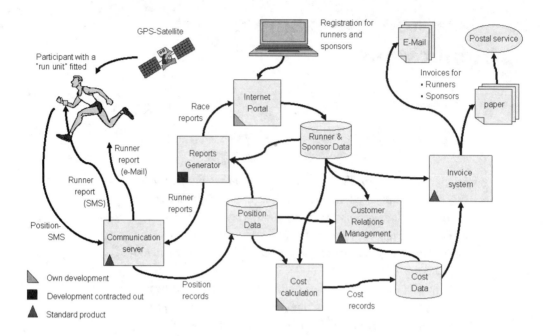

Figure 2–1 application (the arrows represent major data and control flows). Further-
The Marathon system more, some of the software components are standard products (sometimes referred to as commercial off-the-shelf, or COTS, systems), some
are to be developed in-house, and some have been contracted out for
development.

For the sake of simplicity, the diagram doesn't even touch on the technical architecture used, but we can be sure that a mix of different platforms
(clients, servers, and operating systems), communications protocols, databases, and implementation languages is used. In short, it's typical of the
kind of system we testers have to deal with in the real world.

We'll be meeting our intrepid marathon runner throughout the book
in the "Let's Be Practical" sections. For now though. let's take a closer look
at the functional requirements and outline how the system is used.

2.2   General Requirements

The Marathon application is designed to provide the following features:

- An administration system for the organizers of the race
- A registration system for runners

- A system for sponsoring runners
- Timely and accurate information to runners and the media
- A reporting system for runners and media
- A help-desk for all those with questions about the race
- An invoicing system that allows sponsor money and runner fees to be invoiced.

The system needs to be capable of handling up to 100,000 runners and 10,000 sponsors for a given race without failing. It must be possible to handle up to five races each year.

2.3   Use of the Marathon System

The Marathon system provides support prior to the race, after the race, and, of course, during the race itself. These principal activities are shown in the figure below (which isn't to scale).

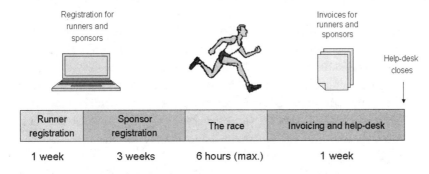

Figure 2–1

Phases supported by the Marathon system

Let's now look at how the Marathon system is used.

Before each race, the system is used for registering runners and sponsors.

- Runner registration starts four weeks before the race commences and lasts for one week. As soon as the registration week starts, a runner may register for the race using an Internet application. Anyone can register for the race, but the maximum number of participants (100,000) may not be exceeded. A first come first served policy is used.
- At the end of the runner registration week, the system administrator starts the invoicing system so that invoices can be issued to all accepted runners for race fees.

Runners and sponsors register

- Sponsoring then takes place over the next three weeks. Sponsors register via the Internet application and can select any runners they wish to sponsor.
- Response time to the registering runners and sponsors must never exceed eight seconds from the time the submit button is pushed to the time the confirmation screen is displayed.
- All information concerning runners and sponsors is held in a database, which is used as a central source of information for all other software components in the Marathon system.
- Race information can be viewed via the Internet application prior to the race and specific questions are handled via a Customer Relations Management (CRM) system with a help-desk.

Ready, set..,.   **During the race**, the system tracks the position of each runner.

- The tracking is enabled using a strap-on "run unit" carried by each runner. This unit receives position information via GPS satellite and transmits a runner's position as a Short Message Service (SMS) message every minute.
- *Heavy loads are handled during the race*   A communications server receives the SMS messages sent by the run units, constructs position records from them, and writes them to a position database.
- A cost calculation system calculates cost records for sponsors using their entered details and the current position of runners they have sponsored. It is assumed that not everyone is going to finish the race, but they can still receive sponsorship money for the distance they cover.
- A reports generator generates an online race report for the Internet application every 10 minutes and also constructs individual runner reports every minute. These individual reports are currently prepared as an e-mail and sent to the communications server for transmission. Runners may then receive and read this during the race via Black-Berry®.
- This method is already known to be unpopular with runners, so a future extension is planned where the reports generator also provides the individual reports via SMS messaging. The communications server will then be able to send these messages directly to the run units for display.

After the race the final reports are created and financial aspects are finalized.

- The reports generator creates an end-of-race report for publishing via the Internet application containing final positions and various race details, such as numbers of starters and finishers, weather, oldest and youngest runner, etc. The preliminary report is generated one hour after the first runner has crossed the finishing line and is updated five hours later (when the race is officially declared over).
- The invoicing application is started by the administrator one day after the race. This application reads records from the cost database and prepares invoices for sponsors according to the runners they sponsored and the distances those runners completed. Completed invoices are sent via e-mail to the sponsor.

Collect the sponsoring money

- Invoices are provided as hard copy only by special request and are sent to a postal service for dispatch (manual system).
- Payment receipt is an outsourced function which is not covered in our application.
- The help-desk stays open to handle queries and complaints.

2.4 Availability of the Marathon System

The system must be available 24/7 during the runner registration week, during the sponsor registration weeks, and on race day itself.

After race day, all data must be available to the help-desk/customer relations system between 08:00 and 20:00 local time for a week, after which the data must be archived for at least two years.

2.5 Caveats About Marathon

As you can see, there are interesting testing challenges associated with this project. But, be aware that in order to be sure we are applying our testing techniques to a realistic situation, we reserve the right to "complicate" this project with late change requests. Welcome to the real world!

3 Management Issues

While management issues are, by definition, the realm of the test manager, there are still areas in this category that are of concern for the test analyst and the technical test analyst. We need to understand the types of systems we are dealing with and how they might affect our testing approach. We also need to understand the overall test process and what our contribution will be at each step. In addition, a good understanding of risk-based testing and risk management in terms of project and product risk is an asset for any test analyst.

3.1 Types of Systems

The types of systems we may need to test are many and varied. Each represents different levels of risk that may lead to particular testing strategies being proposed. In a book on test analysis, a full coverage of specific types of systems and their architectures would be inappropriate. However, certain specific types of systems are described in the following sections because they have significant and direct influence on the software quality characteristics to be addressed in testing strategies. We'll consider the following system types:

Testing strategies are influenced by the type of system under test

- Systems of systems
- Safety-critical systems
- Real-time and embedded systems

3.1.1 Systems of Systems

Today, we are frequently involved in testing systems of systems. As you will see from the summary points outlined later, the very nature of such systems represents a particular challenge for all those with testing responsibilities.

The architecture that makes up a system of systems features several individual components that themselves may be considered systems. They cooperate to provide benefit to a particular stakeholder (e.g., business owner). The components of the overall system of systems typically consist of various software applications or services, communications infrastructure, and hardware devices. These may themselves be driven by software applications.

The Marathon example is a system of systems

Systems of systems are developed using a "building block" concept. Individual component systems are integrated with each other so that entire systems can be created without having to develop applications from new. A system of systems frequently makes use of reusable software components, third-party applications, commercial off-the-shelf (COTS) software, and distributed business objects.

On the upside, this concept may result in cost reductions for the development organization but there is a downside when we consider the cost of testing, which may increase substantially. Why is this?

- High levels of complexity
  Complexity is inherent in systems of systems. This arises from a number of sources, including system architectures employed, the different software lifecycle development models that may be used for individual application development efforts, and complex compatibility issues of both a technical and functional nature (i.e., do the building blocks actually fit together?) Testing professionals know that complexity is a major driver of product risk; where we have high levels of complexity we generally expect there to be more defects in the product, both from a functional (domain) and a non-functional (technical) perspective.
- The time and effort needed to localize defects
  Within a system of systems, the localization of defects can be a technical and organizational challenge. It may take a long time and considerable effort to localize defects since the testing organization typically does not have complete access to all system components. As a result, it may simply not be possible to perform detailed analysis or set up monitors where we would like to.

System integration tests play a critical role

- More integration testing may be required
  Whereas the development of an individual system normally calls for an integration testing stage, with systems of systems we have an additional "layer" of integration testing to perform at the intersystem level. This

testing level, which is often called system integration testing, may require the construction of simulators to compensate for the absence of particular component systems.

▨ Higher management overhead

Who's in charge here?

More effort often results from managing the testing among the many organizational entities involved in developing a system of systems. These could include various product suppliers, service providers, and many supplier companies that are perhaps not even involved in the project directly. This may give rise to a lack of a coherent management structure which makes it difficult to establish ownership and responsibilities for testing. Test analysts need to be aware of this when designing particular tests such as "end-to-end" tests of business processes. For example, when a user initiates a transaction, the technical and organizational responsibility for handling that transaction may change several times and may be completed on systems that are totally outside the control of the originating organization.

▨ Lack of overall control.

Because we may not always have control over all system components, it is common for software simulations to be constructed for particular component systems so that system integration testing can be performed with some certainty. For the same reasons, the test manager will also need to establish well-defined supporting processes such as release management so that the software can be delivered to the testing team from external sources in a controlled manner. Test analysts will need to work within the framework of these supporting processes so that, for example, tests are developed to defined releases and baselines.

Many of the characteristics exhibited by a system of systems are present in the Marathon example:

▨ Individual components like the customer relations management system can be considered systems in their own right.
▨ System components used consist of various software applications (e.g., invoice system) and software-driven hardware devices (e.g., run unit).
▨ Two of the applications (the customer relations system and invoicing system) are commercial off-the-shelf applications that may not have been used together in a system of systems like Marathon before. This highlights the need for system integration testing.

3.1.2   Safety-Critical Systems

A safety-critical system is one that may endanger life or lead to other severe losses in the event of failure. Normally the criticality of a project is estimated as part of the project's feasibility study, or as a result of initial risk management activities. The test analyst and technical test analyst must be aware of how the project's criticality has been assessed and, in particular, whether the term safety-critical applies.

Safety-critical systems require more rigorous testing

The strategies we apply to testing safety-critical systems are generally comparable to those discussed throughout this book. For safety-critical systems though, it is the higher level of rigor with which we need to perform test tasks and which shape our testing strategies. Some of those tasks and strategies are listed here:

- Performing explicit safety analysis as part of the risk management. Failure Modes and Effects Analysis (FMEA) can support this task (refer to section 3.10 in the Advanced syllabus for more details).
- Performing testing according to a predefined software development lifecycle model, such as the V-model.
- Conducting failover and recovery tests to ensure that software architectures are correctly designed and implemented.
- Performing reliability testing to demonstrate low failure rates and high levels of availability.
- Taking measures to ensure that safety and security requirements are fully implemented.
- Showing that faults are correctly handled.
- Demonstrating that specific levels of test coverage have been achieved.
- Creating full test documentation with complete traceability between requirements and test cases.
- Retaining test data, results, or test environments (possibly for formal auditing).

Industry standards often apply to safety-critical systems

Often theses issues are covered by standards, that may be specific to particular industries, as in the following examples:

- Space industry:
  The European Cooperation on Space Standardization (ECSS) [URL: ECSS] recommends methods and techniques depending on the criticality of the software.
- Food and drug industry
  The US Food and Drug Administration (FDA) recommends certain

structural and functional test techniques for medical systems subject to Title 21 CFR Part 820.

■ Aircraft industry

The international Joint Aviation Authorities (JAA) defined the levels and type of structural coverage to be demonstrated for avionics software, depending on a defined level of software criticality.

The test manager will convey the level of safety criticality of the system and software under test and whether particular standards need to be applied. We must ensure that the tests we design comply to any such standards and that we can support the test manager by demonstrating compliance not only within the testing project but also possibly to external auditors.

3.1.3   Real-Time and Embedded Systems

In real-time systems, there are usually particular components present whose execution times are critical to the correct functioning of the system. These may be responsible, for example, for calculating data at high update rates (e.g., 50 times per second), responding to specific events within a minimum time period, or monitoring processes.

Software that needs to function in real-time is often "embedded" within a hardware environment. This is the case with many everyday consumer items such as mobile phones and also in safety-critical systems such as aircraft avionics.

Embedded systems are all around us

Real-time and embedded systems are particularly challenging for the technical test analyst. For example:

■ We may need to apply specific testing techniques to detect, for example, "race" conditions.

■ We will need to specify and perform dynamic analysis with tools (see section 8.2, "Dynamic Analysis").

■ A testing infrastructure must be provided that allows embedded software to be executed and results obtained.

■ Simulators and emulators may need to be developed and tested to be used during testing (see section 18.3.3 for details).

3.2   Test Process

Test processes may consist of many individual activities, but there are five steps into which these activities generally fit. These five steps to the generic test process are shown in the following diagram:

Figure 3–1
The fundamental test process

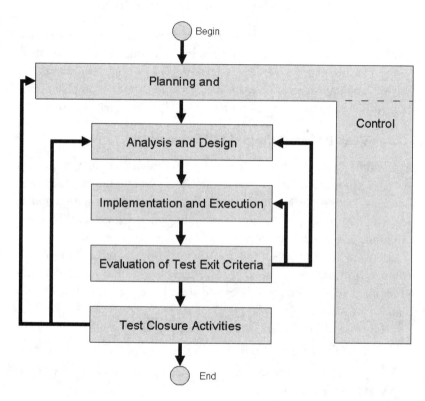

Managing the test process is the job of the test manager. So why include this diagram? Because the test analysts and technical test analysts are critical to implementing the test process and a general understanding of the process is required if we are to do our job the right way at the right time and supply the right documentation. The process will break down if steps are skipped and we will soon find ourselves reacting rather than approaching a project with a planned effort.

Test analysts and technical test analysts are a critical part of a successful test process implementation

Let's look at each of the steps in the test process more closely.

3.2.1 Test Planning and Test Control

At the test planning stage, the test manager is determining the testing approach, planning the resources, setting the strategy, creating the test schedule, and determining the metrics that will be needed for adequate control and monitoring of the project. In terms of resources, at this point we are considering equipment, software and people resources that will be needed to accomplish the testing. The test manager is looking at training needs and hiring requirements in order to be sure the staff is in place when the project begins. Most of this information is documented in the test plan document. The IEEE 829 Test Plan Specification provides the following outline for the test plan document:

If a project isn't planned, it can't be controlled

1. Test plan identifier
2. Test items (including version/revision and documentation such as requirements)Introduction
3. Features to be tested
4. Features not be to tested
5. Approach (activities, techniques, tools)
6. Item pass/fail criteria
7. Suspension criteria and resumption requirements
8. Test deliverables
9. Testing tasks
10. Environmental needs (facilities, hardware, software, network, supplies, level of security, special tools)
11. Responsibilities
12. Staffing and training needs
13. Schedule (test milestones and item transmittal events)
14. Risks and contingencies
15. Approvals

Caution! Everything may be assumed to be in scope unless you state otherwise

Notice that there is a section to identify risks and mitigation plans for those risks. When we are looking to control a project, we are hoping to control the risks. When a risk is identified, we have to deal with it by creating a mitigation plan, transferring the risk elsewhere, or deciding to ignore it. In the case where we can identify risks at the beginning of a project, we are better able to make plans to deal effectively with those risk items should they occur.

Risk management is usually the responsibility of the test manager. Test analysts and technical test analysts must contribute information for risk identification and possible mitigation plans as part of the planning process. When we are looking at the risk of the project, we need to consider the two risk types: project risk and product risk. Project risks are sometimes called planning risks and are oriented toward anything that could cause the overall project to fail to meet its objectives. Project risks include such things as personnel issues (vacations, training, availability), vendor or third party issues, or delivery schedule issues. Product risks are the risks within the product itself, such as unfound defects. Testing and following good quality practices are ways we mitigate product risk.

Before we go any further into the test process, let's look at figure 3-2 to see how all the IEEE 829 Standard Test Documents fit together.

3.2.2   Test Analysis and Test Design

In the test analysis and design step, we are considering the details of the testing project. This is where we are figuring out what to test, how much effort to expend, what types of testing we should do and any tools that will be required for this effort. For example, after reviewing the requirements documents, we may determine that performance testing is warranted. In that case, we need to be defining performance test cases, purchasing performance testing tools and procuring the resources we will need to do this testing.

Start static testing as soon as you have something to read

As we review the test basis, the documents from which we are determining what to test, we are doing static testing. We are examining each document, and we should be documenting any problems we find both to ensure resolution and to use for future process improvement initiatives (reviews are discussed in depth in chapter 17). During these reviews, we also gather the data needed to write the test specification. This document, cleverly named, specifies what we are going to test. The IEEE 829 test design specification document consists of the following information:

1. Test design specification identifier
2. Features to be tested (test items, features, and combinations of features that will be covered by this spec)
3. Approach refinements (refinements from the test plan)
4. Test identification (list of the test cases associated with this design)
5. Feature pass/fail criteria

Is it wrong, or just practical, to plan to run out of time?

As we work on building the test design specification, we should also be building the risk analysis that will be used to guide a risk-based testing

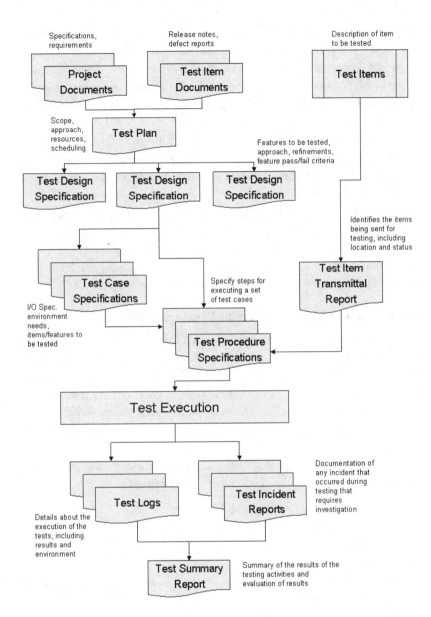

Figure 3–2

IEEE-829 document tree

effort. This risk analysis defines the testable items of the project, some-times categorized by the ISO 9126 quality characteristics, and is used to record the business risk (how important is the correct operation of this item to the business) and the technical risk (how likely is it to fail) for each item. By recording this information now, in the analysis phase, we can organize our actual test execution so that the highest risk items are addressed with the appropriate amount of testing. Risk-based testing is used to deal with situations in which there is not enough time to test everything (which, in our experience, is most of the time) by prioritizing our testing and test development. This gives us a strategy that allows us to use the time we have in effective risk mitigation.

A good risk analysis is a result of the contribution of the project stakeholders. The business interests have to be represented by someone who truly understands the business and the customer concerns. The technical risk can be determined only by the people who know what is likely to fail—the developers who know that some parts of the code are excessively complicated, the testers who know that some pieces of functionality will be extremely difficult to test well. It's the test manager's responsibility to coordinate and see to the creation of the quality risk analysis. It's the test analyst's job to ensure that the testing concerns are well represented.

3.2.3   Test Implementation and Test Execution

Our old familiar friend, the test case

Now that we have our test design specification, it's time to create our test cases and test procedures. Logical test cases are the high-level test descriptions that do not define the data that is to be used for the tests. Concrete test cases include the actual data that is to be used during testing. Since many test cases refer to spreadsheets that contain the actual data, they become concrete only when the instructions are actually joined with the data.

The IEEE 829 test case specification is commonly used in industry. That specification includes the following information:

1.   Test case specification identifier
2.   Test items
3.   Input specifications
4.   Output specifications
5.   Environmental needs (hardware, software, and other environmental needs for this case)
6.   Special procedural requirements (special constraints on the test procedures that will apply to this case)
7.   Intercase dependencies

Notice that we are specifying the output from our test case. This means we have to know what the outcome should be based on the test condition (the item or event that we are testing) in the test case. The expected outcome is usually determined by some form of an oracle that tells us what the software should do. This oracle should be defined in the test basis in order for us to define accurate test cases.

The IEEE 829 Test Procedure is the document that explains how to run a particular test case or a set of test cases. This procedure is often, in practice, actually included in the test case itself. Officially though, it should be considered a separate document containing the following information:

1. Test procedure specification identifier
2. Purpose (including list of applicable test cases)
3. Special requirements
4. Procedure steps (log, setup, start, proceed, measure, shutdown, restart, stop, wrap-up, contingencies)

When test cases are being designed, consideration should be given to test execution automation potential. If automation is a viable option, the automation coding should be underway at this stage of the project, creating automation scripts (which are actually self-contained test procedures often called test scripts). If we wait until the end to actually create the automation code, we won't get the benefit of using it for this version of this project. That may be acceptable if the project is to live a long time and repeated regression testing will allow the use of automation. Whether we will develop it now or later, we need to be thinking about automation right now (please refer to chapter 18 for more on automation issues).

So what about test execution? Will those tests run themselves? Probably not (unless you have some really amazing automation code!). This is the time for the manual and automated (if available) execution of the test cases we have so carefully designed. But wait, before we start running the test cases, it would probably be good to actually have something to test. The IEEE 829 Test Item Transmittal Report provides the information we need to locate and install the software we will be testing. It consists of the following information:

1. Transmittal report identifier
2. Transmitted items (including version, revision and person responsible)
3. Location
4. Status
5. Approvals

Now we know what we are testing, we know how to install it, we know what changes/fixes we are receiving, and we are ready to execute our test cases. As we run the test cases, we want to be sure we are recording the execution information in the IEEE 829 Test Log. This document is used to record particular information for each test case execution. This information tracking capability may be built into your test management system, but you will want to track the same information as that specified in the test log.

1. Test log identifier
2. Description (including items being tested and environments used)
3. Activity and event entries (dates and times, execution description, procedure results, environmental information, anomalous events, incident report identifiers)

IEEE 829 has you covered! BS-7925-2 is another source for the type of data that should be logged. But what if we find a defect? IEEE 829 has us covered there too. We can fill out an IEEE 829 Test Incident Report that contains the following information:

1. Test incident report identifier
2. Summary
3. Incident description (inputs, expected results, actual results, anomalies, date and time, procedure step, environment, attempts to repeat, testers, observers)
4. Impact

Of course, your defect tracking system may track different information, or you may choose to follow the IEEE 1044 defect specification (discussed further in chapter 19).

The work at this stage tends to be iterative. As we receive new releases of the software, we will rerun test cases. This is usually the longest step in the generic test process, time-wise, because this is where the actual testing occurs.

3.2.4   Evaluation of Exit Criteria and Reporting

Our last IEEE 829 test standard document appears in this step of the process—the IEEE 829 Test Summary Report. The test summary report can be prepared periodically as a type of test progress report at the conclusion of a level of testing (after integration testing, for example), but it is commonly done at the conclusion of the testing effort. The test summary document includes the following information:

1. Test summary report identifier
2. Summary (evaluation of test items)
3. Variances
4. Comprehensiveness assessment
5. Summary of results
6. Evaluation (per test item)
7. Summary of activities
8. Approvals

How do we know when we are finished testing? We determine test completion based on meeting the exit criteria we defined in the planning phase. This is often considered the Ship/No Ship decision point, where the information found in testing is returned to the project team for the release decision.

You're not finished until the test closure activities complete

3.2.5   Test Closure Activities

The test closure activities occur after the release has been shipped out. Now is the time to do any wrap-up reporting, document and archive the test environments, archive the test documents and data, and generally clear the decks for the next project. These test closure activities are often under-budgeted and receive inadequate attention because the next project is already waiting. It is important for the test manager to hold firm on these activities and to ensure that they are done correctly. Only in this way will we be able to return quickly to this project for maintenance releases or patches. Inadequate time spent on the test closure activities also reduces the effort we can spend looking for ways to improve our processes.

If we don't learn from our mistakes, we are very likely to do the same things wrong in the next project.

3.3   Learning Check

The following checklists will help you judge the knowledge you have gained from this chapter.

Terms Used

BS-7925-2, exit criteria, FMEA, IEEE 829, product risk, project risk, risk analysis, risk-based testing, risk identification, risk management, risk mitigation, risk type, safety- critical system, software lifecycle, system of systems, test case, test closure, test condition, test design, test execution, test implementation, test item transmittal report, test log, test plan, test procedure, test progress report, test schedule, test script, test specification, test summary report

Test Analyst and Technical Test Analyst

- Recall the essential features of systems of systems
- Explain the factors influencing the testing of systems of systems
- Recall the essential features of safety-critical systems
- Recall the testing tasks that are particularly significant for testing safety-critical systems and give examples of industry-specific standards
- Recall the essential features of real-time and embedded systems
- Explain the criteria that influence the level of test condition development
- Explain and provide examples of test oracles and how they can be used in test documentation
- Describe the conditions that must be in place prior to test execution, including the testware, configuration management system, defect tracking system, and test environment
- Determine if the test completion criteria have been fulfilled based on a set of measures

Test Analyst (Specific)

- Analyze and breakdown a requirement specification into a test specification based on IEEE 829, focusing on functional and domain test cases and test procedures
- Explain the stages in the software lifecycle at which functional testing is appropriate
- Understand how test analysis and design are static testing techniques that can be used to discover defects
- Prioritize test case creation and execution based on risk and be able to document this appropriately in the test documentation
- Outline the activities of risk-based testing for domain testing

Technical Test Analyst (Specific)

- Explain the stages in the software lifecycle where non-functional tests and structure-based tests may be effectively applied
- Outline the activities of risk-based testing for technical testing

4 Specification-Based Testing Techniques

Testing techniques are the core of the test analyst's and technical test analyst's work focus. Most of the time at work, we are designing, implementing and running various tests. The test techniques we use, and our ability to use them effectively, will determine the contribution of the testing toward producing a quality product.

In each section in this chapter, we provide a summary of what we learned at the Foundation Level for each technique. We then expand on that information by providing examples, comparisons, practical uses and potential pitfalls of the described technique.

4.1 Introduction

Specification-based test techniques derive the test conditions and test cases from the system or software requirements specifications. Because the terminology for requirements varies widely in industry, the input documents from which the code is designed and developed are collectively termed the test basis" since these are the documents from which we are determining what we need to test. Specification-based testing relies on the documentation we can obtain rather than an inspection of the code as in structure-based testing.

The specifications used for testing can be in the form of models, feature lists, text documents, diagrams, or any other documentation that explains what the software is expected to do and how it is going to do it. Test coverage is determined by the percentage of the specified items that have been addressed by the designed tests. Coverage of all the specified items does not necessarily indicate complete test coverage, but it does indicate that we have addressed what was specified. For further coverage, we may need to look for additional information.

These specification-based techniques are used by both test analysts and technical test analysts, but primarily by test analysts. Techniques such as orthogonal arrays and state transitions may require knowledge of the hardware or the various configurations and so may require the input and expertise of a technical test analyst. To effectively apply each of these techniques, good knowledge of the domain is required to effectively apply the technique.

4.2   Individual Specification-Based Techniques

In the ISTQB Advanced Level syllabus, seven different specification-based techniques are discussed:

Table 4–1
Specification-based
techniques

Techniques	Description
Equivalence partitioning	Grouping test conditions into partitions that will be handled the same way
Boundary value analysis (BVA)	Defining and testing for the boundaries of the partitions
Decision table testing / cause-effect graphing	Defining and testing for combinations of conditions
State transition tables	Identifying all the valid states and transitions that must be tested
All pair testing / orthogonal array testing	Determining the combinations of configurations to be tested
Classification Tree Method	Using a graphical notation to show the test conditions (classes) and combinations addressed by the test cases
Use case testing	Determining usage scenarios and testing accordingly

In the following sections we'll look at each of these individually and then demonstrate how these techniques could be used in various examples.

4.2.1   Equivalence Partitioning

Equivalence partitioning is a test design technique that lets us ensure that our testing will be efficient. In equivalence partitioning, we search for test conditions that will be handled identically and put them together into a partition (sometimes called a class). It's called an equivalence partition because we expect every value or condition within that partition to be treated equivalently. For example, if we were testing an order processing system and the user can order from 1 to 100 items, we might have a reasonable expectation that the same code will be exercised whether the user orders 27 items or 65 items.

In fact, we can make the reasonable assumption that all quantities from 1 to 100 will be handled the same way. Since all the values from 1 to 100 are in the same equivalence partition, meaning that each test condition using one of those values will receive the same processing, we need to test only one value in that partition. Instead of needing 100 test cases, each with a different test condition or input value, we need only 1 to test the correct handling of any value in that partition.

Is that good enough? Alas, we have only considered what is known as a *valid* partition. There are also *invalid* partitions, which are the partitions that contain values that should be considered "invalid" by the software being tested. So, in addition to our valid values, we must also consider the partition of invalid values above 100 (we'll deal with zero and the negative numbers in a moment).

Don't overlook the invalid partitions when testing the valid partitions

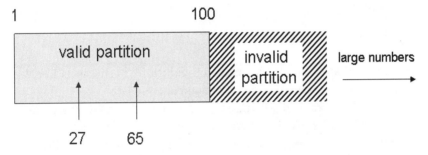

Figure 4–1
Equivalence partitioning

Another way to look at this is to think of all possible values as a set. In this case, since we are dealing with integers, our set would include all possible integers, that could be represented by the software (back to those negative numbers). From that we create subsets that are actually the partitions. Note that partitions must be disjoint, meaning that in order to be a member of a partition you couldn't be a member of another partition made from the same set. If we were to draw this, it would look like figure 4-2.

Coverage in equivalence partitioning testing is determined by the number of tested partitions divided by the total number of partitions, but partitions can exist in many places. It's important to remember that partitions are not limited to ranges. Partitions can also be made for sets of discrete items, in which case the partition would be either in the set or out of

Figure 4–2
Equivalence partitioning sets

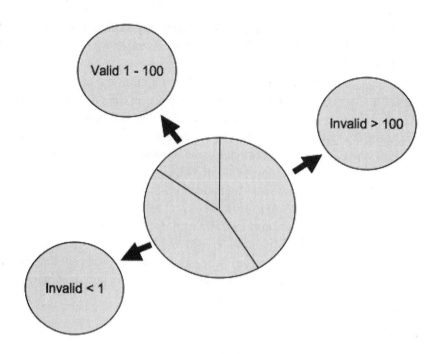

the set. Partitions can also be made for something as simple as Boolean values—yes in one partition, no in the other.

Partitions exist in many places—save testing time by finding them!

But it gets even better. Partitions don't just exist with GUI inputs as in the preceding example. Partitions exist with inputs from files and other systems. And, partitions can also exist for outputs. For example, if we are testing to see if we provide the proper result for a college entrance exam, we might have the two partitions, pass and fail. When we are testing, we want to be sure we generate output that will fall in each partition. If all our input values result in outputs in the same partition, we have completely missed the other partition. Partitions exist in many areas of our software. We can significantly and safely reduce our testing effort by identifying and testing for these partitions. Let's look at some examples of other partitions.

In the Marathon application, sponsors enter their information during the valid time frame before the race. So, in order to allow the sponsor to enter information, we have to determine if he is in the valid sponsor time frame—a valid partition consisting of three weeks based on the date of the race—or outside the time frame. Outside the time frame actually consists of two partitions–dates before the three-week sponsor window and dates after the three week sponsor window. In the example, we have chosen a start date for the race of 9 AM on 21 April (you would have to supplement this with a year and a time zone to be absolutely precise).

Figure 4–3

Valid and invalid equivalence partitions

What if we enhance the Marathon system so that sponsors can enter credit card information? Then our invoicing process will limit itself to billing the credit card (much easier than sending an actual invoice and waiting for payment). Do we have any partitions there? We would have to check our specifications to be sure. Maybe we accept only Visa and MasterCard but nothing else. Then we would have two partitions at this level; valid credit cards (Visa and MasterCard) and invalid credit cards (all others). Below that, we might have a lower-level partition where we divide up Visa and MasterCard. This means that if we are testing to see if American Express is accepted, we don't have to try 100 different American Express cards–one should be sufficient.

Equivalence Partitioning Strengths

By default, we tend to overtest. We do this because we don't know what we can safely exclude. Equivalence partitioning reduces the number of tests we need to run. That's a good thing, at least in our world when time is always a constraint. It requires an intelligent analysis of the software and the available specifications so we can determine what is truly handled equivalently. Once we know that, we can significantly reduce the number of tests we need.

EP can significantly reduce the numbers of tests needed

In order to do the analysis required, interaction between the testers and developers can be very helpful. Developers should know where the partitions exist. I emphasize the *should* here. Developers don't always know. In fact, sometimes they think they know and they are wrong. I can help find inconsistencies by talking with the developers and by testing. I have found that by encouraging this interaction, it builds an appreciation for the enormity of the testing task on the part of the developers.

That said, in some cases, you may not be able to talk to the developers. As test analysts we have to use our skills at doing specification-based test design and our domain skills to extract information from the specifications (test basis). If we can talk to developers, that's a valuable source of information too, but it shouldn't be our only source.

Experience Report: Testing those #&@%$* characters

One of my favorite examples of this is testing the ability to accept special characters in an input field. There are a lot of special characters! The code can specifically include and exclude individual characters. Now what do we do? Do we need to test for all possible special characters? What if we're testing a name field? Dash (-) should be valid. Apostrophe (') should be valid. Should the percent sign be valid (%)? Not in any names I know. With the percent sign we also have to be concerned about SQL injection vulnerabilities (but that's covered in section 13.3.1, "Typical Security Threats"). What about a period (.)? That might be valid if we accept titles in our name field such as Dr. or Jr.

If we have to test for every special character, we better hope we have automation. If we can talk to our developers and determine that they are excluding sets of special characters based on ranges of the ASCII values of those characters, then we can form some equivalence partitions. This can significantly reduce our testing efforts, particularly if one partition includes 50 special characters that we would otherwise have to test individually.

Equivalence Partitioning—Weaknesses

As mentioned earlier, we do want to talk to the developers and maybe the designers and architects (depending on who wrote the specifications). If they are not available, we will have to be careful about the assumptions we make regarding where the partitions fall. We can use the reasonableness test. For example, if we know we can order items costing $1.00 up to $1,000, then we probably don't have to test every dollar value in between. We will, however, test a couple values in there to be sure my partition assumption is correct. There might be a partition we didn't know about. Maybe $499.00 is accepted on an e-commerce web site without requiring that the user enter the CCV (the magic code on the back of a credit card that proves you have the actual card in your hand), but for $500 and above, the CCV is required. That's another partition because the $499 purchase is not handled the same as the $500 purchase.

Experience Report: There aren't 49 states in the United States?

Just to make you nervous, I'll relate a partitioning error I committed one time. We were creating a web application that required the user to enter information about themselves and their credit card, a delivery address for a product, and an installation address (which could be different from the delivery address). Fairly straightforward (you might think). On each of these screens, the user was prompted to enter their state (this product was only available in the United States). On each of these screens, there was a drop-down that listed the states. How many of those drop-downs would you test?

I assumed that if I tested one to be sure it was correct (and had all the states), that would be sufficient. I spot-checked the others to be sure they dropped down and allowed selection, but I didn't verify that every state was in every drop-down—that would be silly, right? Not if you live in Missouri. It turns out that in one of the windows (the delivery address window), the drop-down did not include Missouri. It had the other 49 states, just not Missouri. The people from Missouri were not amused when technical support asked them if they'd mind picking up their purchase in Mississippi.

It seems reasonable to assume that the states would be handled the same way, as long as they appeared on the list, but be careful when picking your partitions. Some partitions are actually high-level partitions that contain lower-lever partitions. Take, for example, months and the days with the month. If we are testing the valid days in a month, we have to know which month we are testing. Are months all the same? January certainly has a different number of days than April. And February itself has a different number of days on leap years (so it is dependent on the higher level partition of "year"). How many hours in a day? Twenty-four, right? Not if you live in an area that changes the clocks twice a year for daylight savings time. On one of those days, the day actually has 25 hours. On the other one, it has 23. This is why testers are never bored; they can always think of more things to test!

Another easy mistake to make with equivalence partitioning is to combine several invalid partition tests into one test case. When this happens, we run

Don't mask errors—test invalid partitions separately

the risk of one error masking another. For example, if we want to test several invalid partitions in an application, ordering a quantity of –1 while also entering an invalid item number, we would expect to get an error—but which error? We might get an error that says "invalid value". Which value was detected as invalid? When building test cases using invalid partitions, it's important to be sure that there will a clear result from the test that will show the proper handling of all the partitions. Remember, when testing the values in the valid partitions, we can usually combine several together because none of them should return an error. In cases where we should generate multiple errors, it's best to test each error condition separately.

4.2.2   Boundary Value Analysis (BVA)

BVA only works on ordered partitions

Boundary value analysis (BVA) is a refinement of equivalence partitioning, which means that we first have to identify the equivalence partitions. Once we have defined our partitions, we can then employ BVA to be sure we create test cases for the boundary values. Boundary values are those values or conditions that occur on the edges of the partitions. Because we are looking at the edges, the items in the partition must be in some order, otherwise we can't find them. In our previous example, if 1 to 100 are in the same (valid) partition, we would use BVA to look at the edges of that partition. When we employ BVA, we see that we also need to test 0, 1, 100, and 101. If our partitions were valid credit cards and invalid credit cards, we can't use BVA because there aren't defined edges of the partitions. You are either in it or not.

> **Defect Report: "You owe me $0"**
>
> A bank issued a letter to a customer demanding payment for $0 (that was the first BVA problem). The customer ignored it until the bank threatened legal measures. The customer diligently submitted a check for $0 which promptly crashed the entire application (second BVA problem). The bank shall remain nameless.

Why are we interested in the boundaries? Because bugs frequently occur in the handling of the edge conditions. It's very easy for a developer to say < 100 rather than <= 100. For any one boundary, we need at least two cases to test the "on" condition (on the boundary) and the "out" condition (outside the boundary). In some cases, we might also want to test the "in"

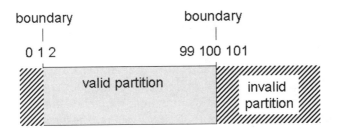

Figure 4-4

Boundary values

condition. In our example (see below), 0 is "out", 1 is "on", and 2 would be considered to be "in".

Coverage in boundary value analysis testing is determined by the number of distinct boundary values that are tested divided by the total number of boundary values. You might want to differentiate between the boundaries that fall in the "valid" versus "invalid" partitions if that would make more sense in determining coverage.

There are two schools of thought on BVA. One is that to do true BVA, you need to look at only the "on" and "out" conditions. In the preceding example, that would mean you need to test only the 100 and 101 and the 0 and 1. The reasoning behind this is that the 2 and 99 are part of the same equivalence partition as 1 and 100. Technically this is true. In my experience, I've found too many issues with 99 and 100 being handled differently, so while they are technically part of the same equivalence partition, they aren't being handled equivalently. If you select to test one value that is greater than 1 and less than 100, you will have this case covered. I like to show the three values (in, on and out) on my chart so I remember to be sure I have them all covered.

Boundary Value Analysis—Strengths

It's very easy to forget to test the boundaries. Boundaries occur everywhere in our software. By taking the time to consider and create tests for these boundaries we can significantly reduce those "edge" bugs that might otherwise slip by. Boundaries exist everywhere in the software, not just on the input values. Some looping code is expected to loop a certain number of times. Does it? Temporary storage tables may have a set size. What happens if they overflow?

Bugs love boundaries

Experience Report: "Flying south for the winter"

When Graham was a flight test engineer he did a flight trial where the aircraft had to fly very low and follow the terrain for awhile. The route took the aircraft on a track which headed due south. A BV problem occurred and the automatic terrain-following software decided the aircraft was now in the Southern Hemisphere. The aircraft was commanded to turn upside-down, which it did, and then continued on its way. The pilot and navigator were not amused.

The trick to doing good boundary testing is in knowing where the boundaries are. We have to use all available resources, including combing through the specifications, gathering and applying domain expertise, and drawing on experience. After all, you only have to fly upside down once before you always remember to check that hemisphere decision!

If you can get to the software developers involved, do so. We have had good luck with this, when we've been able to do it. Our biggest returns in boundary testing have come from the conversations with the developers to identify the boundaries. Invariably, as we are discussing what we will test, their hands edge over to the keyboard and they make a quick check to be sure they have correctly handled those boundaries. We've had a significant number of bugs fixed this way–without even having to find them!

Boundary Value Analysis—Weaknesses

The only drawback to doing boundary value analysis is the risk of putting too much emphasis on the edges and not enough on the rest of the functionality. As with all testing we do, we have to balance the time we spend against the risk we can mitigate. Historical data will help guide your decisions regarding how much time and effort to expend in this area. If we had done better boundary value analysis in the experience report below, we would have caught the problem. Instead, we just did equivalence partitioning, assuming that moving any of the items 1 to 99 would have the same results. We chose the lower numbers, thinking that was a more reasonable test (as it probably was), but we missed the boundary fault.

> **Experience Report: "The silly sort"**
>
> We had a particularly difficult boundary bug on a project. We missed it during testing and it was found in production. When we took the escalated support call, the customer explained that the software was always aborting when they tried to sort a batch of inputs. We tried and tried and could not reproduce the failure. We finally had the customer walk us through every step. It turned out that they had a batch of 100 items and they wanted to put the first one at the bottom of the batch. Easy enough, right? Obviously you take the first item and move it to end. Not if you were that customer! Instead of moving the 1 item to the bottom, they moved the 99 other items to the top. It aborted every time. On further analysis we discovered the developer had reasoned that no one would ever move more than half the items at a time because they would always move the smaller set. As a result, he sized his temporary table to be half the size of the batch. So, when our customer moved the 99 items, the software tried to put it in a table that would hold only 50, resulting in a fatal error. You can see the logic the developer used. You can also probably see how we would have missed this in testing, thinking, "no one would ever do that; it would be silly!"

4.2.3   Decision Tables and Cause-Effect Graphing

A decision table lets us examine the combinations of conditions that can occur and ensure that we test for all possible outcomes. When looking at the conditions, we have to consider relationships between the conditions as well as any constraints. Cause-effect graphing is a graphical representation of the testing effort showing the various possible "cause" scenarios with the resulting effects. In practical usage, these diagrams quickly become too complex to be useful with software that has any degree of complexity.

Collapsed decision tables are a risk-based technique by which we reduce the full decision table that has recorded all possible combinations and concentrate on the most likely and highest-risk conditions and outcomes and remove combinations that are simply not possible. Any reduction or elimination of combinations requires strong domain knowledge to minimize the risk of eliminating something we actually need to test.

Coverage in decision table testing is determined by the number of combinations of conditions covered divided by the maximum number of condition combinations. Let's look at an example of using decision tables.

In my early life, I had the questionable privilege of working in the customer service department of a large department store. One of my jobs was to deal with "credit inquiries" that came from the point-of-sale terminals spread around the store. When a "credit inquiry" would appear on the register during a purchase transaction, the sales clerk brought the customer to us along with the credit card that was used for the transaction. We then had to figure out what was wrong with the card.

There were three checks that were made on a card that received a credit inquiry: Was it over the limit? Was the address out-of-date? Was it stolen? All three checks were made. Depending on the results, different actions were required. Now in the days of automation, we have a program that does this for us. We enter the card number, and the program checks these conditions and displays the proper response. What are the conditions we need to test? Over limit, address update, and stolen status. What are the expected results from these conditions? Let's look at the business rules we received in the requirements:

Decision tables help clarify condition combinations

If the card is only over limit, call credit to increase limit. If card is over limit and needs an address update, get address update and then increase limit. If card is marked stolen, take the card and call security.

It's nice to have requirements, but never assume the requirements are complete. In this example, they have identified only three conditions that need to be tested, but we know that these three conditions can occur in any combination, so we actually need to test not just three condition combinations but eight combinations (Yes and No for each of the three conditions = $2 \times 2 \times 2$).

There are a few rules of thumb we can apply to decision tables. The first one is to pick the most frequently used condition first. The most likely condition in this example is that the card is over its limit (we know this based on our domain knowledge). The most unlikely condition is that the card is stolen. From that point on, we need to consider all the other conditions, again in the order of frequency. It makes the table much easier to read that way.

The second rule of thumb is how large the table should be. The number of columns in the table should equal the number of the conditions as explained. We will need to have eight columns in this table to provide complete coverage. We can later collapse the decision table to remove

Conditions (Causes)	1	2	3	4	5	6	7	8
Over limit	Y	Y	N	N	N	Y	N	Y
Address update required	N	Y	N	Y	Y	N	N	Y
Card stolen	N	N	N	N	Y	Y	Y	Y
Actions (Effects)								
Increase limit	Y	Y						
Update address		Y		Y				
Call security					Y	Y	Y	Y
Approve transaction	Y	Y	Y	Y				

Figure 4-5

Decision table

unlikely combinations, (based on the risk of these items) or those that are just plain impossible.

So what should our table look like?

This decision table shows all the conditions we need to test for to get complete test coverage. In this layout, the columns reflect the most frequently occurring combinations of conditions starting from the left. As an alternative, we can adopt a regular pattern that might help us check that we haven't missed any combinations. This might be a good idea if there are more than three conditions involved. The following table contains the same information as the preceding one, it's just presented differently. It's your choice which style you want to use.

Using patterns can help check condition coverage

Conditions (Causes)	1	2	3	4	5	6	7	8
Over limit	Y	Y	Y	Y	N	N	N	N
Address update required	Y	Y	N	N	Y	Y	N	N
Card stolen	Y	N	Y	N	Y	N	Y	N
Actions (Effects)								
Increase limit		Y		Y				
Update address		Y				Y		
Call security	Y		Y		Y		Y	
Approve transaction		Y		Y		Y		Y

Figure 4-6

Decision table: alternative style

Can we collapse this table? In order to collapse it, we look for conditions that result in the same action. We have a clear situation here that if the card is stolen we will always call security, and that is our only action. What does that mean in terms of test cases? If we want to collapse our testing effort, we might decide to use only combinations 1 and 2. Is this safe? As always, it depends. Is there a risk that the software will act differently when the address update is required and the card is stolen (conditions 6 and 8)? It shouldn't, but it could. So, when collapsing decision tables according to risk, be careful to ensure that you will be providing adequate testing with the minimal number of test cases. Don't forget also to use your domain knowledge to eliminate any conditions that might be impossible (in the example, we didn't need to do this because all combinations are possible).

Could we make a cause-effect graph? We could, but it wouldn't be fun, and the value added by doing this would, to be honest, be questionable. Even in this simplistic case, the graph is not easy to read. Trust us and stick with decision tables. You'll be much happier.

Decision Tables—Strengths

As we already admitted, this is one of our favorite techniques. Decision tables are good for taking complicated business rules and sorting out the conditions we need to create to verify all the testable results. They are readily understandable by technical and nontechnical people, making the tables valuable for review by domain experts as well as developers. A side benefit to creating decision tables is the ability to guide the testing even if there isn't time to make detailed test cases. Decision tables can be used as checklists for unscripted testing.

One of the most difficult problems with determining coverage is being able to look at all the possible conditions to see if we have addressed every one. Coverage for black-box testing is usually determined based on coverage of the requirements. As testers, we know that you can claim coverage of a requirement by just running the test cases you have created for that requirement. In fact, most test management tools report that if you ran all the tests you created for a requirement, you have achieved 100 percent coverage. While this makes for pretty charts that are predominantly green, it may not accurately reflect the real coverage. A good decision table is an easy way to determine all the possible conditions to be tested and lets us make a more accurate assessment of coverage.

Decision Tables—Weaknesses

But what if my requirements are terrible?

Decision tables are easier to build if you have well-defined business rules and requirements. They are an excellent tool for finding holes or contradictions in the requirements. It is difficult to design comprehensive decision tables if you don't know what the software should do—so, the better the requirements, the more accurate the decision tables. Decision tables can be built as we experiment with the software and can be used to document exploratory tests. There is always the concern that when we do this, we may be documenting what the software is doing without knowing if this is the right thing. Again, this is why domain knowledge is so important, particularly when the requirements are less detailed than we would prefer.

So maybe none of these are really weaknesses but rather non-typical uses. As a technique, it takes practice to become proficient with creating good decision tables. You may find that it takes several drafts to accurately show all the conditions and results that must be tested. Of course, very complicated business rules may result in very complicated decision tables, but then any technique becomes more difficult to implement as the software becomes more complex.

4.2.4   State Transition Testing

State transition testing focuses on all of the states that the software under test can encounter and the transitions to and from those states. State transitions are sometimes shown as models or diagrams that can be documented using state transition tables. The purpose of state transition testing is to ensure that the software can move correctly from state to state and that invalid state transition attempts are prevented. State transition testing is commonly used when testing embedded software, but it can be used for application software as well.

If we take a simple example application for state transition testing, think of how you would change the time on a digital clock.

- When the time is displayed, you can change it by clicking the Change button. You can then change the digits and press Accept when you are happy with the new time. This returns you to the time display.
- You can switch back and forth between the time display and a date display by pressing Change Display.
- When the date is displayed, pressing the Change button allows the date to be changed. Once you are happy with the date, press Accept and you are back at the displayed date.

Let's take a look at the state transition diagram for this:

A word on notation here: The states are in square boxes and the transitions are the arrows. Each transition is labeled with the event that triggers the transition (above the dividing line) and the effect this should have (below the dividing line). The effect doesn't always have to be the

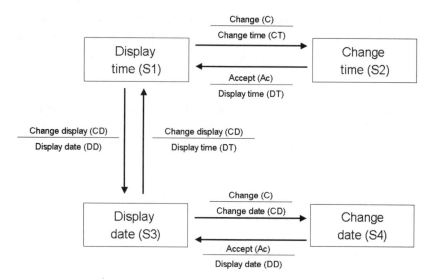

name of the next state as in this example. All of the items are labeled so that we can refer to them more easily. This is just one way of drawing your state transition diagrams. Later on you'll see an example where we use a slightly different notation to convey the same information.

Having drawn our state transition diagram, it's helpful to put the information into a table. We can choose a variety of formats for this; it all depends on what we want to cover. The following table assumes we want to cover transitions, which are represented in the table by the columns.

	T1	T2	T3	T4	T5	T6
Start state	S1	S2	S1	S3	S3	S4
Event	C	Ac	CD	CD	C	Ac
Effect	CT	DT	DD	DT	CD	DD
End state	S2	S1	S3	S1	S4	S3

Coverage in state transition testing is determined by the percentage of all valid transitions exercised during the test. If these are single transitions (i.e., from one state to another), this is also known as 0-switch coverage. In the preceding example, if we decided to go for 0-switch coverage, we would simply create six test cases, one for each column in the table.

As so often happens with major failures, the cause turns out to be an unforeseen sequence of events. If we cover more than single transitions we have a better chance of finding these sequences and the confidence we have in our test coverage will be higher. It will cost us a lot more test cases though. If we test chains with three states we have a start state, an end state, and a state in between called a *switch* state. Between the start state and the switch state is a transition, and from the switch state to the end state, a further transition. This is why testing sequences with N transitions achieve what is known as N-1 switch coverage (also sometimes called Chow's coverage measure).

Which switch is which?

Let's extend our example now to achieve 1-switch coverage. We simply have to identify where two transitions follow each other. Here's the list, this time showing just the transitions:

Test case	Start state	Switch state	End state
1	S1	S2	S1
2	S1	S3	S1
3	S1	S3	S4
4	S2	S1	S2
5	S2	S1	S3
6	S3	S1	S3
7	S3	S1	S2
8	S3	S4	S3
9	S4	S3	S1
10	S4	S3	S4

Table 4–3
State transition table with 1-switch coverage

So we needed 6 test cases to achieve 0-switch coverage and 10 cases for 1-switch coverage. By the way, the states in a sequence don't all have to be unique; we can return to states already visited in the sequence

State Transition Diagrams/Tables—Strengths

For software with a known set of states and possible transitions between states, this is a strong technique. The state transition diagrams allow a clear portrayal of all the testing paths that must be exercised. Analyzing the possible paths through the states will help eliminate some redundant

State diagrams/tables help visualization for the tester

end-to-end tests and will help encourage thinking toward transactions rather than functionality. State transition tables can also include all the invalid state transitions, and this is a good place to start with security testing as well as error handling. By creating a comprehensive state table, you can visualize all the possible transitions that must be tested or should at least be considered for testing.

State Transition Diagrams/Tables—Weaknesses

Some software doesn't have clear states. Some software has many, many transitions possible from each state. For example, web software usually allows the user many transition options from every screen. Diagramming software with many transitions can become very complex very quickly. Even creating state transition tables can be a considerable undertaking for complex software. If you want to achieve high switch coverage levels, you may end up with a test case explosion! That said, just because it's complex doesn't mean we shouldn't test it.

Ways to fill your white board

State transition testing is primarily used for embedded software but it certainly can be used for application software. It can be very useful for testing the navigation within a GUI to be sure that you can actually get everywhere you need to go (and get out too!) . Business cases can be traced through the state diagram to ensure that a reasonable number of steps is required to complete a transaction. This is actually a form of usability testing. State diagrams are flexible and have many uses. Just be sure you have a lot of room to create your drawing!

4.2.5 Orthogonal Arrays and All-Pairs Tables

These test design techniques are all oriented toward determining the representative sample combinations to be tested. Testing in a complex environment often results in test combinatorials in the hundreds or even thousands. If we look at a client/server system, we need to think about server operating systems and service packs, client operating systems and service packs, database versions, browser versions, and any number of other configuration options. The more "open" and configurable our product is, the more configuration options need to be tested. Since we don't usually have endless time to test, we need to reduce the combinatorial explosion down to a manageable set.

All-pairs testing looks at taking pairings of the options, eliminating the combinations that are impossible or unlikely to occur, and testing all realistic pair combinations.

Let's look at how we would apply this technique (we'll look at orthogonal arrays later). Let's say we have been assigned to test a web application. We have been told this application needs to run on Windows and Mac clients and must support the three most recent releases of each. We also need to support four different server configurations due to an anticipated change in our production server configurations. We will be supporting four different browsers. Oh, and did I mention the database products? There are three of those. Too easy? That's right, I left out localization. Fortunately, for this first release we only need to test five languages.

Given these parameters and their values we can build up a data table (sometimes called an input parameter model or IPM). Our IPM in this case has five parameters with up to six possible values each and is shown here.

Clients	Browsers	Languages	Databases	Servers
Windows A	Browser A	English	Database A	Unix
Windows B	Browser B	French	Database B	Linux
Windows C	Browser C	German	Database C	Solaris
Mac A	Browser D	Arabic		HPUX
Mac B		Mandarin		
Mac C				

Table 4-4

All Input parameter model

If we do the math and if all combinations are valid, we would need $6 \times 4 \times 5 \times 3 \times 4 = 1440$. That's a lot of combinations. Let's see—if it took us just half an hour to specify and run these 1,440 tests (not to mention writing protocols and bugs reports), you would need 90 days to test this. How many people have that kind of time? And how many people would want to suffer the mind-numbing boredom? Do we really need to test all of them? Probably not. But, before we get out our felt pen and start striking through configurations, let's see if we can apply the all-pairs technique to reduce the number of cases.

We used the decision table technique to deal with factors that affected each other. All-pairs and orthogonal arrays work on factors that shouldn't interact (like the browser you use and the database the backend uses). All-pairs works on the basis that if we have tested the possible pairings of the adjacent variables, we will have created a representative sample.

The assumption with all-pairs is that not every item affects the other items, so we don't have to consider the giant number of test cases that we would get if we simply rotated through all the possible combinations. The great news is that once we have our IPM, we can use a tool that will create the all-pairs table for us. A valuable source for both all-pairs and orthogonal array tools is [URL: Pairwise].

By running this IPM through the all-pairs tool found on [URL: Satisfice] the following results were produced.

From 1,440 to 31?
Sign me up!

A total of 31 test cases certainly sounds more feasible than 1440! The larger the IPM, the more substantial are the savings.

Is this a perfect technique? Running the 1,440 test cases will give us complete coverage. What we do see with all-pairs is that if a defect exists when one value is paired with any of the other values, we will find it. For example, we can see that Windows A is paired with Browsers A, B, C, and D (test cases 1, 2, 3, and 27). We can also see that Windows A is tested with each supported language (test cases 1, 2, 3, 20, and 27). Windows A is tested with each database (test cases 1, 2, and 3). Windows A is also tested with each operating system (test cases 1, 2, 3, and 21). What the all-pairs technique does not cover are specific combinations of the variables. This is considered a safe assumption because the variables should be independent and not influence each other. If they do, there is chance that a particular combination that is affected by the influence might be missed.

One other note. In the preceding table, you see that some of the values are prepended with a ~. This means that this value is not required and you can substitute a different one if you want. For example, if you know that one configuration is more common than another, you might substitute those more commonly used values where the ~ occurs.

Could we have used orthogonal arrays? Orthogonal arrays are another method used to deal with large numbers of combinations of parameters. They work on the basis of ensuring that every parameter is compared with every parameter in the neighboring column. In this way, we can be sure that problems with one particular value (for example, the type of database in the previous example) are detected. This is also known as a single-mode fault. We can also detect the interaction between two parameters, known as a double-mode fault. We cannot guarantee that we will detect all multiple-mode faults (greater than double) across multiple

Table 4-5
All-pairs for the input parameter model

Case	Clients	Browsers	Languages	Databases	Servers
1	Win A	A	English	DB A	Unix
2	Win A	B	French	DB B	Linux
3	Win A	C	German	DB C	Solaris
4	Win B	B	English	DB A	Solaris
5	Win B	A	French	DB C	HPUX
6	Win B	D	German	DB B	Unix
7	Win C	C	English	DB B	Linux
8	Win C	D	French	DB A	Solaris
9	Win C	A	German	DB A	Linux
10	Win C	B	Arabic	DB C	Unix
11	Mac A	D	English	DB C	HPUX
12	Mac A	A	Arabic	DB B	Solaris
13	Mac A	C	Mandarin	DB A	Unix
14	Mac B	C	Arabic	DB A	HPUX
15	Mac B	B	Mandarin	DB C	Linux
16	Mac B	D	French	DB B	Unix
17	Mac C	D	Mandarin	DB B	HPUX
18	Mac C	B	German	DB A	HPUX
19	Mac C	D	Arabic	DB C	Linux
20	Win A	A	Mandarin	~DB B	Solaris
21	Win A	C	French	~DB C	HPUX
22	Win B	C	Arabic	~DB A	Linux
23	Mac A	B	French	~DB A	Linux
24	Mac B	A	English	~DB C	Solaris
25	Mac C	C	English	~DB B	Unix
26	Mac C	A	French	~DB A	Solaris
27	Win A	D	Arabic	~DB A	~Unix
28	Win C	~ B	Mandarin	~DB B	HPUX
29	Win B	~ A	Mandarin	~DB C	~Unix
30	Mac A	~ A	German	~DB B	~Linux
31	Mac B	~ B	German	~DB C	~Unix

parameters because we don't test every possible combination. We will find a large number of these faults, but we can't guarantee we will find all of them.

Let's start with a simple example. If we have three parameters, each of which can have two values, we would have the following table if we tried to test every combination:

Table 4-6

All combinations for all

parameters

Test	Parameter A	Parameter B	Parameter C
1	0	0	0
2	0	0	1
3	0	1	0
4	0	1	1
5	1	0	0
6	1	0	1
7	1	1	0
8	1	1	1

If we apply orthogonal arrays, we need to be sure we have tried all the possible pairings of the parameters. This results in the following table:

Table 4-7

Reduced set of tests

Test	Parameter A	Parameter B	Parameter C
1	0	0	0
2	0	1	1
3	1	0	1
4	1	1	0

You can see that all pair combinations are covered (all possible pairings between Parameters A and B, A and C, and B and C). A combination like 1, 1, 1 is not covered using this array. That case is not included because we have already tested the combinations of 1, 1, 0 and 0, 1, 1 and 1, 0, 1. As with all-pairs testing, we would miss a bug if it occurred only when A and B and C were all set to a particular value, but the chances of this occurring are considerably smaller than the possibility that we can't run all the possible combinations. Since we have to reduce the number of test cases, it's good to have a proven formula to do it.

We can find links to various repositories of orthogonal array tables at [URL: Pairwise]. The tables at [URL: ATT] are publicly available and have been proven to work in the telephony field. There are arrays of various sizes available. You then take their values and substitute the parameters you need to test.

Let's use the preceding orthogonal array for the Marathon application. Let's say we're creating test cases that need to be run with the following parameters: Runner gender (male or female), Experienced runner (yes or no), and Runner age classification (youth or mature).

Test	Gender	Experienced	Age
1	0 = male	0 = no	0 = youth
2	0 = male	1 = yes	1 = mature
3	1 = female	0 = no	1 = mature
4	1 = female	1 = yes	0 = youth

Table 4-8

Example for Marathon

Or, to simplify the notation a bit:

Test	Gender	Experienced	Age
1	Male	No	Youth
2	Male	Yes	Mature
3	Female	No	Mature
4	Female	Yes	Youth

Table 4-9

Simplified example for Marathon

Even in this simple example, we reduced the number of test cases by half. The larger the number of parameters, the higher the savings.

So you may ask, what's the difference? Honestly, not much. Both are test case reduction methods. Both look at pairings of options. The pairing methodology is a little different between the two, but the results are not substantially different.

What about coverage? For the first example we looked at, complete coverage would require 1,440 test cases, but we think we can provide adequate coverage with 31 test cases. Is this complete coverage? No, but it's

Bigger is better for orthogonal arrays, at least in terms of test case reduction

probably "good enough", and it's certainly better than starting at the beginning of the 1,440 tests cases and testing until we run out of time! So to determine coverage we would look at the number of test cases we ran divided by the number of all-pairs combinations or the orthogonal array tests indicated by our test design technique. As always, when reducing the number of test cases or when filling in the optional values, we should use risk as the basis of the decision. Some combinations are higher risk, maybe because they have higher usage, maybe because they're new, maybe just because they tend to be buggy. We will want to favor those when picking the optional values to fill in the matrix.

These are very powerful techniques, but as with all techniques, their use must be weighed against the realities of the product you are testing, the skills of the testing team, and the acceptability of the technique. You may need to "sell" the technique to your management before you reduce the number of tests from 1,440 to 31.

There has been a lot of good research performed into the techniques described in this section. A thorough examination of their use is described by Mats Grindal in [Grindal07]. Lee Copeland also covers the techniques and gives worked-through examples in [Copeland03].

Orthogonal Arrays/All-Pairs—Strengths

These are really the only effective methods for dealing with combinatorial explosions caused by multiple configuration items. In practice, when faced with thousands of possible test configuration combinations, the testers usually select the ones they believe are the most common. This may be based on risk analysis information, "common knowledge" within the organization, or sales/support information regarding installed customers. Sometimes testers test the configurations that they happen to have in the lab or can easily create in the lab and hope those are representative of the real world. Orthogonal arrays and all-pairs tables allow us to make an intelligent choice of which configuration combinations to test and which ones can be safely ignored.

Orthogonal Arrays/All-Pairs—Weaknesses

These methods significantly reduce the number of test cases we will need. Each is a statistically sound method to determine how to reduce the test cases and still cover the important combinations. Is it 100 percent safe? No. There may be a case where there is unexpected interaction between components, and that one configuration combination might be one that is excluded. To minimize risk with these techniques, it's important to review the selected combinations and augment as needed with knowledge of customer preferences, previous failure information, and known common configurations.

4.2.6 Classification Trees

Classification trees provide a graphical representation of the combinations of conditions to be tested. The items to be tested are created as classes and classifications within the classes. You could take this information and build your own test cases based on these combinations, but that would be silly when there are perfectly fine free tools available. Using the same example as used in the all-pairs discussion, the first step is to create a classification tree from the following table of configuration information:

Free tools can be wonderful things

Clients	Browsers	Languages	Databases	Servers
Windows A	Browser A	English	Database A	Unix
Windows B	Browser B	French	Database B	Linux
Windows C	Browser C	German	Database C	Solaris
Mac A	Browser D	Arabic		HPUX
Mac B		Mandarin		
Mac C				

Table 4-10
Configuration data

The next step is to construct a classification tree diagram that shows the relationships between the options to be tested. The free tool available at [URL: Systematic Testing] has been used to create the following tree.

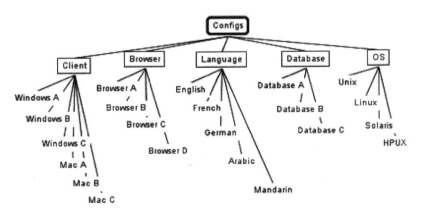

Figure 4-8
Classification tree for configuration data

Figure 4-9
*Classification diagram for
configuration data*

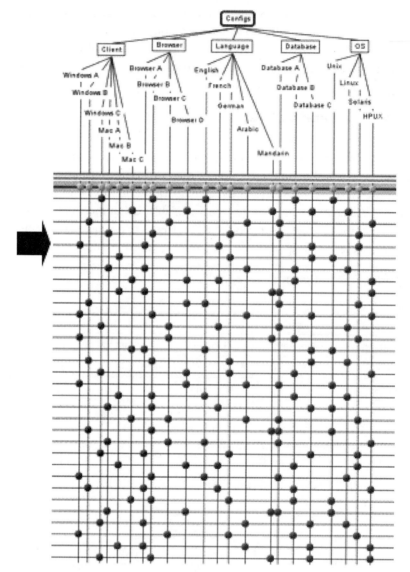

Figure 4-9
Classification diagram for configuration data

Using combination rules (e.g., pairs, three-wise), you then ask the tool to construct a chart showing all the test cases you need to run. I requested all the combinations of pairs (test every pairing of each option) which resulted in the 32 test cases shown in figure 4-9.

A circle indicates that option should be used for the test case. Test cases are formed by combining all the indicated options in a given row. For example, if we picked test case 5 (the fifth row in the chart is shown by an arrow), we would need to test a configuration consisting of Windows A, Browser A, French, Database C, and Solaris.

If you request three-wise test cases, you get 151 test cases. Three-wise looks at all combinations of three options.

Classification Trees—Strengths

The tool provides a strong set of rules that let you select combinations (such as two-wise for some options and three-wise for others). This is particularly useful if you know some combinations are higher risk or more likely to occur (or both!). This is where the classification trees are more powerful than the all-pairs technique since all-pairs is limited to only pair (or two-wise) combination testing.

The use of classification trees has one other big advantage over combinatorial techniques such as all-pairs; visualization. Any technique that is strong on visualization is likely to have advantages when designing tests, especially where documented specifications are weak and we need to talk to stakeholders to find out their requirements.

Classification Trees—Weaknesses

Care has to be taken when using this technique. The strength of having good visualization can quickly become a weakness if we end up creating huge, cumbersome diagrams. Always work top down when designing your classification trees. If your trees get too big, split them up into several smaller trees that reference each other (make sure the tool you are using can manage this).

4.2.7   Use Case Testing

Use cases are scenarios that depict actual usage of the software in the customer environment. Use cases are oriented toward transactions rather than functional areas. Only someone with good knowledge of the customer and the customer's usage can create accurate and valid use cases.

When we make use of use cases to design tests, we are simulating real user interaction with the system. If we look at a typical ATM application we could have the following use cases:

- The customer withdraws cash
- The customer checks balance
- The customer makes a deposit
- The customer makes multiple transactions (makes a deposit, checks balance, withdraws cash)

Never trust a user to stay on the primary path

Each of these use cases would contain a primary path and some number of alternate paths. The primary path is the series of actions that would result in the user achieving the objective with the least number of steps. The alternate paths would consider error conditions, transaction cancellations, and other events that could occur off the primary path.

Use cases, like code, can call other use cases. This helps to reduce redundancy both in use case design and in test design.

When tests are designed from use cases, we attempt to create a test that will follow the transactions that are outlined in the use case. One use case with alternate paths may result in many test cases in order to cover the primary as well as all the alternates. One individual path may require multiple test cases in order to provide complete and thorough coverage of that path. At a minimum, there will need to be one test created for each possible path, primary and alternate. Coverage is determined by the coverage of the various defined paths.

Use Cases—Strengths

The major strength with a use case is that it tells us what a user will really do. It helps us align our testing and double-check that we are addressing the users' needs. Good use cases need to include the alternative paths as well as the common paths in order to provide adequate test coverage. Good use cases also include an example. This example can be used as the basis for test case design.

Use Cases—Weaknesses

Use cases are only valuable if they reflect realistic usage scenarios

The major strength can turn into a major weakness if the use case does not accurately reflect the customer's usage of the software. We can expend test effort on unrealistic scenarios at the cost of not testing more reasonable and likely scenarios. Another common issue with use cases is that they may contradict the functional requirements that have been written in a separate document. This is why it is so important to create a traceability matrix that spans all the requirements documents (business requirements documents, functional specifications, design documents, architectural documents, use cases, and mock ups) to be sure we are testing everything. It is not unusual for a requirement to make its first and only appearance in a use case. When this happens, it's very easy for the developer to miss the feature (particularly if the use case is very wordy) during implementation and easy for testing to miss it unless there is comprehensive traceability.

Use cases are a wonderful thing, but it's smart not to assume that they will contain all the requirements you need to test. Take them as input to the testing, but not as the sole authority of how the software should work.

4.3 Selecting a Specification-Based Technique

In terms of practicality, all these techniques have their applicability. It always helps to have multiple techniques. Even with our simple examples, we can see that the different techniques approach test design from different angles. Each one of these techniques yields a set of test cases, some of which overlap with others and some of which are slightly different.

Generally speaking you should always consider using equivalence partitioning. Even if you only use the positive partitions, you will still be able to demonstrate basic confidence that the software functions correctly for the "normal" conditions that most frequently occur. If you are looking to find more defects than positive equivalence partitioning can give you, extend your techniques to include negative equivalence partitions and boundary values. This will give you additional confidence that your software is robust and handles exceptional conditions well.

Other techniques depend on the nature of the software application to be tested. Try to model the software's behavior with your stakeholders (customers, developers and, yes, maybe even marketing). Draw diagrams, discuss, challenge. Afterwards step back and look at what you have. In amongst all those scribbles, sticky notes, cards, or whatever, you may notice a couple of fundamental patterns. Do we have lots of states that our application can take? Does it wait in certain states until some event pushes it to another? If the answer is yes, we ought to think about state transition testing as a technique to apply. Does the behavior of our application depend on lots of rules? Do we see statements like "if A and B are true then perform action C, but only if there is an "r" in the month"? If the answer is yes here, then we should think about using cause-effect analysis as our technique. If we are challenged by the complexity of large numbers of input parameters and values, each of which could theoretically be combined with each other, take a look at modeling the input parameters and then using the all-pairs technique or orthogonal arrays.

Take care when selecting your techniques. You may have to comply with specific standards that insist that particular techniques are applied and a specific level of coverage demonstrated. This is particularly the case for real-time and safety-critical systems (ask your test manager about any applicable standards if you are unsure).

The more techniques you master, the more testing challenges you can conquer

If you are able to choose the techniques to be used yourself, you may not have the luxury of time to employ all of them. Personally, I'm really slow at drawing the state diagrams but I'm willing to rough one out on a white board to make sure I've got all the transitions covered (I erase my artwork quickly so no one finds out that I can't draw a freehand circle and that I crossed my arrows!). Use the techniques that work for your problem—you'll find you get faster with the various techniques the more you use them. At first though, it may be painful to wrap your mind around creating a decision table or using orthogonal arrays, but once you get the hang of it, they are really very straightforward techniques (and do not require drawing circles!). Practice is the key to making these techniques usable. Read books with worked examples, go to training courses, get coaching, and then practice using them in your own context. Share your experiences with others. Improve!

4.4   Let's Be Practical

Marathon: Specification-Based Techniques

Can we use some of these techniques for our Marathon project? Let's make this a little more like real life.

Take a look at the Marathon system diagram below. We just received updated requirements for the Internet Portal. When the developer began to work on the registration function, there were too many undefined issues. Clearly we should have had a requirements review before coding started!

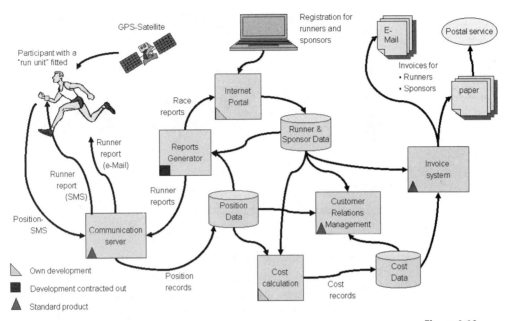

Figure 4-10
The Marathon system

Here are the new requirements:

- Sponsors must create an account that includes their email address and physical mailing address
- Sponsors must be checked against the "no pay" list before they are allowed to sponsor a runner
- Runners to be sponsored must be selected from the list of registered runners
- Multiple selections are allowed
- Sponsors are allowed to sponsor up to 10 runners
- Sponsors are allowed to sponsor a runner for up to $1,000 per mile

Can we apply the techniques we just covered? Let's see what we can do with what we've learned.

Marathon: Equivalence Partitions and Boundary Value Analysis

Do we have any equivalence partitions here? There are at least two. One is the number of runners that can be sponsored and the other is the amount of money per mile.

A sponsor can choose to sponsor from 1 to 10 runners. If we look at this as partitions, we have the following:

Figure 4-11

Equivalence partitions for

numbers of runners

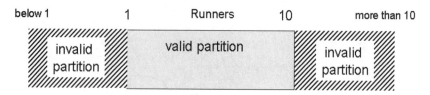

With these partitions, we are making the assumption that we have some testing on the user interface to detect nonnumeric characters and non-whole numbers. We could make an additional partition that just includes all invalid characters, but, for simplicity sake let's assume that is being tested elsewhere (always a dangerous assumption!).

With the previous partitions, we have one valid partition, 1-10, and two invalid partitions, less than 1 and greater than 10. Now it's time to do a sanity check. Is it reasonable for us to assume that all the values within these partitions will be handled the same way? With the "below 1" invalid partition, we just have to be sure we test a value that would be accepted if it were positive so we know it's rejected for the right reason. A negative value between –1 and –10, say –5, is good for that check because if the software has a bug and accepts it as a 5, we will see the problem and can assume that problem applies to all negative numbers. If we tested with –2500, and it's rejected, we don't know if it was rejected because it's a negative number or because it is being treated as a positive number that is greater than 10.

The 1-10 partition warrants more attention. Is it reasonable to assume that the code will follow the same path when you want to sponsor 1 runner as when you want to sponsor 2 or 3 or 4 runners? While we can never be absolutely sure that the developer didn't code different handling for runner 7 for some reason (probably just to drive us crazy), we can be reasonably sure that the behavior will be the same. So this is a good partition.

The "greater than 10" invalid partition is also a good partition. It's reasonable to expect that a sponsor trying to sponsor more than 10 runners (12, 25, 525, and so on) will get the same error and the processing will be the same.

So we have three partitions. How many test cases do we need to cover these partitions? No, it's not a trick question—we need three, one for each

partition. If we select to try −5, 7, and 207, we have adequately tested each
partition.

Now wait. If sponsors can only select these runners from a list, how
can they get a negative number? Maybe they can't. Right now, we don't
have the user interface. There might be a place where they can enter the
number of runners they plan to sponsor. Until we can verify that this is not
possible with the user interface, it's better to leave it in as a test case.

It's easier to remove unneeded test cases than to remember the ones we skipped

Now that we've seen we can use equivalence partitioning, can we
refine that with boundary value analysis? Being suspicious testers, we
know that it would be really easy for the developer to have a mistake in the
code at one of the boundaries. So, we'll test for those values.

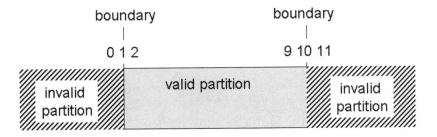

Figure 4-12
Boundary values for numbers of runners

We're going to test for the valid boundaries at 1 and at 10 and for the invalid
boundaries at 0 and 11. This will help us catch bugs that might occur when
the code says > 1 instead of >= 1 and the same with <10 instead of <= 10.
We might also catch initialization bugs that occur only when one runner
is selected and that runner is the only runner. By doing boundary value
analysis, we have added two more test cases for the valid boundaries and
two for the invalid boundaries, but we have probably allowed ourselves a
more restful night of sleep since we won't be worrying about those pesky
boundary defects anymore!

Marathon: Decision Tables

Could we use decision tables for Marathon? What if our ever-vigilant business analyst has determined that there is a significant revenue opportunity
if we sell Marathon T-shirts.

We have received the following new requirements:

- T-shirts will be available for sale
- T-shirts are available to runners and nonrunners

■ If a nonrunner buys a T-shirt, we want to know why they are interested in Marathon

■ If the buyer is a man, we will always sell a large T-shirt. If the buyer is a woman, we will prompt for size small, medium, or large

■ Some buyers may be eligible for a discount provided by our "purchase assistance" program. If the buyer is eligible, a discount will be applied to their purchase amount.

■ Nonrunners will be sent an application for our next all-male or all-female race, as appropriate

We have several things to consider before we build our decision table. We have three conditions (runner/nonrunner, male/female, and discount/no discount), so we should end up with eight sets of conditions (2×2×2). We also want to look for the if/else combinations because that tells us where we should look for relationships between the conditions (if female, prompt for size; else no prompt).

Figure 4-13

Decision table: Marathon

T-shirt sales

Conditions	1	2	3	4	5	6	7	8
Runner	Y	Y	Y	Y	N	N	N	N
Male	Y	Y	N	N	Y	Y	N	N
Discount applicable	Y	N	Y	N	Y	N	Y	N
Results/Actions								
Prompt for Interest category	N	N	N	N	Y	Y	Y	Y
Prompt for size			Y	Y			Y	Y
Apply discount to total	Y		Y		Y		Y	
Send app for women's race					Y	Y		
Send app for men's race							Y	Y

The table indicates that we need eight test cases. Do we? Can we collapse any of these? In this case, we actually have no test cases that result in the same actions as another test case, so no collapse is possible. Do we need to consider any boundary conditions? None of these items depends on an ordered set, so no we don't need to worry about boundaries.

We're going to need a T-Shirt warehouse! But that's not a testing problem.

What if we get another requirement? I hate those late requirements, don't you? But our marketing department has just determined that we could make lots of money if we allowed people to buy multiple T-shirts in one transaction. In fact, they want to give a discount (in addition to the one the buyer may already be entitled to) for those who buy more than 10 T-shirts. In the case of the women's T-shirts, they all have to be the same size in the same order.

What does this do to our decision table? Now we need to add two more conditions, one for buying fewer than 11 T-shirts and one for buying more than 10 T-shirts. These are two equivalence partitions (1-10 T-shirts and 11-x T-shirts). There is probably a partition that contains the maximum number of shirts one can buy, but that isn't in our requirements so we'll worry about that later. What about boundary conditions? Are you worried about the purchase of exactly 10 T-shirts? You should be, because it is clearly a boundary. So now we need to add three new conditions. That would mean instead of our initial three conditions, we now have six. $2 \times 2 \times 2 \times 2 \times 2 \times 2 = 64$ test cases. Oh my! But these conditions are mutually exclusive, so in truth, we don't need all 64 test cases. We can collapse the decision table anywhere it has a test case that tests more than one quantity. That reduces the number of test cases to 32. We can also eliminate the cases where no T-shirts are ordered because that's not what we're testing here (that's another area of testing). That gets rid of another eight test cases. So now we're down to 24 test cases. Does that make sense? We originally needed eight test cases and for each one of those we have to add testing for the > 10 case, the < 11 case and the = 10 case. That means our test cases increase from 8 to 24. Here are the conditions in our extended decision table:

Conditions	1	2	3	4	5	6	7	8	9	10	11	12
Runner	Y	Y	Y	Y	Y	Y	Y	Y	Y	Y	Y	Y
Male	Y	Y	Y	Y	Y	Y	N	N	N	N	N	N
Discount applicable	Y	Y	Y	N	N	N	Y	Y	Y	N	N	N
<11	Y	N	N	Y	N	N	Y	N	N	Y	N	N
>10	N	Y	N	N	Y	N	N	Y	N	N	Y	N
10	N	N	Y	N	N	Y	N	N	Y	N	N	Y

Conditions	13	14	15	16	17	18	19	20	21	22	23	24
Runner	N	N	N	N	N	N	N	N	N	N	N	N
Male	Y	Y	Y	Y	Y	Y	N	N	N	N	N	N
Discount applicable	Y	Y	Y	N	N	N	Y	Y	Y	N	N	N
<11	Y	N	N	Y	N	N	Y	N	N	Y	N	N
>10	N	Y	N	N	Y	N	N	Y	N	N	Y	N
10	N	N	Y	N	N	Y	N	N	Y	N	N	Y

Figure 4-14

Extended decision table: Marathon t-shirt sales

You might be able to figure this out logically, but there is always a risk of losing a test case. If you make the decision table and then do the collapse, you'll know you didn't miss anything. You'll also be ready when someone changes the requirements and adds an additional discount for an order > 20. By adding to and collapsing our full decision table, we can always be sure we have covered all the possible combinations.

Exercise:

You have just received a new requirement to allow people to also purchase Marathon coffee mugs and they receive a discount if they purchase both the coffee mug and a T-shirt. Create the decision table.

Marathon: State Transition Tables

Let's look at those requirements again. A new one has been added! Is this beginning to seem like one of your own projects?

- Sponsors must create an account
- Sponsor is connected to a credit agency and must supply additional information to obtain approval. The credit agency verifies the sponsor information and checks that the sponsor is not on the "no pay" list.
- Runners to be sponsored must be selected from the list of registered runners
- Multiple selections are allowed
- Sponsors are allowed to sponsor up to 10 runners
- Sponsors are allowed to sponsor a runner for up to $1000 per mile.

Could we make a state diagram for our new requirements? Sure we can. Here it is.

Note that the notation used in the diagram is slightly different than the example shown previously. Here we are using circles for the states and the transitions are labeled Event[Condition]/Action. Choose the notation that suits you best.

Is this a perfect diagram? Well, first we'd need to determine if we have perfect requirements. One thing that bothers me is that we haven't given the user a way to cancel out once they have started to pick runners and amounts. Perhaps this was by design? Once we have the sponsor captured we will not release them!!! In reality though, they can always just close their browser. Since there are ways for them to get out, we need to check that we will clean up properly if they do select to terminate their session.

The diagram would be more accurate if it looked like figure 14-6 (this time the states have been given an identifier for ease of reference) We often

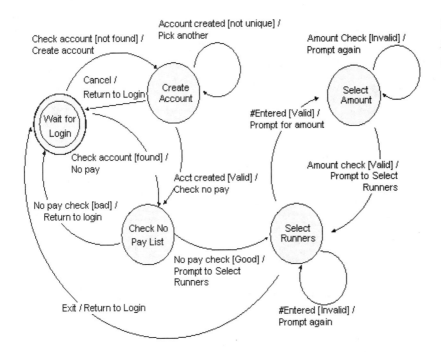

Figure 4-15

State transition diagram:

Marathon sponsors

represent the information in these diagrams as a state transition table like the one in table 4-11.

For Marathon we have decided to cover all transitions. To cover all the transitions, we can follow four paths. The state identifiers shown in the preceding diagram are used to describe the paths; you might like to trace them through on the diagram:

1.   WL-CA-CA-CNP-SR-SA-SR-WL
2.   WL-CNP-WL
3.   WL-CA-WL
4.   WL-CNP-SR-SA-WL

We would define a test case for each of these paths to achieve full transition coverage.

If we cover all the transitions, have we done all the testing we need to do? This is always a problem for testing. It's one thing to cover all the transitions once, but what if there is a cascading effect that is seen only in a certain combination? What if there is a bug that occurs only after we have selected and sponsored three runners and then we make a multiple selection of 10 runners? We probably won't find that bug, unless we

Figure 4-16

Extended state transition diagram: Marathon sponsors

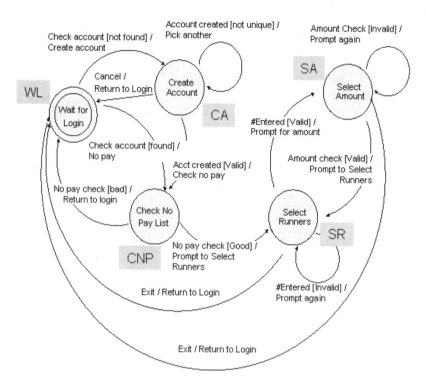

Figure 4-16

Extended state transition diagram: Marathon sponsors

increase the "switch coverage" we talked about previously, but that could be expensive.

It's reasonable to assume that we should mix a single selection with multiple selections as that could be a problem (for example, the developer might set a value somewhere in the code to accommodate the number of entries from the multiple selection and might forget to clear that value before the single selection, causing an internal error). This is why good testers have trouble sleeping at night. There's always a chance that Missouri got left off the list! Or, in this case, that there is an interaction between actions that influences subsequent actions.

The more complex the code, the more complex the testing

For example, is there a hidden defect that occurs only when the sponsor selects exactly four runners and sponsors them for the amounts of $1, $2, $3, and $4? And what if this insidious defect actually corrupts the sponsor's account. What if the corruption results in the sponsor values being subtracted from the invoice instead of added to it when the invoice is created? Would we catch it? Only if we tried that exact series of transitions.

Current State	Event [Condition]	Action	Next State
Wait for Login	Check account [not found]	Create account	Create account
	Check account [found]	No pay	Check No Pay List
Create account	Account created [not unique]	Pick another	Create account
	Cancel	Return to Login	Wait for Login
	Account created [Valid]	Check no pay	Check No Pay List
Check No Pay List	No pay check [Bad]	Return to login	Wait for Login
	No pay check [Good]	Prompt to Select Runners	Select Runners
Select Runners	#Entered [Valid]	Prompt for amount	Select Amount
	#Entered [Invalid]	Prompt again	Select Runners
	Exit	Return to Login	Wait for Login
Select Amount	Amount check [Valid]	Prompt to Select Runners	Select Runners
	Amount Check [Invalid]	Prompt again	Select Amount
	Exit	Return to Login	Wait for Login

Table 4-11

State transition table

The more techniques we use to attack the testing, the more likely we will find issues like this. That's why we want to have multiple techniques in our arsenal. Remember though, there is no substitute for experience and the natural suspicion that experienced testers develop.

Marathon: All-Pairs

Could we use orthogonal arrays or all-pairs techniques? Sure. An example was given above during the orthogonal arrays description.

Marathon: Use Cases

What about use cases? Use cases are always useful as long as they represent what a user would do. Let's look at a sample:

Table 4-12

Use Case example.

UC Name	Accept Sponsor Selections	UC-20
Goal in Context	A registered user is allowed to select runners to sponsor and to indicate sponsor amount on a dollar per mile basis	
Scope	Primary Use Case	Version: 1.0
Referenced Use Cases	Register Sponsor (UC 12) Register Runner (UC 5)	
Referenced UI Messages	Message 12, Message 15, Message 17, Message 18, Message 22, Message 25	
Preconditions	The sponsor must have already been registered in the system (see UC 12). The runners must have already been registered in the system (see UC 5).	
Post Conditions	The actor selects from zero to 100 runners to sponsor and provides a sponsor amount from $1 to $1000 per mile for each runner.	
Actors	✍ Sponsor	

Table 4-13

Main flow of use case.

Main Flow Steps	Action
1	The actor logs into the system
2	The actor enters the selection criteria to display a set of runners
3	The actor selects several runners from the first list
4	The selected runners are displayed and the actor is prompted to enter an amount for each runner
5	An amount is entered for the runners and the actor submits the amounts

Table continues

Main Flow Steps	Action
6	The actor repeats this process several times, entering different selection criteria and selecting different numbers of runners.
7	Actor selects Finished. Display message 25 and log user off.

Alternative Flow Steps	Alternative Flow That Define Paths That May Be Triggered and Take the Place of the Normal Flow
1a	The sponsor does not have an account. Display message 12. Call UC 12.
2a	No runners are found for the selection criteria. Display message 15. This use case continues with step 2.
5a	The actor clicks submit without entering values for each runner. Display message 17. This use case continues with step 5.
5b	The actor enters an amount greater than $1000 for a runner. Display message 18. This use case continues with step 5.
6a	The actor has selected a number of runners that will exceed 10 for his sponsorship. Display message 22. Use case continues with step 6.
Frequency of use	Use case is performed each time a sponsor decides to register an amount for a runner.
Specific requirements	If the system is not available, the generic system offline message must be displayed.
Outstanding Issues	Will credit card verification be required before sponsorship is accepted?
Explanation of terms	<Enter explanations here as required>

Table 4-14

Alternative flow for use case

From this use case, we can derive a number of test cases. At a minimum, we need to address every step in the main path as well as all the steps in the alternate paths. That means we will need at least one test case for the main flow steps. Notice how the use case spans several areas of functionality—login, entering selection criteria, multiple and single selection, assignment of amount, repeat selections and logout. Each one of these areas would also be tested in functional testing, but this is a nice end to end test case that we can use for defining load profile for performance and load testing as well as smoke testing (smoke testing is type of testing that is conducted using a relatively small set of tests that are run to verify basic functionality of the software).

In addition to the main flow, we also need to test the alternate flow conditions. Notice that these all have messages associated with them. We can verify that we get the message and that it's the right message (assuming these message numbers reference something sensible that the reader can understand; we have known developers who would code it so the software would popup a message box that would say "Display Message 15").

Does this use case help you think of test cases that you might not have considered? Would you have tried selecting multiple runners and then going back and selecting just one? If you're an experienced test analyst, you would probably think of that. If you're new to testing, you might not. Either way, the use case helps to ensure that you are testing realistic scenarios.

4.5 Learning Check

The following check lists will help you judge the knowledge you have gained from this chapter.

Terms

*all-pairs, boundary value analysis (BVA), cause-effect graphing, classification tree method, decision table testing, decision testing, equivalence partitioning, *orthogonal array, *orthogonal array testing, pair wise testing, requirements-based testing, specification-based technique, state transition testing, use case testing

Test Analyst and Technical Test Analyst

List examples of typical defects that would be identified by each of the specification-based techniques. Indicate coverage criteria as applicable.

Test Analyst (Specific)

■ Demonstrate the ability to write test cases using the following test design techniques :

- Equivalence partitioning
- Boundary value analysis
- Decision tables
- State transition diagrams and tables
- Classification tree method
- Orthogonal arrays and All-pairs tables
- Use cases

■ Analyze a system via its requirements specification to determine which specification-based techniques should be applied to achieve specific objectives. Outline a test specification based on IEEE 829, focusing on functional and domain test cases and test procedures.

Technical Test Analyst (Specific)

■ Demonstrate the ability to write test cases using the following test design techniques :
  - Equivalence partitioning
  - Boundary value analysis
  - Decision tables
  - State transition diagrams and tables

■ Analyze a system via its requirements specification to determine which specification-based techniques should be applied to achieve specific objectives. Outline a test specification based on IEEE 829, focusing on component and non-functional test cases and test procedures.

5 Structure-Based Testing Techniques

Technical test analysts must be skilled at using structural testing techniques to increase the effectiveness of testing. This chapter first considers the principal benefits, possible drawbacks and areas where structural-based testing techniques can be applied. An explanation of each technique is then provided with examples. The chapter concludes by considering the factors that influence the selection of specific techniques including the coverage goals, practicality and relative merit of the techniques.

5.1 Benefits

When we looked at specification-based testing techniques in chapter 4 we looked at various techniques that would enable the software, as specified, to be covered by the test cases we designed. This is a perfectly acceptable approach to take, except that there are a couple of questions we left unanswered: Does specification-based testing give us effective testing? If we get full coverage using a specification-based technique like, say, equivalence partitioning, could there still be defects left undetected in the software? If you're still unsure about the answer, consider the following piece of pseudo-code for a module in a financial application called PayMoney (line numbers inserted for reference):

Does specification-based testing alone give us effective testing?

PayMoney (Integer: AccNumber, Sum)

```
1    if EnoughMoney (AccNumber, Sum) then
2            PayMoney(Sum)
3    else
4            ShowMessage ("Sorry, no money in account")
5            if AccNumber = Sum then
```

6	PayMoney (AccNumber)
7	end if
8	end if

The specification for PayMoney may have been as follows (additional details given in brackets):

Check the account corresponding to the account number (AccNumber) received (line 1) to see if it has enough money in it to cover the value requested (sum). If it does (line 2), pay it, otherwise issue a friendly message (line 4) and don't pay it.

A specification-based technique like equivalence partitioning (EP) may have been selected for testing this PayMoney module as a black box. Remember, with black-box techniques like EP we are interested only in the inputs and outputs, but not the internal structure of the module. Using EP we would have defined various test cases using input variables AccNumber and Sum and we would have set up the account to be used before executing the tests to give us the required test conditions.

There's something horribly wrong with the PayMoney module

Now, as we can all see (this is an example, OK), there's something horribly wrong with this module. If the account doesn't have enough money but the sum requested just happens to match the account number, money does actually get paid—the same amount as the account number in fact (lines 5 and 6). Perhaps the developer had been distracted when writing this code or had used copy and paste incorrectly. Since account numbers can be quite big, this could become a high impact failure, but what are the chances of requesting a sum that isn't in the account and is exactly the same value as the account number? Pretty remote you might think. Well, actually, if this module takes values from a user interface and the user gets confused by entering the account number in two adjacent fields (maybe the layout or the labeling of the interface was confusing), this may not be so unlikely at all, especially if the user base includes the general public (e.g., using Internet applications like home banking).

Question: Using EP, would we have chosen the right values of the variables sum and account number needed to locate that defect (be honest with yourself now)? I suspect not. Enter structure-based testing techniques.

Increase coverage levels using structure-based techniques

One of the big advantages of structure-based techniques is their ability to supplement the tests designed using black-box techniques to increase levels of coverage and increase testing effectiveness (i.e., defects found in testing). Consider the following diagram:

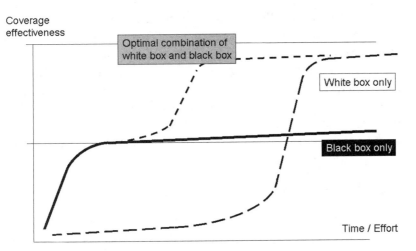

Figure 5–1
Coverage effectiveness

The diagram shows that a test strategy using only black-box techniques (equivalence partitioning, state transition testing etc.) provides a certain level of coverage relatively quickly in comparison to a white-box-only strategy. The level of coverage effectiveness provided by a black-box-only approach "tops out" though and increasing effort does not really give us a good return in terms of finding more defects. Consider the white-box-only curve now and the situation is reversed. More investment is required at first, but this pays off later with a high level of coverage effectiveness. The optimal "golden line" represents a combined strategy where black-box techniques are applied first and are then supplemented by white-box techniques to raise coverage levels. Many thanks to BJ Rollison for the illustration. We should take care though when using this diagram; it only illustrates a general point and should not be used literally. As always, the actual tracks followed by the curves shown will vary according to your own project context.

Even using a fairly weak structural coverage measure, such as statement coverage, would helped us find the problem at lines 5 and 6 of the PayMoney example. We might have performed black-box testing techniques using the module specification and then noticed that statement coverage was not 100 percent. On examination of the missing coverage we might have designed white-box tests to take us through lines 5 and 6 or, as so often occurs, we would have first analyzed the reason for the lack of coverage and simply "seen" the problem in the code. It's not always as easy as this though; very often we will need to design specific white-box tests to

Obscure parts of the code often contain defects

take us down paths in the code that are not exercised by black-box tests. This may take us into the more obscure parts of the code (exception handlers, for example) where we often find clusters of defects.

To round off the discussion of benefits, it's worth mentioning that code reviews and other static analysis methods can also be used to supplement dynamic testing, regardless of the particular approach used. In fact the defect shown in our PayMoney example at the start of this section would have been detected quite easily if we had performed a code review.

5.2 Drawbacks

Just as specification-based techniques rely on a specification of the software to be usefully applied, structural testing techniques rely on some form of testable structure (see figure 5-2 below for an example).

Some drawbacks may result from this:

- Availability of structural information. Perhaps the development is performed by a different organization and we have no access to the code. Perhaps our relationship with development is not good enough to allow analysis at this level.
- Skills levels. Do we have the technical skills to understand the structural information? Can we understand flow diagrams? Do we have a grasp of basic coding principals such as decisions, loops etc?
- Effort required to achieve required coverage levels. Again, depending on the type of structural coverage we require and the tool support available, we may be in for a surprise regarding the effort required. This is closely related to the complexity of the structure to be tested and the levels of coverage required. If we require high levels of path coverage for example(see section 5.4.7 below), we may find the number of test cases required to be impractically high.
- Inability to detect faults which are sensitive to data. As Lee Copeland points out [Copeland03], test cases may not detect defects which are sensitive to the data used. For example, the statement

$$x = y/z$$

may execute without failure in all cases except where $z = 0$, and if the statement

$$p = q^2 \text{ is incorrectly implemented as } p = q*2$$

we will not detect the fault if we select data inputs q=0 or q=2.

- Assumption of structural correctness. When testing the structure we make the general assumption that the structure itself is correct. The task is to ensure that our tests cover this structure, but we are unlikely to find certain defects with the structure, such as parts of it that may be missing.
- Calling order. A module may work correctly when called in a particular order but may fail dismally if called differently. The module itself may not be at fault, but there may be a dependency that is hard to detect.
- The testing focuses only on structural issues. Designing structural tests may, of course, reveal defects in the functionality of the software. We should be aware, though, that if we were to apply only a structure-based approach to our testing, major defects will more than likely be missed. In fact, structural testing will not detect a missed requirement. Once again, this highlights the need for a balanced approach between structure-based techniques and other techniques available to us.

Structual testing will not detect a missing requirement

In section 5.5, we will compare the various structure-based techniques according to a number of specific factors. In discussing these factors a number of other potential drawbacks will be mentioned.

5.3   Application of Structure-Based Techniques

Nearly every description of structure-based testing techniques focuses on code, just as in the example earlier. Of course, covering the structure of code is of major importance for module/unit testing, but there are also reasons for not just focusing on the code:

Structural techniques don't just apply to code

- As test analysts we may start to think of structural techniques as only being useful for developers (i.e., "nothing to do with me").
- We may ignore the possibilities offered to us for using structural techniques in other testing levels.

So where else could we apply structure-based techniques?

- Procedure testing (e.g., backup procedures, recovery procedures, maintenance procedures).
- Testing of control scripts that may, for example, be used to control batch processing.

■ Testing of any design or requirements that are represented as a structured sequence. A good example here is the use of Unified Modeling Language (UML) activity diagrams which can be used to model designs or requirements.

■ And, naturally, code.

In short, structure-based testing techniques have wider applicability to testing than we sometimes realize. Testing strategies that do not consider these techniques are frequently "one-sided" and may miss critical defects, even if they can demonstrate 100 percent coverage of some other factor, such as equivalence partitions or states.

Experiences and Lessons Learned: Who tests the batch jobs?

Many large financial applications used by banks and insurance companies, use batch processing to handle high volumes of transactions or regulate time-based activities (e.g., a monthly check on unpaid invoices). Sometimes there can be thousands of these batch programs. In fact, there can be so many that answers to simple questions like, "What batch programs do we have and what do they do?", are sometimes surprisingly difficult to answer. The batch programs themselves are called by special programs (sometimes called "batch jobs") that are written using machine-dependent languages (e.g. JCL) and that implement the required business logic.

Like any software program, batch jobs can be trivial or complex. In my experience they are generally quite complex, and yet (here comes the lesson learned), I have often noticed that these programs rarely receive the same testing attention as other programs.

Dear technical test analysts; try not to consider batch jobs just as black boxes. Some structural testing could help considerably here. We would know what batch programs are called by our tests, which batch programs are not called (maybe they are "dead code"), what coverage levels we have achieved in the batch jobs, and so on. This is valuable testing information that is too often missing.

5.4   Individual Structural Techniques

Those of us who studied the Certified Tester syllabus at the Foundation level have already learned the various structural testing techniques available to us. To make this book valuable for those without this prior knowledge (and to give the rest of us a gentle reminder), the following sections provide a summary of the techniques.

Once we have completed the review of techniques, a few words of guidance are given regarding the relative strengths and weaknesses of the techniques. This will help you select an appropriate technique and be able to explain its contribution to the test strategy.

To demonstrate the use of the techniques, an example will be used. This is shown below with a piece of pseudocode and a corresponding control flow graph. (If you are unfamiliar with using control flow graphs, I recommend referring to [Spillner 07] or [Copeland 03] for helpful examples).

Here is the pseudocode for our example; it represents a module that receives values for three integer variables x, y, and z (maybe from the user or a database) and might change one of them (variable z) according to two decisions points. The value of variable z is written (to a screen or file perhaps) at two points in the code.

```
// get values for variable x, y and z
read (x)
read (y)
read (z)

// decision point 1
if (x>1 and  y=0) then
     z=z/x
endif

write z

// decision point 2
if (x=2 or  z>1) then
     z=z+1
endif

write z
```

Figure 5–2

Sample code

Here's the corresponding control flow graph (some people use circles instead of rectangles and diamonds; it really doesn't matter). Note that sequences of code statements that are not interrupted by any decisions (e.g., read x, read y, read z) are grouped together in one rectangle.

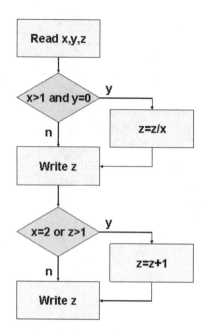

The following structure-based techniques will now be described using this example:

- Statement testing
- Branch/decision testing
- Condition testing
- Multiple condition testing
- Condition determination testing
- Path testing
- LCSAJ testing

5.4.1 Statement Testing

With statement testing we design tests that cause executable (non-comment, non-whitespace) statements to be executed at least once. The number of statements executed as a percentage of the total number of statements gives us the level of statement coverage.

How many test cases would we need to ensure that we "touch" each element of the diagram as we go from top to bottom? The following diagram shows the path (as a dotted line) on which a test case would take us if we selected the following values for the three variables:

Inputs: x = 2, y = 0, z = 4; expected result: write z = 2 and then z = 3

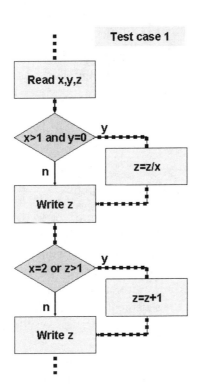

Figure 5–4

Statement coverage

The dotted line representing our test case "touches" all statements. With this single test case we have achieved 100% statement coverage.

We'll be looking at the relative merits of structure-based techniques later, but at this stage I would just like to restate the powerful arguments made by Boris Beizer and Lee Copeland relating to statement coverage levels below 100%. Here goes:

Some thoughts on the value of statement coverage

Boris Beizer [Beizer90] wrote, "Testing less than this [100% statement coverage] for new software is unconscionable and should be criminalized.... In case I haven't made myself clear,... untested code in a system is stupid, short-sighted and irresponsible."

Lee Copeland [Copeland03] defined testing below 100% statement coverage as "test whatever you test; let the users test the rest," and goes on to say that "the corporate landscape is strewn with the bleached bones of organizations who have used this testing approach."

Get the message? If we don't exercise the code, we really have no idea what it may do to the user.

5.4.2 Decision/Branch Testing

Branches result from decision points in the code, where each decision point can have a true or a false outcome. The decision statements themselves could be any of the following and may vary according to the programming language used:

- if – end if
- if – else – end if
- switch, case
- loop statements: for, do-while, do-until

Coverage is determined here by the number of decision outcomes executed as a percentage of the total number of decision outcomes (case statements would have test cases for each possible exit point).

Returning to our example, we are interested in covering all the "true" and all the "false" outcomes with our test cases. We already have one test case to cover 100% of the statements. Let's take a look at that one first and see how much decision coverage that test case would give us.

Figure 5–5

Branch coverage test case 1

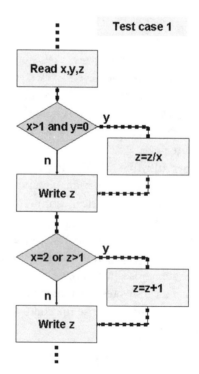

Well, we covered the two "true" conditions here (labeled "y" for "yes"), but what about the "false" conditions (labeled "n" for, you guessed it). So far we have covered only two out of the four conditions, giving us only 50% condition coverage with test case 1. We need to cover the other conditions.

The following diagram shows the path (as a dotted line) of a second test case if we selected the following values for the three variables:

Inputs: x = 1, y = 1, z = 1; result: write z = 1 and then z = 1

Test case 2 now covers the two "false" conditions. Test cases 1 and 2 together would achieve 100% decision coverage.

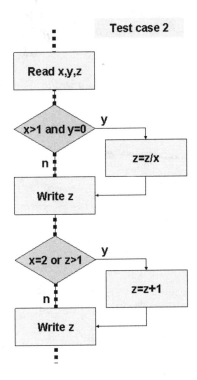

Figure 5–6

Branch coverage test case 2

5.4.3 Condition Testing

To explain condition testing the term *condition* first has to be explained. Take a look at the decision points in the preceding control flow diagram. They each contain two conditions that are combined with a logical operator (e.g., and, or, not).

Decision 1: if $(x > 1)$ and $(y = 0)$ then

Decision 2: if $(x = 2)$ or $(z > 1)$ then

The individual conditions (e.g., $x > 1$) are sometimes called *atomic* or *partial* conditions because they are the simplest form of code that can result in a "true" or a "false" outcome. They have no logical operators (e.g., and, or) and contain relational symbols like $<$ and $=$. It's possible to combine more than two atomic conditions together into one decision, but this is considered bad programming practice (in fact, many coding guidelines do not recommend more than one per decision).

To achieve 100% condition coverage, we need test cases that ensure that each atomic condition that makes up a decision has a true and a false outcome. Let's consider the two decision points in our example and construct a table for each representing the outcomes of each individual condition.

As a reminder, here are the inputs for test cases we have defined so far that gave us decision coverage:

Test case 1: $x = 2$, $y = 0$, $z = 4$

Test case 2: $x = 1$, $y = 1$, $z = 1$

Decision 1: if $(x > 1)$ and $(y = 0)$ then

Table 5–1

Conditions for decision 1

Condition 1 (x > 1)	Condition 2 (y = 0)	Decision 1 outcome	Input Values	Covered by
True	True	True	x = 2, y = 0	Test case 1
False	False	False	x = 1, y = 1	Test case 2

Decision 2: if $(x = 2)$ or $(z > 1)$ then

Table 5–2

Conditions for decision 2

Condition 1 (x=2)	Condition 2 (z > 1)	Decision 2 outcome	Input Values	Covered by
True	True	True	x = 2, z = 4	Test case 1
False	False	False	x = 1, z = 1	Test case 2

The two atomic conditions in each of the two decisions each deliver a true and a false outcome, so we have achieved 100% condition coverage here with the test cases we already defined for decision/branch testing.

If we take a closer look at the table for decision 2, we can maybe spot a weakness in this form of condition coverage (which is sometimes called *simple* condition coverage). To explain this, let's consider a different example from the one we've been using so far.

Consider the following decision:

if (x<3) or (y<5) then

...

end if

To ensure 100% (simple) condition coverage, we might design the following tests:

Condition 1 (x<3)	Condition 2 (y < 5)	Decision outcome	Input Values
True	False	True	x = 2, y = 8
False	True	True	x = 6, y = 3

Table 5–3

Test cases for 100% decision coverage

The table shows that both conditions take both true and false values but that the outcome of the decision is "true" in both cases. The "false" decision outcome remains untested.

A weakness in simple condition testing

5.4.4 Multiple Condition Testing

To compensate for the deficiency mentioned earlier, simple condition testing can be extended to multiple condition testing by considering all possible *combinations* of true and false outcomes for the individual conditions within a decision.

Now consider all combinations

Returning to the example used so far, we can extend the table of conditions to include all combinations. For two conditions per decision (it probably won't be more), we should consider the combinations true/false, false/true, false/false and true/true. On a following page, we can see the resulting tables for the two decisions in our example.

As a reminder, here are the inputs for test cases we have defined so far:

Test case 1: x = 2, y = 0, z = 4

Test case 2: x = 1, y = 1, z = 1

Decision 1: if (x > 1) and (y = 0) then

Table 5–4

Multiple conditions for decision 1

Condition 1 (x > 1)	Condition 2 (y = 0)	Decision 1 outcome	Input Values	Covered by
True	False	True	x = 2, y = 1	Test case MC3
False	True	True	x = 1, y = 0	Test case MC4
False	False	False	x = 1, y = 1	Test case 2
True	True	True	x = 2, y = 0	Test case 1

Decision 2: if (x = 2) or (z > 1) then

Table 5–5

Multiple conditions for decision 1

Condition 1 (x=2)	Condition 2 (z > 1)	Decision 2 outcome	Input Values	Covered by
True	False	True	x = 2, z = 1	Test case MC3
False	True	True	x = 1, z = 4	Test case MC4
False	False	False	x = 1, z = 1	Test case 2
True	True	True	x = 2, z = 4	Test case 1

We have to define two additional test cases to cover the combinations of conditions not yet covered by test cases 1 and 2:

Test case MC3: Inputs: x = 2, y = 1, z = 1; Outputs: write z = 1 (twice)

Test case MC4: Inputs: x = 1, y = 0, z = 4; Outputs: write z = 1 (twice)

5.4.5 Condition Determination Testing

Reducing the number of test cases

Multiple condition testing has closed the potential weakness of simple condition testing but at the expense of more test cases and the potential masking of defects. The objective of condition determination testing is to only consider the condition combinations if each of the conditions has an impact on the result. If one of those conditions were to be incorrectly implemented, we would not detect this in the form of a different result than expected. Test cases in which the result does not depend on a change of an individual condition are not therefore considered when applying condition determination testing (also called modified multiple condition testing).

If we take a look at the table we created earlier for multiple condition testing of decision 2, we can see an example of this.

Here is the table again:

Condition 1 (x=2)	Condition 2 (z > 1)	Decision 2 outcome	Input Values	Keep or delete?
True	False	True	x = 2, z = 1	Keep
False	True	True	x = 1, z = 4	Keep
False	False	False	x = 1, z = 1	Keep
True	True	True	x = 2, z = 4	Delete

Table 5–6
Multiple conditions: keep or delete

Take a close look at the last combination of the conditions 1 and 2. If condition 1 were to evaluate "false" due to an incorrect implementation, the overall result of decision 2 would still be "true". The same can be said of condition 2. Using this technique we would not design a test case for this combination of conditions.

If a test case adds no real value, away with it

5.4.6 Path Testing

Path testing covers the independent paths through our code with test cases. Sounds easy, doesn't it? Certainly this technique is less complicated and more intuitive than the condition determination technique outlined earlier, but with path testing it's easy to be misled into designing an impractically large number of tests. How could this happen?

There are dangers in using path coverage

- If our code is structurally complex the number of independent paths through it can quickly become enormous, especially if the code contains loops (each time through the loop theoretically counts as an independent path).
- If the required path coverage (i.e., the number of paths covered as a percentage of the total number of paths) is set too high we are forced into designing large numbers of test cases to achieve those coverage levels.

It's somehow tempting to commit to a high level of path coverage without appreciating the consequences

Considering the control flow diagram for the example, we have the four paths shown in figures 5-7 and 5-8.

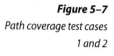

Figure 5–7

Path coverage test cases

1 and 2

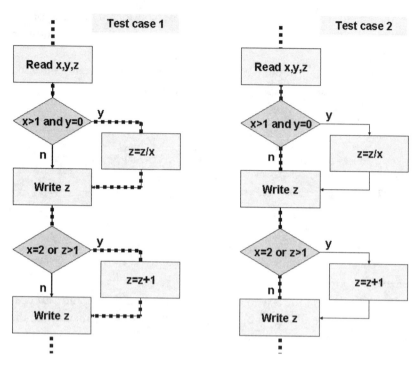

The first two we already covered with test cases 1 and 2. We still need two further test cases to cover the remaining paths.

Now we have two further test cases (see figure 5-8):

Test case 3: Inputs: x = 3, y = 0, z = 9; Outputs: write z = 3 (twice)

Test case 4: Inputs: x = 2, y = 1, z = 1; Outputs: write z = 1, write z = 2

As you can see, we have four test cases for path coverage. With other, more complex, examples, the number of test cases to cover all paths can rapidly grow very large. Take care when using this structural coverage technique!

5.4.7 LCSAJ (Loop Testing)

Linear Code Sequence and Jump (LCSAJ) is a technique that covers sections of code. The beginning of the sequence can be the start of a module or after a decision statement (including loops). The end of the sequence is either another decision or the end of the program. These *linear code*

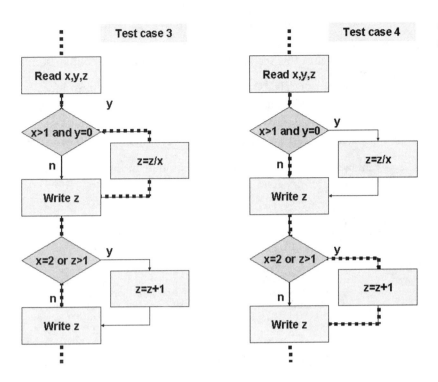

Figure 5–8

Path coverage test cases 3 and 4

sequences are also known as DD-Paths (for decision-to-decision paths). The term *linear*, or sometimes *in line*, refers to a set of code that is in line and unbroken by a decision statement.

The LCSAJ technique is used to define specific test cases and the associated test data required to exercise the linear code sequences. A more detailed explanation of this infrequently used technique is provided at [URL:IPL].

5.5 Selecting a Structure-Based Technique

Just like the specification-based techniques discussed in chapter 4, structural techniques offer a range of possibilities for detecting defects and providing coverage information.

The general benefits and drawbacks of using structural techniques were considered in sections 5.1 and 5.2. The big question now is, If I decide to apply structural techniques, which one is best for me? It will probably come as no surprise to learn that there are no clear answers to

So many possibilities. Which one is for me?

this question, but certainly comparisons between the techniques can support our decision making.

The remainder of this section considers three forms of comparison:

- A summary of general advantages and drawbacks of the techniques
- A diagram that demonstrates which types of coverage implicitly include other types of coverage (i.e., one "subsumes" the other)
- A comparison of techniques based on a check list of evaluation criteria

The advantages and drawbacks of each technique are summarized in the following table:

Table 5–7

Advantages and drawbacks of techniques

Technique	Advantages	Drawbacks
Statement	Easy to understand and apply. Can isolate "dead" code. Relatively low maintenance required.	Limited value for code containing structural elements such as decisions and loops. Many paths through the code remain untested. Using ad-hoc testing can achieve 60–75% statement coverage.
Branch/decision	Easy to understand and apply. Gives a reasonable level of confidence for the effort required.	Doesn't take account of any combinations within decisions.
Condition	No real advantages over branch/decision	Branches may get omitted.
Multiple condition	Thorough handling of complex decisions.	Multiple conditions may simply have been coded as two consecutive single conditions. Number of test cases needed higher than other condition-based techniques.
Condition determination	Reduces the number of test cases needed for multiple condition coverage.	Can be more difficult to understand.
Path	Very thorough. Appropriate also for procedure testing	Achieving high levels of coverage may be practically impossible.
LCSAJ	Offers an alternative technique that may give a different "angle" on structural coverage.	Can be difficult to apply. Highly sensitive to changes.

During the discussion on individual structure-based techniques, the test cases we designed were often re-used. For statement coverage, we designed one test case and added one more for decision coverage and a further two for path coverage. This would imply that providing coverage using some techniques guarantees the coverage obtained from others. The word used here is *subsumption* (i.e., technique X subsumes technique Y). The following diagram describes the subsumption relationships between the different structure-based techniques we have covered (except LCSAJ).

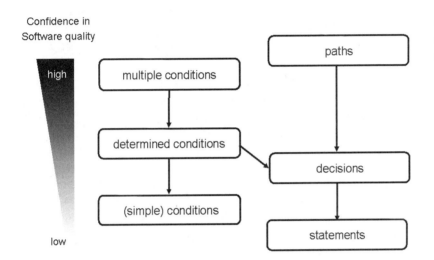

Figure 5–9

Structural techniques: subsumption diagram

The arrows in the diagram indicate which coverage technique subsumes others. For example, if our test cases can demonstrate 100% path coverage (generally not an easy task, by the way), we automatically achieve 100% decision coverage. Achieving 100% decision coverage automatically ensures 100% statement coverage.

Note that this diagram applies only where we are talking about 100% coverage. We cannot say things like "50% path coverage ensures 76% decision coverage" or "95% statement coverage automatically ensures 38% decision coverage." The rules are fairly intuitive to follow, perhaps with the exception of the "crossover" between determined conditions and decisions. With a little thought we can maybe accept the rule that 100% coverage of determined conditions also gives us 100% decision coverage.

Different coverage type—
different confidence

Perhaps the discussion on subsumption rules might appear a little academic at first, but there is a practical side to this too; just consider the level of confidence we can have in software quality by achieving 100% of a given coverage. Statement coverage, for example, is right down at the bottom. If you proudly announce that you achieved 100% statement coverage in your tests, don't be surprised if one of your stakeholders says, "So what." That might be a bit cruel because achieving 100% statement coverage is definitely better than showing no structural coverage at all, but please be aware of these issues when setting testing goals and reporting levels of confidence in software quality. Even though the test manager is usually tasked with doing this, the (technical) test analyst must be in a position to provide advice to the test manager on such issues and give objective comments on structural testing during reviews.

Moving on from subsumption rules now, here is a practical check list of factors with which to evaluate the relative merits of structural techniques. Note that in section 5.2 we considered general drawbacks that relate to all structure-based techniques. Here we consider the factors that can apply to particular techniques.

- Thoroughness
  A technique that provides a greater depth of testing may have a higher chance of finding defects, and as shown in the previous diagram, it will certainly give us more confidence in the quality of the software.

There's usually a good
reason why some
techniques aren't used
much

- Ease of understanding
  Can we make sense of the technique? Ease of understanding is especially important when we need to know why achieved coverage levels are below the levels we require. What tests do I need to design now to raise the levels? Why can't I achieve 100%? Of course, in attempting to answer these questions we may hit upon defects, so it's important to focus our efforts on detecting defects rather than the technique we are using to find them. If the technique gets in the way of testing because it's too difficult to understand, then we should find an expert or leave it well alone! Industry usage of certain techniques—or, more accurately, lack of usage—has borne this out.

- Maintainability: Sensitivity to change
  Once we have the tests designed, how easy it to maintain them when changes take place to the software structure? With some techniques we are faced with considerable effort to maintain coverage levels and with others it's easier. For example, depending on the type of structural

coverage we require (statements, branches, paths, etc.) a single change to the code structure can alter possible paths through the structure completely and result in redesigning many tests.

▪ Automation

Stand by for a potentially controversial statement: If the structure-based technique is being applied to code and the technique cannot be applied using testing tools, forget it. We're working in the real world here; with specification-based techniques the use of tools needs careful consideration and we may still opt for a manual approach (see section 18.6, "Should We Automate All Our Testing?"). Compared with structure-based techniques being applied to testing code; the use of tools here is, practically speaking, essential.

Tools for structural techniques are a "must have"

The preceding factors were among those considered in a study (see [URL:IPL]) that ranked the factors for each technique on a scale from 1 (bad) to 5 (good). The results of this study are combined with the remarks of a number of authors on the subject in the following table.

The values in the table are the result of qualitative evaluation. Please treat the table as a guideline that can help us answer the difficult question, "Which structural technique should I choose?"

	Thorough	Understandble	Tool support	Maintainability
Statement	1	5	5	5
Branch /decision	2	5	5	5
Condition	2	5	4	5
Multiple condition	3	4	4	5
Condition determination	4	5	3	5
Path	5	2	1	2
LCSAJ	3	1	4	2

Table 5–8

Evaluation of structure-based techniques

As we've seen in this section, selecting the "right" structural technique is not always easy. In some situations we may be relieved of this task by being obliged to apply standards that define the techniques to be used and the coverage levels to be achieved. This is particularly common with industry-specific standards in safety-critical areas.

Making the Right Decision

We've spent quite a bit of time in this chapter considering the overall benefits and drawbacks of structural testing techniques as well as their relative merits. This reflects the learning objectives of the Advanced Level Certified Tester syllabus and emphasizes the move away from simply learning the techniques and toward a better understanding of how best to use them. There is no question that these can be powerful testing techniques when well applied, but, as with all techniques, we need to understand the cost/benefit tradeoff in order to make an intelligent decision.

5.6   Learning Check

The following checklists will help you judge the knowledge you have gained from this chapter.

Terms

branch testing, condition determination testing, condition testing, LCSAJ, multiple condition testing, path testing, statement testing, structure-based technique

Technical Test Analyst

- List examples of typical defects that would be detected by each of the structure-based techniques
- Create test cases that will provide the following levels of coverage:
  - Statement
  - Decision
- Condition determination
- Multiple condition
- Analyze a system to determine which structure-based technique should be applied to meet specified test objectives
- Understand each structure-based technique, its coverage criteria, and when to apply it
- Compare and analyze structure-based techniques to determine the best one to use in a situation

6 Defect-Based Testing Techniques

Defect-based testing is a useful technique for focusing on and detecting particular types of defects. This chapter considers defect taxonomies and their role in implementing this technique. It also looks at the benefits and drawbacks of the technique and coverage expectations.

6.1 Introduction

Depending on the type of defect being sought, the test cases will vary in depth, skill required for development and execution, and tool usage. When the tester is performing defect-based test design, the target defects are determined based on taxonomies (a *taxonomy* is a hierarchical list) that list root causes, defects, and failures. Unlike specification-based or structure-based testing, test case coverage is determined by the test designer in a systematic way. Adequate coverage is achieved when sufficient tests are created to detect the target defects and no additional practical tests are suggested. It should be noted that the coverage criteria for defect-based tests do not imply that the set of tests is complete but that sufficient detection will be provided for the target defects.

Targeting specific bugs can help focus testing efforts

6.2 Taxonomies

There are published taxonomies, or classifications, of bugs that we can use to help us identify possible areas for defect-based tests. Taxonomies vary in the level of detail from the very broad classification of "user interface bugs" to the detailed list supplied in IEEE Std 1044-1993, where, for example, possible input problems are broken down into the following areas:

- Correct input not accepted
- Wrong input accepted

- Description incorrect or missing
- Parameters incomplete or missing

Boris Beizer's *Software Testing Techniques* [Beizer 90] contains one of the more widely recognized defect taxonomies. It goes through four levels of increasing detail, the highest two of which are tabulated here:

Table 6–1

First two levels of Beizer's defect taxonomy

Level 1	Level2
Requirements	Requirements incorrect
	Requirements logic faulty
	Requirements incomplete
	Requirements not verifiable
	Presentation & documentation
	Requirements changes
Features & Functionality	Feature or function incorrect
	Feature incomplete
	Functional case incomplete
	Domain defects
	User messages and diagnostics
	Exception conditions mishandled
Structural defects	Defects in control flow and structure
	Processing
Data	Data definition and structure
	Data access and handling
Implementation & coding	Coding and typing faults
	Violations of style guides & standards
	Poor documentation
Integration	Internal interfaces
	External interfaces, timing, throughput
System and software architecture	Operating system calls and use
	Software architecture
	Recovery and accountability
	Performance
	Incorrect diagnostics & exceptions
	Partitions & overlays
	Environment
Test definition and execution	Test design defects
	Test execution defects
	Poor test documentation
	Incomplete test cases

Taxonomies can be used to classify defects that are found as well as to determine the types of defects for which we should test. Here are some other taxonomies:

Reference	Description
[Kaner 93]	General taxonomy more than 400 defects
[Binder 00]	Object-oriented taxonomy
[URL:Vijayaraghavan]	Taxonomy for e-Commerce applications

Table 6–2
Other taxonomies

The more detailed the taxonomy used, the more exacting the testing will be. As with all checklists though, we don't want to become so fixated on the list that we forget to consider items that are not on the list. For example, we might want to expand the list to include input too long, input too short, invalid characters, and so forth. Test analysts know what types of things break. The taxonomy serves as a checklist to be sure nothing gets skipped when the testing is being planned and executed. Remember though, the taxonomy is probably not a perfect match for your product. When using the taxonomy as a checklist, remember to remove items that are not applicable and add any items that you know are likely to occur based on your hard-learned experience.

Don't assume that even a good taxonomy will cover everything.

6.3 Let's Be Practical

Marathon: Defect-Based Testing

Let's see if we can apply this defect-based technique to Marathon. Rumor has it that a previous version of Marathon had a large number of usability issues. There is a strong desire not to make the same mistakes in this release. This seems like a good candidate for defect-based testing. You know your users are very, very, very picky about the formatting of their reports. Since you now know you are looking for report formatting issues, you can target your test cases accordingly. You will design tests that look at the format of individual lines of data and multiple lines of data and at paging, sorting, and saving in different formats. You will also create tests for the "look and feel" of the reports, including presentation, title alignment,

Augment the taxonomy with your own experiences.

bolding and highlighting, consistent access to the search criteria, and consistent placement of information on the page. As a double check, you will look at defects that have been reported previously for other reports and ensure that you have covered those conditions.

How good is your coverage? If you have experience with similar products, a comparison of your test cases against the bugs found is a good check. In this case, you have a list of reported bugs from the previous version. Would your test cases have found all the bugs previously reported? If so, that's a good sign. Test case coverage is rarely perfect and generally improves over time, but even when writing brand-new tests, we can use our experience with report testing (and our domain knowledge of reports) and our knowledge of what has broken in the past to verify our coverage.

As noted earlier, coverage criteria for defect-based tests are based more on the tester's knowledge than any independent measurement.

6.4 Learning Check

The following checklists will help you judge the knowledge you have gained from this chapter.

Terms

defect-based technique, defect-based test design, defect taxonomy

Test Analyst and Technical Test Analyst

- ◼ Describe defect-based techniques, including the reasons for their use, and differentiate from specification- and structure-based techniques.
- ◼ Provide examples of defect taxonomies and explain their use.

7 Experience-Based Testing Techniques

Experience-based techniques are based on the tester's experience with testing, development, similar applications, the same application in previous releases, and the domain itself. The tester brings all their knowledge to bear when designing the test cases.

In this chapter, the four principal types of experience-based testing techniques are described and the strengths and weaknesses of these techniques are outlined.

7.1 Introduction

Experience-based test design techniques also consider defect history, but unlike defect-based test design, these techniques do not necessarily have a systematic way of verifying coverage and may not have any formal coverage criteria.

Because the tester employs his knowledge gained from experience, this can be a very high-yield technique for error detection. These methods are not as effective at achieving a specific level of test coverage and tend to be light on documentation, making repeatability secondary to accomplishing the goal of finding defects.

When executing tests using experience-based techniques, the tester is able to react to events and adjust future tests accordingly. Executing and evaluating the tests are concurrent tasks. In some cases, the tests are actually created at the same time they are executed, making this a dynamic testing approach. In some cases, tests are created in advance, but testing is later adjusted depending on the findings, making this a more structured approach.

There are four major types of experience-based testing discussed in the syllabus:

■ Error guessing
■ Checklist based
■ Exploratory
■ Attacks

Lesson Learned: Experience counts!

Experience-based testing can have huge benefits, as can be seen from the examples. But use these techniques wisely. Experience-based testing isn't an excuse to have poor testing documentation or to jump into testing with no plan. This type of testing is most effective in the hands of experienced testers who will bring their knowledge to bear in the most productive ways possible. Experienced testers know what needs to be documented to assess coverage and ensure some level of repeatability. They also know what to target to find the biggest bugs quickly and return a high yield during their testing time. These are not techniques for novices—but they are definitely appropriate and productive techniques for the advanced tester.

7.2   Error Guessing

It doesn't sound very official, but it works.

Error guessing is commonly used in risk analysis to "guess" where errors are likely to occur and to assign a higher risk to the error-prone areas. Error guessing as a testing technique is employed by the tester to determine the potential errors that might have been introduced during the software development and to devise methods to detect those errors as they manifest into defects and failures.

Error guessing coverage is usually determined based on the types of defects that are being sought. If there is a defect (or bug) taxonomy available, that can be used as the guideline. If a taxonomy is not employed, the experience of the tester and the time available for testing usually determine the level of coverage.

Experience Report: Error-guessing

How about error guessing? Does that work in real life? Have you ever received a new release of some software, rubbed your hands together, and said, "Hmmmm. I bet I can break this." Now, we know that's not a politically correct thing to say out loud, but you've thought it, haven't you? What did you do next? Did you start right in on scripted testing, or did you poke around a little to see how solid it was? Did you go after areas that had previously broken or were problem prone? If so, that's error guessing. You're using your experience to hone in quickly on the likely problem areas. You can do error guessing as a group exercise and turn it into a bug hunt. While this may not be the most organized technique (or the easiest for metrics tracking), it is very high yield in the hands of experienced testers.

One thing to remember about error guessing: we should always be focusing on quality rather than quantity in our bugs. We had an error-guessing exercise on a project that had just received a release that contained the reporting functionality. There were five different reports the software could generate. We had a meeting to determine which areas were most likely to yield the most bugs. We determined we should have two major focuses: the presentation of the data (a historically bug-ridden area) and the validity of the data.

Bug quality is more important than quantity.

On previous projects, we had found that the data presentation would have many, many bugs but the data validity issues were harder to find and harder to fix and had a much higher impact on the customer. When we guessed where our bugs would be, we divided into two teams, did some further analysis, and launched our effort. In the course of the next two weeks, we logged over 200 defects, 75 percent of which were in the data display area and 25 percent in data validity. This was actually a higher proportion of data validity bugs than we had found on previous scripted efforts. Because this was our initial test effort, the developers were happy (well, as happy as developers ever are to get bugs) to get the data bugs so early in the process. Traditionally, our scripted testing bogged down in documenting all the data presentation issues and we didn't get to the data validity issues until much later in the testing.

7.3 Checklist-Based Testing

Checklist-based testing is used by experienced testers who are using checklists to guide their testing. The checklist is basically a high-level list, or a reminder list, of whdeeds to be tested. This may include items to be checked, lists of rules, or particular criteria or data conditions to be verified. Checklists are usually developed over time and draw on the experience of the tester as well as on standards, previous trouble-areas, and known usage scenarios. Coverage is determined by the completion of the checklist.

Experience Report: Checklist-based testing

Checklist testing can provide fast feedback with low preparation time.

Since I normally do risk-based testing, checklist testing is a natural byproduct of the quality risk analysis (QRA). I use the QRA as the checklist. If I have time to develop the test cases (and that varies from project to project), I may end up with 20 test cases for a single item on the QRA. But, if I don't have time to write the test cases, I use a double checklist system. The QRA is the primary checklist, and then I use my handy test case coverage checklist to remind me about what I need to check for each item on the QRA. My checklist is simple and is a combination of the quality characteristics and lessons learned. My list includes user interface, security and access control, data integrity, configurations, installation/upgrade, internationalization, performance/stress/load, recovery/error handling/failover, and business cycles (testing for functionality that is used weekly, monthly, yearly as part of the normal cycles of the business).

As I get more time in the project, I develop the detailed test cases from my checklists. Checklist testing is an easy, fast way to get to testing while still maintaining some information regarding coverage.

7.4 Exploratory Testing

Exploratory testing is not ad hoc testing.

Exploratory testing occurs when the tester plans, designs, and executes tests concurrently and learns about the product while executing the tests. As testing proceeds, the tester adjusts what will be tested next based on what has been discovered. Exploratory tests are planned and usually guided by a test charter that provides a general description of the goal of the test. The process is interactive and creative, ensuring that the tester's knowledge is directly and immediately applied to the testing effort. Documentation for exploratory testing is usually lightweight, if it exists at all.

Coverage for exploratory testing can be very difficult to determine. The use of the charter helps to define the tasks and objectives of the testing. The charter is used to specify what is to be tested, what is the goal, and what is considered to be in and out of scope, and sometimes it also indicates what resources will be committed (including time allocated for the test session). If there is a clear charter, coverage can be determined based on adherence or expansion of the charter. In some cases, coverage is also

---

Experience Report: What? Our scripts aren't perfect?

I managed a large testing group for a company. We had a large contractor staff (about half of the testers in fact), and we had an average contractor longevity of six months. In this high-turnover environment, we had developed very detailed test cases that included every step required. The employees were generally responsible for developing the scripts and, in their spare time, doing exploratory testing.

I was relatively new to the company and had just launched a process to audit these detailed test cases, on which we were dependent, to assess our test coverage. In the middle of this process, one of my people came to me looking particularly horrified. We were in the process of testing printer drivers for complex copier/printer machines. We had what we thought were exhaustive test cases that covered all specified conditions that were to be tested. On this particular device, we had just completed all testing and I was working on the release notes to attach to my approval for release notification.

What had my horrified tester found? It turned out that we had complete test cases for the collate function. We had complete test cases for the staple function. She had attempted, in an exploratory test, to collate AND staple. We didn't have a test case for that very common combination of functions. It failed. In fact, it didn't just fail, the driver crashed. My tester wasn't the only one who was horrified! After this incident, we put a concerted effort into reviewing our test case coverage. We found that we were covering only about 85 percent of the specifications. Most of our test case development time had been devoted to maintaining the existing test cases rather than developing new ones, at a significant cost to our declining coverage.

A user would never do that!

determined based on defect or quality characteristics that have been addressed by the testing.

7.5   Attacks

You have to admit, "attack testing" sounds fun.

Software attacks (sometimes called fault attacks) are focused on trying to induce a specific type of failure. When performing attack testing, you should consider all areas of the software and its interaction with its environment as opportunities for failures. Attacks target the user interface, the operating system, interfacing systems, database interfaces, APIs, and any file system interaction. Anytime data is being exchanged, it is potentially vulnerable to a failure and consequently is an excellent target for an attack.

Coverage for attack testing is usually measured by determining if all the potentially vulnerable interfaces have been tested. For further information on security testing using attacks, see section 13.4.1.

Good guys vs. bad guys

Experience Report: Attacks

What about attacks? Can we learn anything from using attacks? It all depends on who does it (as is true with any experience-based technique). Attack testing requires technical expertise, usually more than the other techniques. One of the scariest people I know is an expert security tester. I'm pretty sure he can get into my bank account anytime he wants to access it. Fortunately, he is one of the good guys. We procured some of his time to do some security testing for us. He did unimaginably bad things to the software as he tried to gain access to restricted areas of our code, interfaces, and data. And, he found some exploitable security vulnerabilities. This is what attack testing is all about. To be a good security tester, you have to think about all the evil things some malicious person could do to your system. It's sometimes a frightening experience when you find out how vulnerable your software is. But better to find out during testing than after production release!

7.6 Strengths and Weaknesses

Experience-based testing techniques require good knowledge of the software being tested. The more the tester knows, the better he will be in applying these higher-level techniques. These techniques can be very high yield when done well and methodically. They are fast and focused and will tend to find the more obvious bugs first. These techniques work well in time-restricted situations (as most projects are!) and on projects where the documentation may be less than desirable. Exploratory testing is often used for taking an "initial look" at a new code delivery before testing proceeds to a more systematic approach. This helps to minimize downtime by not propagating a potentially problematic and untestable release. Exploratory testing is often used during maintenance testing when time for testing may be severely restricted.

That said, there are some downfalls. Inexperienced testers will not get the same bug yield as an experienced tester. They may become distracted by relatively low yield areas and miss major sections of the code. They may not know the likely vulnerable areas to target for an attack. They may not be able to "guess" the types of errors that will occur. They may not be able to follow a checklist because there aren't enough details.

Because these techniques require little documentation, the tests tend to lose repeatability. This is both an advantage and disadvantage. Less repeatability means there is more flexibility in the range of software that will be covered and so we expand our bug-finding potential. Less repeatability also means that we may "lose the magic formula" to induce a failure. In some cases, testers may run a tracing tool that will record their interactions with the system. This can be very helpful when searching for the steps required to reproduce a failure. The tracing tools should be selected carefully though, as some put a considerable load on the system and may affect the actual testing due to memory usage.

Sometimes repeatability is sacrificed to improve flexibility.

Worse, we are dependent on our experienced testers to know what to test. If they leave, we will have difficulty training incoming testers since we have little or no documentation (although some methods can lead to developing scripted tests, which would lead to more repeatability in those cases).

7.7 Let's Be Practical

Experience-Based Testing of the Marathon Application

Could we use these techniques on Marathon? Let's look at each technique for possible application. We will assume that we do have an experienced test team whose members will be able to use these techniques correctly.

How about error guessing? Let's imagine we had to list the first three areas we would target for testing based on our experience. Each of us could come up with a different list, but these are my top three:

- Communication speed for the 1-minute updates to the runners
  I expect to see that the 1-minute updates are occasionally missed due to an inability to gather and process all that information. I expect this problem to be much worse at the beginning of the race than toward the end when runners have dropped out. I'm worried that this data might not be coming in at random intervals within that 1 minute. I'm going to target load testing for this area.
- Performance of the system
  As everyone is signing up for a new marathon, I would expect to see the system slow down when we have a large announcement and a lot of interest in our marathon. Again, I would target load testing in this area.
- GPS reporting capability
  I don't mean the GPS itself here, but the ability to gather the information across all the runners. I'm worried about our interface between our application and the GPS software. We have to be able to communicate quickly and accurately and identify which GPS we have gathered information from. We also have to know to stop gathering information from a runner who has dropped out of the race. I'm going to test the individual communications first, then start to increase the load to see if we can still keep up. Experience tells me to be cautious regarding the integration between the software components. I visualize having the entire office staff walking around with GPS monitors while we are doing testing. That should reduce the number of trips to Starbucks!

Could we use checklists? As I mentioned earlier, I often use my decision tables as checklists for testing. I would also use a checklist to verify that the GUI objects act properly (radio buttons allow only one selection, and so forth).

Exploratory testing would be likely to be done when every code drop is received to ensure that effective systematic test progress can be made. In addition, to ensure that there are no significant gaps in the testing, I would assign my test team to spend a portion of each day on exploratory testing. This will help them build new test cases and will provide time for some interesting work rather than just scripted test execution.

Attacks? Ah yes. Those are always fun. I suspect we might not have error recovery that is as solid as it should be. So, I plan to shut down the database server and see if the application detects it and returns a proper error.

This is only a handful of the experience-based testing we could do. The opportunities are almost limitless and are usually, in reality, limited by schedule. Never allow yourself to become so fixated on completing the scripted testing that you forget to do the experience-based work. You have that experience for a reason—use it!

Experiences and Lessons Learned

In my test teams, I use all of these methods to complement the scripted manual and automated testing that we regularly perform. Scripted tests are never perfect. We need to use the experience-based testing to fill in the holes and find new opportunities for testing. Releasing a product without doing any experience-based testing is equivalent to saying your scripted tests provide complete coverage and no further testing is needed. I sure wouldn't want to say that!

7.8 Learning Check

The following checklists will help you judge the knowledge you have gained from this chapter.

Terms

attack, dynamic testing, error guessing, experience-based technique, experience-based testing, exploratory testing, fault attack, software attacks, test charter, test session

Test Analyst and Technical Test Analyst

- Understand when and why to use experience-based techniques.
- Explain the specification, execution, and reporting of exploratory tests.
- Specify tests using software fault attacks that target specific defects.
- Analyze a system to determine which specification-based, defect-based, or experience-based techniques should be applied to achieve specified goals.

8 Analysis Techniques

The technical test analyst can find out a lot about the software under test by analyzing it. When we perform analysis, we may be looking for specific types of defects that would be difficult to find using the testing techniques described in the previous chapters, or we may be gathering information that will help shape our testing strategy. If we don't consider analysis, we may be exposing our stakeholders to unnecessary risks. Since most analysis can be performed with tool support, we can reduce those risks at relatively low cost if we are aware of the analysis techniques available.

In this chapter, we will be considering two principal categories of analysis techniques:

- *Static analysis, where code is not executed*
- *Dynamic analysis, where code is executed*

8.1 Static Analysis

As the name implies, static analysis doesn't involve executing a program. We can perform static analysis on a number of software-related items provided they are available in an analyzable, structured form. This typically means code, but we can also perform static analysis on procedures, such as those defined for complex software installations, or on architectural designs, such as those created with standard modeling languages like UML.

The static nature of this form of analysis represents both its primary benefit and its principal limitation. Before we go on to examine the different types of static techniques available, the following sections outline some of those benefits and limitations.

8.1.1 Benefits

Static analysis can find faults when they're less expensive to fix.

The ability to perform any form of testing early in the Software Development Life Cycle (SDLC) is a major benefit. One of the most well-established and valuable principals of testing is that defects found early in the SDLC generally cost less to fix than those found later. Static analysis can be performed before any executable program is available and therefore enables potential or actual faults to be found early.

Since static analysis includes verification that applicable coding standards have been used, our code benefits from being more maintainable and more portable (we will be discussing these quality characteristics later in chapters 15 and 16). In addition, we will be able to demonstrate compliance to coding standards if that is required.

Static analysis is essentially a cost-effective activity that can be performed off-line by a wide range of capable tools. Provided the static analysis is integrated into your development and testing life cycle and performed regularly, the benefits often outweigh the costs of licenses and tool support.

Static analysis provides valuable support to a number of other testing activities:

- Reviews are supported by static analysis when the same items (code, designs, etc.) are in focus. The results obtained from static analysis can be used to indicate where to focus attention in the review and allow valuable review time to be spent on finding other forms of defect. When scheduling code reviews, it may be an effective approach to perform static analysis first to "weed out" as many defects as possible and highlight any other potential defects before embarking on the review itself.
- Risk analysis is supported by static analysis primarily by the metrics that static analysis can provide. These metrics can be used as indicators for risk (e.g., complexity) and are valuable inputs to a risk-based testing approach.

Lesson Learned: Static analysis tools prevent defects

In one particular project in which I became test manager (alas, only once the project had slid into difficulties), a static analysis tool was introduced. A short while after I took over the role, it became apparent that the project's C++ programming guidelines were not being applied and that the development team was suffering the consequences (little reuse of code and poor analyzability being the chief causes of pain). Shortly after announcing that a static analysis tool would be used to help resolve the problems (but before its actual installation), I observed an interesting effect. Code started to be delivered from the developers that conformed much better than before. Developers are generally proud of their work and don't like the idea of being shown up by a tool (especially in front of the new test manager). Once the tool was in place, it was used to good effect assisting the developers in writing high-quality, compliant code. The focus shifted to fault prevention as the dominant motivation and the tool became a success, (although how to practically use some of the more obscure metrics it could generate remained a mystery to us all).

8.1.2 Limitations

Perhaps the biggest limitation of static analysis is its ability to find actual defects. Frequently, static analysis warns us of "suspicious" areas in our code that would need further investigation by the tester or developer before they decide whether a defect is indeed present. Despite the value of such warnings, care has to be exercised in deciding on which warnings to investigate so that valuable developer and tester time is not wasted. Tools help in this sense by allowing lower levels of warnings to be filtered out if desired.

Static analysis points us to potential defects.

Static analysis can become complex for all but relatively trivial pieces of code or design. Tool support is therefore essential. However, you will still need to understand what the tool's results are telling you, and this may require some expertise. The remainder of this chapter will help you in this task by outlining some of the principal static analysis techniques and describing the types of defect they find.

Tool Tip

8.1.3 Control Flow Analysis

Control flow analysis examines structure. The items that make up the structure of code typically include decision points (if-then-else) and loops. Depending on how these logical constructions are used, the code may become more complex or even contain defects. The term *control flow* comes from the understanding that there is a set of statements that are

Examples of control flow diagrams are in chapter 5, "Structure-Based Testing Techniques".

"in control" when being executed. Depending on the path taken from a decision, the flow of control changes.

We try to find the following types of defects with control flow analysis:

- Code that cannot be executed (sometimes called *dead code*) because of some incorrect logic
- Control flow that enters a loop but can never exit (*endless loops*)

Control flow highlights structural complexity. Control flow analysis also highlights areas of excessive complexity, which can help to focus our attention on areas more likely to contain defects. Please refer to [Beizer 95] for more details on control flow analysis.

Consider the following (buggy) piece of pseudocode, which should calculate a value for the variable "sum". Apart from not being especially well written (few comments, bad programming style, etc.), it contains two control flow defects. Can you spot them?

Figure 8–1
Example code

```
integer    sum, count, var1, subtotal1, subtotal2
integer    bonus = 10000

// get the absolute values of subtotal1 and '2
// they cannot take negative values
subtotal1 = abs(calculate_subtotal(1))
subtotal2 = abs(calculate_subtotal(2))

sum   = subtotal1 + subtotal2
count = subtotal1 / subtotal2

if (sum < count) then
        count = 0
endif

do while count >= 0

        sum = sum + bonus
end do

count = count -1

write (sum)
```

Remember, we're interested in the logical flow through the code. In figure 8-1, the control flow is determined by a single decision point and a single loop. Taking the decision point first, we should ask ourselves if the possibility exists for the decision never to be "true", such that the code within the if-endif block never executes. On close examination, variable "sum" can never be less than variable "count". The statement count = 0 can never be executed. We have a *dead code* control flow defect.

Stuck in a Loop?

Now consider the loop. Is it possible to enter the loop and, once inside, to exit the loop? The loop variable "count" can be 0 or more, so it is possible to enter the loop, but how can the loop be exited once entered? The loop variable "count" is never changed within the loop, so an *infinite loop* control flow defect exists. In continuous operation, the value of variable "sum" will eventually exceed the value that can be stored in an integer, which may cause some kind of exception to be raised and perhaps cause the loop to be exited. Either way, we have a clear control flow defect that needs to be corrected.

What We Don't Find with Dynamic Testing

Can defects like this be detected just as easily by executing the code using a dynamic testing technique? In our example, we would certainly have noticed the effect of the infinite loop since our tests would never have completed. We may have noted an error message or the system may even have crashed. The infinite loop itself would have been detected as part of the subsequent defect analysis, which would probably have used control flow analysis to localize the defect.

Defects involving dead code can be less easy to find dynamically, depending on the influence the nonexecuted code has on our expected test results. Using a coverage measurement tool during dynamic testing shows areas of the code not yet executed and can help identify sections of code that may be unreachable. Once again though, the investigation of these areas will probably involve using control flow analysis.

You may be wondering by now what the problem is with having dead code. After all, dead code is just that, dead. It doesn't do anything. There is some amount of overhead associated with having it there to be loaded when the code is executed, but that is probably not interesting unless your memory is severely constrained. The risk with dead code is the

Dead code is a maintenance risk.

maintenance risk. The next time a programmer looks at this code, he has to figure out what that code does before he makes changes. There is always the danger that insufficient analysis may lead him to make that code accessible as part of correcting a problem. So, while dead code itself isn't a risk while it's dead, it is a risk that it may later come to life or just take up space.

8.1.4 Data Flow Analysis

Data flow analysis focuses on the data variables in code. There are two principal questions to be answered here:

- Where are the variables defined (i.e., receive a value)?
- Where are they used?

As with control flow analysis, performing data flow analysis often detects anomalies that suggest that a defect may exist rather than identifying the actual defects themselves. The types of anomalies that data flow analysis can detect are as follows:

- Undefined variables (i.e., those that contain no value) that the program then tries to use
- Variables that are defined but become undefined or invalid before they can be used
- Variables that are redefined before their original values can be used

Anomalies where variables are defined but not used (i.e., the last two in the preceding list) must be detected as soon as possible since they are clear signs that the code is in some way incorrect. The technique used is to examine the paths between the definition and the use of the variables (usually referred to as *du-pairs* or *set-use pairs*). The following pseudocode example (again, not the best programming style, but sufficient for demonstration purposes) shows a module that defines several local variables and uses them to calculate a sales employee's personal bonus payment based on their achieved order entry, their personal target, and the company's profits.

Consider the set-use pairs for the (underlined) variables "CompanyBonus" and "LocalBonus". Both are initially set to 0 as a default value. If an order entry has been achieved by the employee the default value of "CompanyBonus" is reset to a value which reflects company profits. The variable is then used to calculate the "PersonalBonus". The set-use pair is complete and no data flow anomaly is present.

Figure 8–2
Example code.

```
Integer PersonalBonus (integer: Year, Personal-ID)
{
     Integer    LocalBonus = 0
     integer    BonusPoints = 0
     integer    CompanyBonus = 0
     Integer    OrderEntry = 0
     Integer    PersonalTarget = 0

     // fetch personal data from database
     OrderEntry     = GetOE(Personal-ID,Year)
     PersonalTarget = GetPT(Personal-ID,Year)
     LocalBonus     = GetLB(Personal-ID,Year)

     if (OrderEntry > 0) then
          BonusPoints = OrderEntry / PersonalTarget
          CompanyBonus = CompanyProfit(Year)/100
     endif

     if (BonusPoints > 0) then
          PersonalBonus = BonusPoints * CompanyBonus
     endif
}
```

Now consider variable "LocalBonus". Again, the default value is reset but a "use" does not take place. At best this anomaly may reduce the code's maintainability, but at worst this may be an indicator for an actual defect (What was the programmer intending to do with the variable?).

Judging defect severity usually needs further analysis

It will be apparent from this example that when examining set-use pairs we also have to consider control flow. We may even detect control flow anomalies while actually pursuing data flow analysis.

8.1.5 Compliance to Coding Standards

Applying coding standards can be an effective measure that can yield some of the following benefits:

- Ability to easily share code among different developers
- Easier code maintainability, including the ability to efficiently test the code
- More portable code
- More secure code

▨ Ability to practice constructive quality assurance, where the emphasis is on defect prevention rather than detection

▨ Generally less risk of coding errors (especially if the coding standards are part of a developer's Integrated Development Environment [IDE])

▨ The ability to improve over time by applying increasingly more stringent rule sets

Tool Tip Many organizations develop their own coding standards, although there are also industry standards available. By analyzing whether the coding standard adopted by our organization or project has been correctly applied to our code, we can find violations of those standards, and where required, standards compliance can be demonstrated.

Coding practice can be improved by adopting standards. Here is a sample of the kind of bad coding practice we can avoid by adopting coding standards and then performing static analysis on our code:

▨ Absence of comments, in particular before certain coding elements such as loops and decision points

▨ Excessively complex coding structure (levels of indentation)

▨ Poor programming style, which may be a source of defects (e.g., implicit type conversion)

▨ Programming language–specific issues, such as failing to release ("delete") main memory dynamically reserved (with "new") in C++

▨ Use of coding practices that may represent security vulnerabilities (e.g., unconstrained data entries)

Standards may also be applied to designs and architectures. These are subject to static testing in a way that's similar to the way code is, but the focus is on different issues:

▨ Use of standard software libraries instead of new development

▨ Guidelines for interacting with external systems (e.g., only via specific connectivity software [middleware] rather than via direct system-level calls)

Using Tools to Enforce Coding Standards

The tools used for performing static analysis and for generating code-specific metrics (see below) are usually directed at specific programming languages (e.g., C, C++, Java) and may also target particular aspects for analysis (e.g., security, websites).

Tools usually contain a predefined set of rules representing a particular coding standard and apply these against the code of your choice. This means you can perform static analysis of code with a minimum setup effort.

If you need to adapt or extend the rule set included with the tool, care should be taken to make sure the tool will allow this without major effort. Most of the leading tools include a user interface with which the required changes can be efficiently performed.

Some of the tools also have the ability to "learn" about false positives (also called false-fails) via an interface that lets you "teach" it about errors that it can disregard.

Tool Tip

8.1.6 Generating Code Metrics

Performing static analysis enables us to gather information that can contribute to testing in a number of ways. Let's take a look at some of these.

Not everything we can measure is actually useful.

Measuring Structural Complexity

Information about structural complexity helps identify areas of code that are at risk of having defects. If we are following a risk-based testing approach, these areas may be targeted for more detailed testing. Care must be exercised here, however, since other factors such as business value may be considered to be more significant to the stakeholders than complexity-related issues. One of the most widely used metrics for measuring structural complexity is the McCabe Cyclomatic Complexity, which is based on the number of independent paths through a piece of code (refer to section 5.4.7 for details of path testing).

Measuring Comment Frequency

Measurements of comment frequency and many other statically derived metrics may be useful indicators for judging the maintainability of code (refer to chapter 15, "Maintainability Testing").

Measuring Code Size

In general, measures of code size are among the least useful and yet most often used metrics about code. They become particularly meaningless where there is high reusability of code, as in object-oriented coding.

A Structured Approach to Using Metrics

A wide range of metrics may be generated from static analysis; some are generally applicable and some are specific to types of systems or particular programming paradigms.

A bewildering array of metrics at the press of a button

Because they are inexpensive to generate, the inexperienced technical test analyst may be tempted to have the tool generate a large number of metrics (i.e., just to see what we get). The cost comes in having to then understand and apply the sometimes bewildering array of metrics generated.

When using metrics, it is therefore advisable to use a structured approach based on specific objectives (e.g., reduced maintenance costs) and only generate the metrics that support those objectives (e.g., comment frequency). The Goal-Question-Metric (GQM) approach is a good example of an approach that supports this concept. As its name suggests, the first step is to ask the question, What do we want to achieve (goal)? Then we ask questions and make decisions on how this can be measured (question), and only then do we pick the metrics that provide these measures (metric). The GQM approach was first developed by V. Basili, G. Caldiera and D. Rombach in the 1990's. An example of using the GQM approach is given in [Burnstein 03].

8.1.7   Static Analysis of a Website

Tool Tip

Static analysis of websites is a specialized area covered by dedicated tools such as hyperlink tools. Since websites typically experience many (perhaps even daily) changes, these tools are used not only for testing purposes but also by those who maintain the sites (frequently referred to as *webmasters*) and by developers wishing to optimize particular attributes of the sites.

What types of defect do these tools find?

- Hyperlinks used on web pages that do not route the user to the intended website. This may be due to an incorrectly programmed hyperlink or an undesired redirection.
- Hyperlinks that do not link to a website at all (i.e., HTTP error 404).
- Specific content of web pages that is incorrect or not present.
- Excessive time required to display a web page (often caused by graphical content) or to perform a download.

Just as with the static analysis of code, the analysis of websites also allows you to gather information that may be useful to webmasters, developers, and testers. Here is a sample of the kind of information provided:

- The size of web pages (useful if display times are important, as with home pages or pages that are used frequently).
- The overall structure of the website (usually referred to as the *site map*). This can be used to analyze usability issues such as the ease with which a user can "navigate" a website and the overall "balance" of the site regarding the granularity of its structure. If a user needs too many "clicks" to obtain the information desired or if the site structure is too detailed in some places and too high level in others, the user experience will be poor and the user may abandon the site.

Note that tools (sometimes called *web spiders*) usually need to interact with the website and the Internet in order to find the defects and provide the previously mentioned information. In this sense, we are stretching the definition of "static" testing somewhat compared to the "pure" static testing (non-executing) of code discussed elsewhere in this chapter.

Tool Tip

8.1.8 Call Graphs

Analyzing the calling structure within a system design can be useful to the technical test analyst in two main ways:

- Maintainability can be improved by enabling better modularization of the design.
- Information can be obtained that highlights those modules in a program that interact strongly with other modules (i.e., call many other modules or themselves receive many calls). These modules represent the heavily used parts in the system that could become a bottleneck if efficiency is not adequate.

Considering a single software module, the information gathered is generally called *fan-in* (for calls received) and *fan-out* (for calls made). The term *fan* is used to represent the lines (calls) all focusing on the module, which results in a fan effect if drawn as a diagram.

In a similar way, call graphs provide a way of showing the interfaces of complete system architectures, which can also show internal module structure. (See figure 8-3. The original and other excellent examples can be found at [URL: Aisee]).

Call graphs can show the interfaces of complete system architectures.

When we're planning integration tests, call graphs help to identify which modules may be effectively integrated at the same time and assist in deciding on an appropriate integration strategy. We may, for example, decide that a bottom-up integration strategy is appropriate or perhaps top-down. Other possibilities, such as pair-wise and neighboring integration, are mentioned in [Jorgensen 02].

In general, call graphs help us see the "big picture" of our program's architecture. The figure shows modules (large rectangles) and the calls between them. For extra information, the internal structure of the modules is also shown, although a call graph does not always need this.

Figure 8–3

Example of a call graph

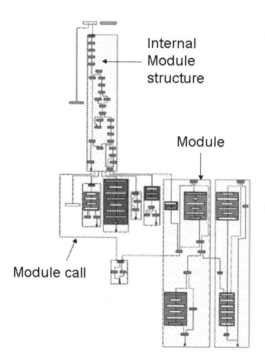

Once the integration sequence has been defined, a sequence of integration can be proposed that can be used when agreeing on the schedule of software deliveries with the development team. Parallel to this, call graphs also help developers and testers to quickly identify any simulations needed (e.g., stubs and drivers) and plan for their implementation.

Further benefit may be obtained from call graphs according to particular system requirements. Here are some examples:

- A real-time system may need to minimize the number of calls made in order to save the CPU cycles that the calling mechanism uses. Call graphs will help identify modules that would be candidates for merging.

- Call graphs can help identify good targets for test automation (mostly in conjunction with dynamic analysis).
- Call graphs may help identify good candidates for testing failure tolerance. These might be modules that, for example, handle communications between systems and should therefore be particularly robust at handling unexpected inputs.

8.2 Dynamic Analysis

Performing dynamic analysis requires that the software program is executed. As with static analysis, it is not likely that we would perform dynamic analysis without the support of tools. These tools provide information for the tester and developer and can detect the following principal types of defects:

- Memory leaks
- Resource leaks
- Pointer problems

Dynamic analysis is appropriate at any test level, but it is mostly applied at the lower levels of unit testing and integration testing. This is because the types of defects found are technical rather than functional in nature and can be more easily scheduled into the master test plan at these testing levels. By detecting and eliminating these problems at an early stage, the system tests also benefit from less disruption caused by leaking memory.

The types of defects found are technical rather than functional in nature.

8.2.1 Benefits

Generally speaking, the big advantage with dynamic analysis is its ability to find defects that would otherwise be very difficult (if not impossible) and expensive to find with other forms of testing.

By the very nature of the defects themselves, they often lead to failures that are hard to reproduce and may even remain unnoticed for long periods of time. These failures sometimes manifest themselves far away from the actual cause of the problem. Since the failures themselves can be critical in nature (e.g., crashes, system malfunctions, and data corruption), this can represent a major risk for reliable operations, especially where safety-critical systems are involved. An appreciation of the types of faults to be found with dynamic analysis is therefore essential for any technical test analyst (these will be discussed in sections 8.2.3, "Memory Leaks," and 8.2.4, "Problems with Pointers").

Tool-based dynamic analysis can be highly cost effective. This is an important factor in test planning when decisions about required tooling should be made. The tools are quite easy to install and use, and the cost of a license can often be recovered from finding just a handful of defects, especially if some of them would otherwise have reached production. Since the tools can also be run "in the background" while functional tests are performed, they represent a viable, low-cost option for frequent regression testing for dynamic analysis issues and for generally increasing levels of confidence in the software's quality. It's not uncommon to find dynamic analysis tools included in a developer's Integrated Development Environment (IDE).

As with static analysis tools, the information provided by a dynamic analysis tool includes graphic presentations (in this case at runtime) that can lead to a better understanding of both the system and the networks it uses. This information can be used to identify areas in the code that would benefit from improvements (e.g., performance) or that might need detailed testing. In some cases, this information can be used to supplement the results of static analysis (e.g., dynamic call graphs), as discussed in section 8.2.5.

8.2.2 Limitations

The benefits of dynamic analysis far outweigh the limitations. However, we need to be aware of a couple of points before performing the analysis.

The benefits of dynamic analysis far outweigh the limitations.

To obtain runtime information, the tools need to have a mechanism for extracting the data. This is often achieved by inserting instrumentation into the code, usually by linking the tool with your application's object code prior to performing the tests. This is an elegant way of enabling dynamic analysis, but it does mean that the code actually executing may be slower than your application would normally be. Generally this is not a problem, but if you are conducting specific performance tests or running timing-sensitive tests on a real-time system, it is highly advisable to check first on the influence your dynamic analysis tool has on system performance (the so-called probe effect).

Dynamic analysis tools are dependent upon the programming language used for your application's implementation. Since certain languages, such as C and C++, are more prone to the defects found by the tools, the cost-benefit relationship may be different when considering less-prone languages, such as Java. These factors need to be considered before purchasing the tool.

8.2.3 Memory Leaks

A programmer cannot always predict in advance of program execution just how much main memory (RAM) the program might need. It may be necessary, for example, to create a "person" object in our program for each record received in a file from an external human resources system. Under such situations, the programmer cannot predict how many "person" objects will need to be created and may be wasting RAM resources by reserving a static amount of RAM big enough to handle the maximum number anticipated (e.g., for 2,000 people). In such situations the developer often arranges for RAM to be reserved dynamically as needed (i.e., for each individual "person" object created) and then explicitly released when no longer needed (e.g., when cumulative statistics for particular categories of people have been calculated). This dynamic reservation and release of RAM provides for flexibility and efficient use of RAM resources, but it can also be the source of memory leaks. Such leaks occur when memory is dynamically reserved but, due to faulty programming, is not released when no longer needed.

Dynamic reservation of memory is a potential source of memory leaks.

Why is this a problem? Well, put quite simply, if a program's available RAM has leaked away in the manner described, it may fail or crash. On the way to this final situation, the program has to "make do" with ever-decreasing amounts of RAM, which may cause the program's execution to slow as it attempts to utilize other memory sources instead of RAM (e.g., hard disk).

Finding Those Leaks

Detecting memory leaks without a tool can be extremely difficult, especially if the amount of memory lost per leak is small and the amount of available RAM is high. The result may be a very gradual degeneration in system performance that progressively builds up over days or even weeks. During testing, our systems are often restarted, and these subtle effects may never get the chance to accumulate before the RAM is reinitialized. If the system delivered into production runs on a continuous basis, the negative effects of RAM will grow until, sooner or later, they become apparent. At this stage, restarting the system may carry considerable financial or safety-related penalties.

To effectively and efficiently detect memory leaks, a tool is indispensable. The tools are normally linked with the executable code of your program and continuously monitor the reservation and release of RAM

Tool Tip

during the course of functional tests. If a memory leak is detected, the tool produces a report that pinpoints the location in the code where this happens. Some tools can even do this for third-party products that your application uses (yes, they can have memory leak problems too).

Even though the discussion in this section has focused on leakages of RAM, it is worth mentioning that practically any limited resource used by a program may be subject to shortages and even failures resulting from incorrect programming. This may be the case, for example, for file handles, connection pools (e.g., for network connections), and semaphores used for program control.

> ### Lesson Learned: Use analysis tools from the outset
>
> In a C++ project I worked on, we encountered a typical memory leak problem where, after the application was used continuously for about three days, the memory loss resulted in poor performance and crashes. Although rebooting the system would fix the problem, this solution was hardly going to be acceptable for a safety-critical application running continuously. Something had to be done.
>
> Even though we were aware of there being a memory leak, it took a maddeningly long time to actually find its source. After several days, we bought a dynamic analysis tool, and within minutes, we had the problem in our sight. A third-party package of graphical objects we were using was leaking about 1KB of RAM each time a particular type of dialogue was opened and then closed. It seems the supplier of the third-party software was totally unaware of the problem and we were unfortunately forced to program our own workaround. We could have saved a lot of effort had we purchased the tool at the start of the project and used it regularly right from the outset of development.

8.2.4 Problems with Pointers

Taming those wild pointers

A pointer is an address in main memory (RAM) that refers to ("points" to) the storage location of instructions, data, and objects the program uses. A number of problems can arise (including system failures) when programming errors cause the pointers to be used in some incorrect way and cause certain rules governing correct memory usage to be violated.

(Pointers that result in these memory-usage problems are sometimes referred to as *wild pointers*).

Some of the typical rules concerning memory usage are illustrated in the diagram in figure 8-4.

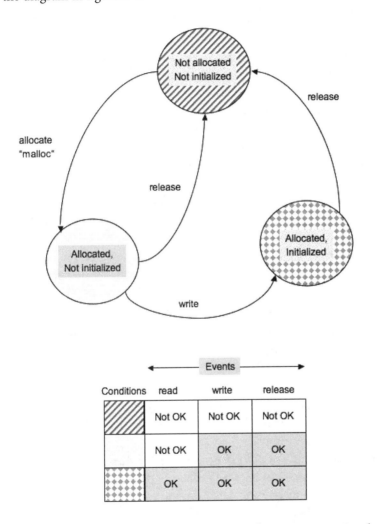

Figure 8–4

Memory states

The figure shows the states in which memory locations can exist, the possible transitions between the states, and the actions that can be correctly and incorrectly performed on memory when in a particular state. In the diagram, *malloc* stands for memory allocation and is the mechanism in the C programming language for dynamically obtaining memory.

In the tabular part of the diagram, a number of actions are shown that should be avoided (Not OK) and that a dynamic analysis tool will detect at runtime. In particular, the act of writing to memory that has not been allocated is of significance because this may result in areas of memory being overwritten with unwanted values. What happens then depends on the intended purpose of that section of memory:

- If the overwritten memory area was not being used, we've been lucky (this time) and the program continues to function as expected.
- If the overwritten memory area is critical for controlling the system (e.g., in an area reserved for the operating system), the system may well crash. If this occurs during testing, the failure will at least be highly visible and we'll be alerted to the presence of a problem.
- If the overwritten memory area is used to store data or objects used by the program, the program will probably keep running but most likely with some form of reduced capability. We may see an error message if an object can't be found, or we may now be using incorrect data. Again, if the effects of these problems are highly visible, we can take remedial action. However, if the effects are subtle (as could be the case with overwritten data), the problem could go unnoticed. We may be able to detect the slight discrepancy between actual and expected results in our functional testing, but there is no guarantee of this happening.

Often we see the symptoms but not the problem itself.

The points listed here reveal the seriousness of undetected pointer/memory defects and the difficulty of locating them, even if we are fortunate enough to notice them in testing. In fact, trying to detect the source of the problem without a tool may be a time-consuming process beset with difficulties. The failure conditions are inherently hard to reproduce and considerable effort may be used chasing down the symptoms of the problem but not the problem itself.

That pointer points at what??

The critical nature of pointer problems are further exemplified in the third case listed, where overwriting memory does not initially affect the program's functioning and the defects in the code do not at first result in actual failures. These are the time bombs in our code just waiting to explode. They may remain dormant and never surface as failures, they may suddenly pop up in testing, or (the nightmare scenario) they may cause our system to fail possibly years after it has been in productive use. This is because even the slightest change we make (e.g., a planned maintenance software upgrade) causes RAM usage patterns to be laid out differently. After a software change is implemented, the locations in RAM

being overwritten may now be highly significant and one of the other failure conditions mentioned earlier may apply. This can also occur when the
developer loads a debug version of the code to try to find a problem; it
moves. Dear reader, if your system is vulnerable to pointer problems and
the consequences if it fails are severe, you avoid doing dynamic analysis
with tools at your peril.

8.2.5 Analysis of Performance

As with tools used for static analysis, the tools available for dynamic analysis also provide a variety of useful information about the software under
test. This is generally in the form of runtime information, which may be
particularly useful in pinpointing performance bottlenecks.

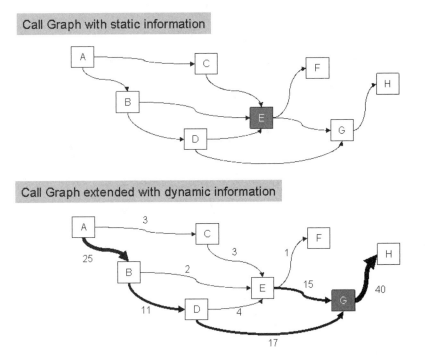

Figure 8–5
*Static and dynamic call
graphs compared*

Recalling the information provided by static analysis on call graphs
(which show the calling relationships between modules), it is possible to
extend that static information to include details of how many actual calls
took place between the modules while running the application. From this
presentation, the tester can identify modules where improvement to

*Static and dynamic analysis
complement each other.*

performance would have maximum benefit. Figure 8.5 shows a call graph
in both static and dynamic forms. The dynamic call graph adds the actual
number of calls made during test execution and scales the width of the
calling interface accordingly. Note that with only static information, we
may have identified module E as the principal bottleneck in this group of
modules, whereas with the additional dynamic information, we would
tend to also place module G in our testing focus.

8.3   Let's Be Practical

How can we apply analysis techniques to the Marathon application? Let's
consider first the system diagram.

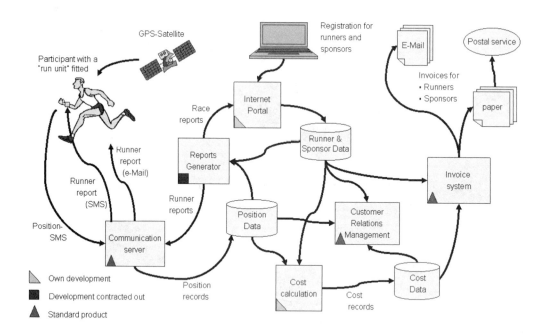

Figure 8–6

The Marathon system.

After an initial analysis of the Marathon system's requirements and specifications, we identified the following aspects that could influence our
approach to using static and dynamic analysis techniques.

- Parts of the system to be developed in-house will use the Java programming language. Java programming guidelines have been established by the development team.
- The communication server, which handles all in-coming SMS messages from the runners, reuses code from an existing development effort and is programmed in C.
- The reports generator, which has been contracted out for development, is known be implemented in C++. We do not have any access to the source code though.
- The communication server needs to handle the SMS messages sent by up to 100,000 runners at the rate of one SMS per minute per runner.

Given these aspects, we may choose to adopt the following approach. Note that technical test analysts may not be able to make the decisions themselves but must be able to advise the test manager and project leader on a suitable approach.

The technical test analyst gives good advice.

- Select a static analysis tool for the Java programming language and ensure that the developers are supported in applying the Java programming guidelines. Consider including this tool in the Integrated Development Environment (IDE).
- Select a dynamic analysis tool for the C programming language and use it to highlight areas where the communication server's performance could be optimized.
- Use the same dynamic analysis tool to regularly check for memory leaks and pointer problems in the C code.
- Request that the project leader negotiate with the suppliers of the reports generator software to ensure that dynamic analysis on the delivered software is performed and the results can be examined. If this risk-reduction measure is not possible, other measures must be considered to mitigate this product risk (e.g., change supplier, purchase own dynamic analysis tool for C++, perform own monitoring).

8.4 Learning Check

The following checklists will help you judge the knowledge you have gained from this chapter.

Terms

Control flow analysis, data flow analysis, dynamic analysis, false-fail, false positive, hyperlink, hyperlink tool, memory leak, pointer, static analysis, wild pointer

Technical Test Analyst

- Use control flow and data flow analysis to detect and interpret anomalies in code or procedures.
- Describe the use and benefits of call graphs for evaluating the quality of software architecture.
- Explain how the dynamic analysis of code can be performed and summarize the types of defect that can be found.
- Be able to explain the benefits and limitations of using static and dynamic analysis techniques.

9 Testing Software Characteristics

Knowing the various software characteristics and being able to develop specific tests for them is a central skill for any test analyst or technical test analyst. But which characteristics are there and which are applicable to which skill set?

In this short chapter, we set the scene for the chapters to come by discussing some fundamental issues relating to software quality characteristics (sometimes called attributes). In subsequent chapters, we will talk about them in some detail.

9.1 Software Quality Attributes

There is a set of principal attributes that are used to describe the quality of software applications or systems. These quality attributes can be assessed using the testing techniques discussed in the previous chapters. Application of the various techniques will vary depending on the ability of the tester, the knowledge of the domain, and the attribute being addressed.

The description of quality attributes in ISO 9126 is used as a basis for describing the attributes. The attributes are considered according to skill set (test analyst/ technical test analyst) rather than the functional/non-functional split proposed in ISO 9126.

9.2 Software Quality Attributes for the Test Analyst

The test analyst would be expected to address the following quality attributes:

- Accuracy
- Suitability

■ Interoperability
■ Functional security
■ Usability
■ Accessibility

Testing these software quality attributs is most commonly conducted at the integration and system level of testing by verifying that the prescribed functionality is available and usable. Chapters 10 and 11 discuss the testing of these attributes in detail.

9.3   Software Quality Attributes for the Technical Test Analyst

The technical test analyst would be expected to address the following quality attributes:

■ Efficiency
■ Technical security
■ Reliability
■ Maintainability
■ Portability

These attributes address "how" the system is delivering the functionality.

Testing of these software quality attributes is conducted primarily at the system test and operational acceptance test (OAT) when a fully integrated application is available. It can also be conducted at the component level for performance benchmarking and to determine resource utilization.

Chapters 12 thru 16 discuss the testing of these attributes in detail.

10 Functional Testing

Functional testing is the cornerstone of testing—it doesn't matter if the software is incredibly fast or amazingly reliable if it doesn't do what it's supposed to do.

In this chapter, we'll be looking at functional testing by considering the following quality attributes:

- *Accuracy*
- *Suitability*
- *Interoperability*
- *Functional security*

10.1 Introduction

Before we jump into the functional quality attributes and how to test them, we need to talk about functional testing in general.

Functional testing focuses on determining if the software does *what it's supposed to do*. The basis for determining what it should do is the information found in the requirements or specification documents, knowledge the tester has of the domain, or an implied need of the customer for the functionality. If we think of the Marathon application, we know our sponsors need to be able to register in our system so they can sponsor runners. This is an implied need. We don't know *how* this will look, we just know the functionality has to be supplied.

Does the software do what it is supposed to do?

The scope of functional testing changes based on the level of the development cycle. If we are doing unit testing (or reviewing unit tests), the concentration is on the functionality of the individual unit. In integration testing, we are doing functional testing across the various interfaces to see if the software was successfully integrated. If we are doing system testing, we are verifying that we have end-to-end functionality within the system. If we are doing functional testing on systems of systems, we are verifying end-to-end functionality across the systems.

Let's take a closer look at the quality attributes that the test analyst with domain expertise would be expected to verify.

10.2 Accuracy Testing

The validity of accuracy testing depends on the correctness and detail of the specifications.

Testing for accuracy requires knowing what the software *should* do. This information may be gleaned from the specifications or it may be based on the tester's knowledge of the domain. Accuracy testing requires that we know how the software should behave in any situation and that the response is correct. This could be as detailed as looking for an exact calculation or as general as making sure a coherent message is displayed when an error occurs.

Accuracy testing is conducted using a variety of the test techniques we have discussed. For example, boundary value analysis verifies that the functional accuracy doesn't break down on the edge conditions. Decision tables verify the accuracy of the implementation of the business rules.

Accuracy testing spans many areas of the software, not just calculations. Screen layouts, report timing, data accessibility, and correctness are all forms of accuracy testing. When performing accuracy testing, we are trying to be sure that the right data is presented at the right time to the right user

Accuracy testing is often one of the core focuses of the specifications and the resulting testing. Testing for accuracy is often considered testing for correctness. This means that we are verifying that the software does the right thing at the right time. Think about specifications you have seen. How much of the specification is devoted to indicating how the software should work and what the "correct" response should be? Usually, it's a good percentage. Certainly we would expect to see more of the specification devoted to accuracy than to suitability (which we will talk about in section 10.3). As a result, accuracy test cases are sometimes more straightforward to create given that we have a specification that contains the accuracy information.

But what if we don't have any "reasonable" people?

So how do we test accuracy if we don't have a specification, or if we have one that is distinctly lacking in information? This is where our domain expertise becomes vital to the success of the project. If the specifications don't tell us what the software should do, then it's up to us to figure out what it should do. We may make this determination based on our expertise, our knowledge of this and similar systems, our knowledge of legacy systems, and information we gather by interviewing the developers, analysts, customers, and technical support people, or if all else fails, we may make it based on what we think a "reasonable person would expect" it to do. When specifications don't exist or don't contain enough information, we can employ experience-based techniques such as exploratory testing, which we discussed in chapter 7.

Let's look at an example. If you are a customer at a bank ATM machine and you request to withdraw $100 dollars from your account, what do you expect to happen? Are you a reasonable person? (If you're not a reasonable person, you should probably skip this section since it won't make sense to you.) Assuming you are reasonable (since you're still reading), if you request to withdraw $100, you would expect to get $100. If you don't have $100 in your account, you would expect to get a message to that effect. If you have only $80 in your account, what would you expect? Should the machine tell you that you have only $80 and ask if you want to withdraw that? Should it just let you guess how much you have and let you keep trying lower amounts? Should it eat your card and tell you you're trying to commit a criminal act by withdrawing more money than you have? Hmmm. Now it's not so clear. OK, we can probably exclude the last one as unreasonable, but the first two are both plausible. Usually, as a test analyst, if the specification doesn't say otherwise, we accept the existing functionality as accurate if it seems reasonable to us.

10.3 Suitability Testing

Suitability testing is testing to verify if a set of functions is appropriate for their set of intended specified tasks. Since this testing is oriented toward the ability of the software to work as is needed by the end user, use cases and user scenarios are usually used to guide the testing.

The validity of the use cases will heavily influence the effectiveness of this testing. If the use cases really reflect how the user interacts with the system, then the testing will be able to verify suitability. If the use cases do not reflect what a real user does, the testing will do nothing toward verifying suitability. In the case where no use cases or user procedures are available, we have to rely on what we know about the intended and expected use of the software and test accordingly.

Suitability testing requires knowledge of the intended or expected use.

Lesson Learned (Suitability): Know your user

A good suitability tester knows the user and knows the user's environment. If that information is not known, it has to be ferreted out. I once had a project where I was testing software that was supposed to track licensing information. It basically tracked how many concurrent users were on the system at a time and also tracked all the individual users who had ever used the system. One of the problems with an early release was that it only tracked up to the number that the license allowed. If more people tried to access the system, it didn't log them because its table was full. Is this suitable to the purpose of the software? Not hardly! But you can see how a developer might have created the software assuming that he just needed to track the valid license users and hadn't considered there might be more people trying to access it. Clearly, there should have been a use case for this situation. There wasn't, but our experience told us there would be people trying to violate the license agreement, so we tested for it.

Good suitability testing is difficult to do because it tends to be somewhat ill defined. How do we determine if a set of functions is appropriate to accomplish the specified task? We've all used software that eventually gets the job done but is awkward or confusing to use, requires too many steps, doesn't work with other software we have installed, requires too much memory or disk space, or has some other factor that makes it unsuitable for the use we intend. Suitability varies with the environment, frequency of use, and the experience of the user. This is where the domain knowledge of the test analyst is so important. Suitability testing requires understanding the user's situation, environment, and skill level. If we don't have good use cases and user scenarios, we are completely dependent on our knowledge to know what to test. It is often a good idea to get the users involved in the testing, particularly if the user information is not available to the test team. Suitability testing is very closely aligned with usability testing and is often done at the same time using the same test basis.

10.4 Interoperability Testing

Interoperability testing is done to verify if the software under test will function correctly in all the intended target environments. This includes the hardware, software, middleware, operating systems, related applications, network configurations, and any other configuration or environmental variable that might affect the operation of the software.

Software is considered to have good interoperability characteristics if it can be integrated easily with other systems without requiring major changes—preferably only requiring that configuration parameters and properties files are changed. The numbers and types of changes required to work in different environments determines the degree of interoperability of a piece of software.

The degree of interoperability is frequently determined by the use of industry standards for communicating information like XML or the ability of the software to automatically reconfigure itself when it detects that it is running on a system that requires different parameters. The higher the degree of manual effort required to run on a different supported configuration, the lower the interoperability of the software. The most interoperable software automatically makes any changes required and runs without manual intervention across all supported configurations and environments. So-called Plug and Play devices are a good example of highly interoperable software.

Interoperable = plays nicely with others

Test Planning Issues

Interoperability testing is commonly used in any software that will run in an environment that must be shared with other software or in a variety of environments in which the configuration is controlled or known. Commercial off-the-shelf (COTS) software must run in a large number of environments with various configuration settings, and each of those must be tested. Systems of systems that require many interfacing components may also span multiple environments and provide data transfer between disparate systems.

Because of the integration nature of interoperability testing, we often see it performed at the system integration level of testing. Interoperability testing is not something that should be left too late though. If a problem is found with a particular configuration, it could result in significant, even architectural, changes to the software—and you sure don't want those arriving late in the testing schedule! Performance problems are another area of concern. Performance issues are sometimes exhibited on some configurations and not on others. Be sure the interoperability and performance/stress/load testing are planned to be complementary, otherwise you risk expending extra effort doing both at separate times and under separate test levels.

Effective interoperability testing requires effective planning of the test lab, equipment, and configurations. Testing of this nature is highly dependent on the environment, and any error in configuration can invalidate a significant amount of testing. As such, it is important to keep your configuration and environmental variables up-to-date. When test cases are executed, they must record exactly which environment was used.

Specified Combinations

Because we are dealing with combinations of configuration elements, we have to consider the possible combinations that are likely to occur and therefore must be tested. Less likely combinations may be considered to be lower in risk (although that's not necessarily true). Because the number of combinations can quickly explode to an unmanageable number, the all-pairs testing technique is perfectly suited to doing interoperability testing. In fact, the example we used to explain all-pairs testing was taken from interoperability testing.

When interoperability test cases are specified, they must clearly indicate the environmental conditions required. Often a matrix is created showing all the environments to be tested and the test cases to be run against those environments. Remember, we spoke in section 4.2.5, "Orthogonal Arrays and All-Pairs Tables", about specifying an input parameter model (IPM) to represent all the parameters (like browsers, operating systems, etc.) and the values they can take. When using the all-pairs technique for interoperability testing, we create the IPM first, then use all-pairs to determine which configuration combinations should be tested. This provides an abbreviated matrix that can then be used for test case mapping.

Frequency of use is not the only determining factor for picking the combinations to test. It is usually the case that some environments are more common than others. It is also sometimes the case that some environments are considered to be more likely to fail than others. Generally, the more common environments should be given the higher priority in testing (assuming we don't have time to test every possible environment), but the environments that are likely to fail must also be considered if a significant amount of the user base will be in that environment. By significant, we don't mean just quantity; it can also mean that it's only one user but it's your most valuable user. I worked in a company where we had "reference accounts." These were the people who agreed to let us use their name in our literature. They also agreed that they would talk to prospects that we sent to them (and would presumably say nice things about us). While some of these customers were not our biggest accounts and were not necessarily the biggest purchasers of our product, they were critically important to the success of the business. These were clearly "significant" accounts in terms of the business.

It is wise to keep an IPM and make it a part of any risk analysis you do. Each possible configuration should be rated to determine that it's important to testing. Two rating values should be used: How much does it matter to the business? and How likely is it to fail? This lets you consider both the environments that are commonly used (or used by significant customers) as well as the environments that frighten everyone. By creating a matrix like this that also rates each environment, you know what equipment you need in your lab and how it should be configured. Remember, you can vary the environments throughout testing—you will probably have to

> ### Lesson Learned: The interoperability matrix won't do the planning for you
>
> Since we know that interoperability issues are unavoidable unless our software runs only in a fully controlled and proprietary environment, we must make the effort to quantify those environments and select a good sample set of tests that will be run on each environment deemed worthy of risk mitigation. Remember though, just making the matrix isn't good enough. We also have to get the equipment and software, know how to configure it, and be sure our lab will support it.
>
> I once talked to a group of very intelligent software developers about the interoperability testing they were doing. They proudly produced their matrix (which wasn't called the matrix of death!) and noted which configurations were always tested, which were occasionally tested, and which were left up to the field to test. I was impressed. I asked them how they had determined which ones they

Why do you test that combination?

were required to test and they explained to me that they tested the ones for which they happened to have the right configuration in the lab. I was less impressed. So I asked them how they had determined which configurations to support in the lab. They told me that they used equipment that was available or had been returned from customers. Uh-oh. I asked if they felt that setup reflected the most common configurations among their customers. They looked puzzled. They looked at each other. They looked back at me. Apparently no one knew the answer. Worse, no one had thought to ask the question.

unless you have a lot of time allocated to testing—but you have to keep track of what you tested in which environments.

Using this risk-based information is invaluable if we need to collapse the number of all-pairs combinations generated for our IPM or when assessing the list of all-pairs to add special configurations and weed out low-risk ones.

Once the configurations to be tested have been determined, some organizations use a technique called *shot gunning* to distribute their test cases across the different configurations (as in the way a shotgun distributes the "shot" when it is fired). You can also select a set of example test cases, usually those that provide end-to-end functionality, and run those against each environment that is to be tested. This takes more time but certainly provides a more organized approach and more measurable coverage.

Interoperability Tools and Automation

Tool Tip   A good test management system should provide a way to easily track the environment configuration used for the execution of a test case and for recording this information in any incident reports issued. The tester should be able to select the configuration from a drop-down list of possible configurations. This information should later be reportable to allow the test manager to determine the test coverage across the various supported configurations. Without tool support, tracking testing against configurations is difficult and often requires building a separate database. Be sure your tools provide the support you need for the types of testing you must complete.

Test execution automation is often a problem in a multiconfiguration environment. If you can insulate your automation from the environment, you can realize tremendous time savings in the interoperability testing. For example, some test execution automation tools will allow you to define configuration items such as the type of browser as variables within the scripts. If the automation is sensitive to the environments and has to be changed for each one, the effort you spend creating and maintaining the automation may be greater than the gains you would realize from having it. As with all automation projects, careful analysis is needed to determine if you will see a positive return on investment from your automation efforts.

Tool Tip

When environments include pieces of hardware, it is sometimes possible to use software to emulate the hardware, thus reducing the need for the actual equipment to be available (and working) during testing. This is particularly useful when there is a problem with equipment availability. Simulators and emulators are discussed in more depth in section 18.3.3. The important thing to remember when testing with emulators is that, in the end, you will still need to run at least a subset of the tests against the real equipment to discover timing issues and problems where the emulator might not exactly match the real hardware.

Life Cycle Issues with Configuration Support

Rarely do we reduce the number of configurations we support. In every job I've ever worked in, the number of supported configurations only

Experience Report: "The matrix of death"

I worked with one company whose employees fondly called their configuration list "the matrix of death." We don't want to grow to fear that the grim reaper will visit us for forgetting a test environment, but we do need to track and be aware of environments that are higher risk. We also need to be able to quantify the testing effort across the environments. That way, when the happy sales guy comes bounding into your office and tells you he just sold a huge contract that will run only on the single most bizarre configuration ever conceived, you will know how much time and effort it will cost to test it. Alternatively, you could just lock the sales guys out of your office, but I've found they somehow manage to sneak in that bizarre configuration anyway.

Just because it's weird doesn't mean we can avoid testing it.

increased over time. So, what might be a manageable manual job in the beginning is likely to grow out of hand as the product becomes more successful. Unless you have the power to drive the market, or the comfort of being able to turn down business that uses a weird configuration, you can bet your list will only continue to grow.

> **Lesson Learned (interoperability): Know what configurations really matter**
>
> If you can't quantify the interoperability testing you need to do, it's time to talk to your field support and technical support people, to marketing and sales (I know, I try to avoid that too) and anyone else who knows what's out there and what matters. Those are the configurations upon which you should focus your efforts. And remember, the predominant configurations change over time. Interoperability testing therefore needs to be a part of any maintenance testing strategy (see chapter 15). The cool environments of a year ago are probably not the same as the ones used today and today's won't be used tomorrow. Think of it as job security! You'll never run out of stuff to test.

Always Challenging

Interoperability is one of the most challenging areas of testing. You need a good lab configuration, strong system administration support, a good awareness of what is likely to be affected by an altered configuration, and an inquisitive test team. Only then will you be able to adequately test, find defects, identify problem configurations, document your findings, and eventually resolve any issues that arise from the various supported configurations.

10.5 Functional Security Testing

Security testing can be divided into functional security testing and technical security testing. Functional security looks at making sure access to data and functionality is granted to those with the correct rights and denied to those without those rights (a form of penetration testing). This can be performed via the user interface by test analysts without special technical

> **Lesson Learned: Question the security**
>
> As a test analyst, one of the most important contributions you can make to the functional security of a product is to ask the security questions during the requirements reviews. Security that is implemented into the software will almost always work better and more efficiently than that added as an afterthought. Security requirements can cause architectural, performance, and flow changes within a product. We don't want these to occur after the software has been implemented.

skills. Functional security requirements are usually stated in the specifications for the software. This information is used as the basis for the development of test cases by the test analyst.

Technical security is discussed in chapter 13 and deals with identifying security vulnerabilities using skills generally available to only the technical test analyst. If you can hack into a system, the system has a technical security risk. If you log on to an application as a normal user and discover you have administrator rights, the system has a functional security risk.

The security scheme of the software can be pervasive throughout the system. As such, security testing requires a good understanding of the software being tested in order to determine all access points that should be tested. Since technical security testing concentrates on checking for the access points that shouldn't be there at all, functional security testing can concentrate on the authorized access points.

Testing for who can do what

Security testing has two different focuses. The first is to see if authorized users are able to get to the functionality and data to which they are entitled. The second is to see if unauthorized users are prevented access. Easy, right? Maybe. It depends on how complex the software is and how many access points there are. Let's look at an example.

Let's say we are creating software that does order tracking for food supplies for restaurants. To make it interesting, we'll make this an online application that restaurant owners can log into and enter their order. They can also arrange payment through this online interface. (Software design is so much easier when it's theoretical and you don't have to worry about those pesky customers!) From this example, what conclusions can we draw about the security testing we need to do?

But, I didn't order all those watermelons!

It seems obvious that we should have security around the payment information. In fact, it makes sense that the restaurant owner will need to have an account and will have to log into that account with a name/password combination. That will help to protect their account information. That makes sense. Now, what about access to information? Should we allow one restaurant owner to order for more than one restaurant? Certainly there could be restaurant chains that would find it more efficient to order all at once—so we'll need a capability for one account to be tied to multiple delivery addresses. Do we need to make sure those delivery addresses are valid? We certainly do if we are going to allow orders to be made COD (Cash on Delivery). Think how much fun restaurant owners would have sending a giant load of watermelons to their chief rival and making it COD. So, perhaps we need a way to validate the addresses that are entered for delivery. Is this a security test? Yes, because without it we would be allowing an account to order for another account, which would be a bad thing.

What about viewing an order? Do we need to add some sort of protection so that owners can view only their own orders? After all, who cares how many loaves of bread restaurant A is using? Maybe no one. But restaurant B might care a lot if restaurant A is ordering prime rib for a special dinner event. So, we need to be sure this data is protected as well. That means that one account can only see the order information for which they are responsible and no others.

This is a relatively simple application, but you can see the security concerns. Ideally, all of these should be clearly stated in the requirements. But don't count on it. Security issues are frequently not addressed, or not sufficiently addressed, in the requirements documents. The test analysts must use their experience and knowledge to determine what should be tested. Because security issues are frequently missed in requirements documents, it is important that the test analysts and technical test analysts be invited to the requirements review meetings and that they ask questions regarding security, whether it be functional or technical in nature. Who is allowed access to what data and what functionality? Do users have the ability to delegate their authority to someone else—for example when they go on vacation? Does someone have to approve access before it is granted? Just asking these simple questions in a requirements review meeting will go a long way toward ferreting out the security requirements. In section 13.3.1, "Typical Security Threats", you will find a whole list of potential security threats that you can raise at these meetings. It's much better to discuss these now than to require a redesign later.

Understanding the security scheme or policy of the software under test is critical to the development of the test environments. We have to be able to create the various circumstances that will test the functional security, which means we need to create users with various levels of access rights. Security testing is one aspect that should be covered in the test plan to ensure that adequate planning and preparation is allocated to the testing (more details on planning security tests can be found in section 13.3).

10.6 Let's Be Practical

Accuracy of the Marathon Application

Does accuracy matter in the Marathon application? As you may have noticed, we don't have the most detailed specifications. In fact, they are a bit vague in some areas. For example, what degree of detail do we need for the time reporting? Does it need to go to hundredths of seconds? Thousandths? I'm not a marathon runner myself, but I do know marathon runners and I've certainly watched marathons on television. So, as a tester, I'm going to assume that time reporting should be to the thousandths of a second. Now, I'm going to write my test cases based on that assumption and I'm going to write defect reports based on that assumption. If I get the software and the time reporting is only to the hundredths of a second, then I have to make a choice. Should I write up a defect report? It may get rejected, but it will open up the discussion and provide a documentation trail. Alternatively, it might be more efficient to contact the system designers or the developer and clarify their expectations. When making this choice, we need to determine if we might later need to reference who made the decision and what it was. When in doubt, write it up. For more information about documenting defects, see chapter 19.

Suitability Testing of the Marathon Application

Do we need to do suitability testing for Marathon? Yes. In fact, we always need to do suitability testing, whether it is specified or not. The good news is, we almost always do it as experienced test analysts. We may not even be aware that we are doing it. If you stop and think about the testing you do, you may be surprised at how often your tests include suitability aspects?

We should always do suitability testing—and we do!

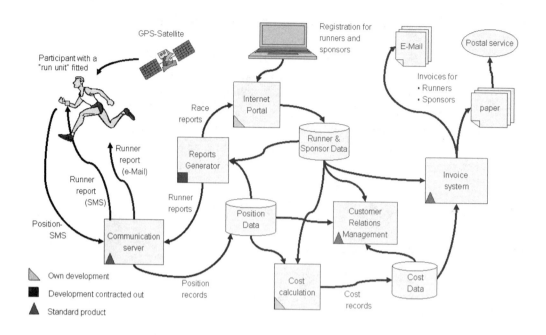

Figure 10–1

The Marathon system

Let's look at our intrepid runner in the system diagram in Figure 10-1. What kinds of suitability tests might present themselves here?

First we need to think about the runner's interaction with the system. The runner interacts when he registers. He also interacts as he is running and receiving his current status information. The runner will also interact with the system when he has finished the race so he can access his statistics and send screen shots of his accomplishments to those he is trying to impress. He might have other interactions too. He might want to log in and see if he has any sponsors. He might want to send screen shots of his race information to his sponsors. He might want to view statistics from other races.

If we think about doing the suitability testing for the runner's registration interaction, that's fairly straightforward. He would need to be able to create an account with minimal steps. We would expect him to be able to access the system via a common browser from a PC. We would not expect our runner to be a computer science major (he could be, but we don't know that), so the interface should be straightforward and easy. We would expect to see some facility for the runner to retrieve his password if he forgets it. We would not expect the user to have to load any new software on his PC to be able to access our system. Ideally, we would have use cases that would document these transactions, but we might not. That doesn't mean we can avoid doing this testing. An application that fails suitability testing will not do what the user needs it to do in a way that is acceptable. This is a critical aspect of validation testing to ensure that our product will be successful.

Interoperability Testing of the Marathon Application

Almost every project needs interoperability testing. If we were to take the simplest interoperability testing problem with Marathon, we would look at the sponsor registration. How many browsers will we support? If we are using a highly portable language like Java, we should remove a number of possible interoperability issues. But, we're not safe. Internet Explorer (IE), Netscape, Opera, and Firefox, all common browsers, work differently. We may see that frames shown on the window look fine in IE but are distorted in Netscape. We may find that certain controls work great on Firefox but refuse to work with Opera. The back button may work fine with Netscape but fail with Firefox. Ah yes, the combinations are seemingly endless. And this is just looking at a relatively portable set of browser software.

Interoperability issues, or potential issues, are everywhere. In Marathon, we are outsourcing the development of some of the components. I hope we clearly specified the languages and operating systems to be used or we may have some communication surprises when we get to the system integration phase (or perhaps even the component integration phase). I've worked on several projects where the outsource specifications allowed the vendor to pick the platform, programming language, database, reports generator, and whatever else they needed. As soon as it came time to integrate, the "glueware" required to get these components to work together was bigger than the rest of the system (and very error prone).

Functional Security Testing of the Marathon Application

Do we need functional security testing for Marathon? What leaps out at you from reading the requirements (see section 2.2)? How about testing to make sure only the sponsor account can enter and change the sponsor amounts? And not just any sponsor account, but the sponsor account's own transactions only. We wouldn't want sponsor A to be able to log in and alter sponsor B's allocations. We certainly wouldn't want runner C to be able to log in and alter any of the sponsor data. So we would need to test for all these combinations.

Who wrote those Marathon requirements??

What about the runner information? Would we want runner A to be able to access runner B's information? That's a tougher question. I know if I were in the marathon, I certainly wouldn't want anyone to be able to view my dismal times! But that's my opinion. It seems likely that runners would want to know how they did compared to others. Maybe we need to make the names anonymous. Now we need to check the requirements. Who should have access to the data of others? Race organizers should certainly be able to view everyone's statistics. Sponsors should be able to view the statistics of their sponsored runners, presumably. An individual runner, though, might not be given access to other runners' statistics—only the requirements can tell us what should happen in this case. Do they? Oh no! They don't clearly state who should access the data. All we know from the requirements is that the data is available.

Now is time for the test of reasonableness. It seems that a valid argument could be made either way. Perhaps we have a legacy system we can check. Perhaps there are competitors' products that we can base our expectations on and that can serve as a test oracle. Barring those options, we will probably have to go back to the requirements people and find out what it should do. Obviously this is an issue that should have been resolved in the requirements review when we asked our well-informed security questions.

One of the problems with a missed security requirement is that it may not be easy to implement later. If our Marathon application was implemented with the assumption that all runner information would be available to everyone and now we get the requirement that the data must be anonymized, more development and testing work is required. Now the

Exercise: Functional security

List the scenarios you would test to test the functional security of Marathon. What access would you expect the sponsors to have and not have? Runners? Observers? Who should be able to change data? Run reports? Access information about others?

software needs to determine who is logged on and anonymize everyone else's data prior to display. That may generate a significant load on the system when these reports are generated. And when will most of the reports be run? Right after the race concludes. This is a potential for a huge load on the server. Now we see a security problem that leads to a performance/load problem.

10.7 Learning Check

The following checklists will help you judge the knowledge you have gained from this chapter.

Terms

accuracy testing, interoperability testing, security testing, suitability testing, quality attributes

Test Analyst

▪ Explain by examples what testing techniques are appropriate to test for accuracy, suitability, interoperability, and functional security characteristics.

Technical Test Analyst

▪ Identify test techniques that are appropriate for testing accuracy, suitability, interoperability, and functional security and where they should be applied in the life cycle.

11 Usability and Accessibility Testing

As software becomes more pervasive in everyone's lives, usability testing becomes more and more important. Our users can be almost anyone, ranging from children to IT experts, from retired people to people with disabilities.

The wider the usage base of the software, the more critical are usability and accessibility testing. These two types of testing are sometimes considered together based on the argument that software that is accessible to everyone will also be easier to use.

11.1 Usability Testing

Usability testing measures the suitability of the software to meet the needs of its users.

Usability testing covers a large range of areas and is designed to measure the effectiveness, efficiency, and satisfaction that will be recognized by the user when using the software.

11.2 Effectiveness

Effectiveness testing looks at the ability of the software to accurately and completely assist the user in achieving specified goals within specified contexts of use. To determine effectiveness, we must have a clear understanding of what the user will be trying to accomplish (goals) and how he will be doing it and in what environment (context).

11.2.1 Efficiency

Efficiency testing looks at how much effort and resources are required to achieve a goal. Effort can be measured in terms of time, keystrokes, think time, and so forth.

While the actual measure of efficiency is a separate testing function under the software quality characteristics (see chapter 12), usability testing looks for problems such as the system locking out all other transactions while one is processing, which would significantly reduce the user's efficiency when using the system.

11.2.2 Satisfaction

We love our software. We just hate the way it works.

Satisfaction testing determines the software's ability to satisfy the user in a particular context of use. Satisfied users are likely to use the software again. Frustrated users are likely to throw things at the monitor and avoid the troublesome software.

Experience Report: It's only an extra keystroke

I have experienced some amazing usability defects in my time. One of the most embarrassing (and show-stopping) defects was one that we had identified in testing and horribly underclassified in priority. One part of our application was used for data entry. Our software allowed the user to find a particular record and add descriptive and classification information for it. Straightforward, right? It seemed that way to us. We tested the application thoroughly, concentrating on the more complex database transactions that were triggered by the user's input. The software was working well at the time we shipped it.

So what's the problem? The user interface for the data entry part of the application was highly customizable. You could rename fields, define the length and type of fields, set rules on the fields, and configure a variety of other cool data-entry-like functionality. One of the features you could set was to make a field "auto-advance", which meant that when it was filled, the cursor would automatically advance to the next field. This didn't work correctly (OK, it didn't work at all). So you could fill up a field, but the cursor would just sit there at the end until you hit Enter or tabbed to the next field. So what?

Well, it turns out that if you are a data entry person and you're used to processing thousands of records a day, you count on some of the fields automatically advancing. In fact, if you are a data entry person, you don't look at the screen at all (unlike we testers who used the mouse to move between fields). It turns out that when the auto-advance doesn'twork and you're not looking at the screen, you end up typing information in all the wrong fields. Not a good thing. This defect came screaming back to us as a priority 1 problem. We had found it but had marked it as an annoyance. Rather a significant misclassification, in retrospect. This is a perfect example of what happens when you don't know your user. We found the defect, but we had no understanding of the impact the problem would have on a real user.

In addition to looking at the effectiveness, efficiency, and satisfaction delivered by the software, usability testing measures the attributes of understandability, learnability, operability, and attractiveness. When testing for understandability, we are looking at the parts of the software that assist the user in recognizing and being able to apply the logical concept of the software. Learnability is determined by the amount of effort required by the user to learn the application. Operability is determined based on the user's ability to conduct his mission effectively and efficiently. Attractiveness is a subjective measure of the capability of the software to be liked by the user.

11.3 Accessibility Testing

Accessibility testing is done to determine the accessibility of the software to those with particular requirements or restrictions in its use. This includes those with disabilities.

With accessibility testing, we must consider the local, national, and industry-specific standards and guidelines. There are Web Content Accessibility guidelines that cover the accessibility standards for web software. There are also legislative requirements that may need to be considered, such as the Disability Discrimination Acts (UK, Australia) and the Americans with Disabilities Act (ADA) as well as section 508 in the United States. These guidelines and requirements can be used to direct the testing that must be done to ensure that the software meets the accessibility requirements of an organization as well as the user base.

Accessibility testing, in an informal environment, is often combined with usability testing. In a formal environment where we must comply with regulations, accessibility testing is often a specialty requiring specific and ongoing training. A good understanding of the accessibility requirements of the software is just as important as understanding the usability requirements—in order for the software to be usable, it must first be accessible. The information in this chapter applies to accessibility as well as usability.

11.4 Test Process for Usability and Accessibility Testing

11.4.1 Planning Issues

Testing strategies for usability can focus on finding and removing actual usability defects (sometimes referred to as formative evaluation) or on testing against the usability requirements (sometimes referred to as summative evaluation).

Part of planning testing is ensuring that the right people with the right skills are available when needed. Usability testing requires expertise or knowledge in sociology, psychology, standards conformance, and ergonomics. The test analysts must have this knowledge as well as the skills required to conduct the other areas of testing. Not everyone must be an expert in each area, but among the team, there must be a solid set of skills.

Being a user doesn't make you an expert usability tester.

One note of clarification: Usability testing is sometimes considered a specialty area. If this is the case, the test analysts on the functional test team are not required to be usability experts, but this doesn't mean they shouldn't document defects they see. Usability is a quality attribute and everyone's responsibility. If software is hard to use for some testers, it's likely to be hard for the users to use as well. Issues like this should be documented. Perhaps these issues will first be reviewed by the usability team (if you have one), but this does not mean that usability is solely the responsibility of the usability team.

One other aspect of planning that should be considered for usability testing: We need to be sure we are testing in an environment that closely resembles the user's environment. This is sometimes done by setting up a usability lab that simulates the user environment and allows real users to use the software while developers and testers observe what they do. Some usability testing labs supply the users with scripts or general guidelines regarding what they are expected to accomplish. Some labs record keystrokes and think time for each user to determine where the interface is confusing or inefficient. Some labs have two-way mirrors or cameras that allow the developers to see the users interact with the system and to observe the facial expressions of the users as they work with the software. Microphones are sometimes used to record comments users make about the interface. These voice recordings capture both positive and negative expressions (sometimes very negative!) as well as discussion and questions among the users.

> **Lesson Learned: Test for the real users**
>
> One suggestion I have for anyone who ever does usability testing is to go to a real usability test lab and watch a test. It's fascinating. When you watch the real user, without assistance, try to figure out your application, you see all the assumptions you have made about the knowledge the user has. Before you sign up to be the resident usability expert, be sure you have a good understanding of your user and usability testing. It seems easy, but it's surprisingly difficult to be good at it.

11.4.2 Test Design

Designing for the User

Test cases must be specifically designed to test for understandability, learnability, operability, and attractiveness. It's difficult for a test analyst to step back and consider the software from the user's standpoint. Often, the tester is so familiar with the software and the domain that they forget it will be new to the user and so must be intuitive, learnable, and welcoming for that user. By creating test cases or even charters for exploratory testing, the tester is reminded to look for the specific usability factors.

Good usability and accessibility testing requires approaching the product from several different angles. We need to inspect or review the requirements documents, mockups, flow diagrams, and use cases, searching for possible usability and accessibility issues. Any documentation that is prepared for the project should be reviewed to determine both usability issues and usability test scenarios. As with any other type of defect, it is faster, easier, and less expensive to detect it before it is implemented in code. Usability defects are one of the most important types of defects to detect in the design phases. Usability can affect many aspects of the software, including the overall design and architecture. Usability concerns may affect the tools used to implement the product as well as the supported platforms. We certainly don't want to find problems in these areas after implementation is completed.

Many Considerations for Usability Tests

Usability testing also includes performing the actual verification (Did we build the product right?) and validation (Did we build the right product?). This is usually done using test scenarios that are developed for usability testing. They may be adapted from existing functional test cases or developed solely for usability attributes like learnability, operability, or attractiveness.

Test scenarios should also be developed to test syntax (the structure or grammar of the interface) and the semantics (reasonable and meaningful messages and output). When testing for syntax, we are looking to see what can be entered into input fields—how the interface is structured, how the user is prompted. When testing for semantics, we are looking to see if the messages given to the user will make sense to that user. We've all seen messages that are written in "programmer-ese" that are unintelligible to the average user but perfectly clear to the programmer.

These test scenarios can be created via the various specification-based techniques such as state diagrams, decision tables, and equivalence partitions. Use cases are, of course, extremely useful in designing usability test cases provided the cases accurately reflect what the user will actually do. Good use cases that specify the messages a user should receive lend themselves to inspection testing as well as becoming the basis for usability test cases.

Don't Forget Information Transfer

When designing tests for usability, we need to consider all the interactions between the software and the user. This includes instructions, messages, navigational aids, screen text, beeps, and any other form of interaction. If representative users are doing some of the usability testing, don't forget to allow time for giving the users instructions, running the tests, and conducting the posttest interviews to gather feedback. Time boxes may need to be established and you may need clarification and guidelines for note-taking or session-logging requirements. This is also a critical time to consider accessibility. If your software should work for the hearing impaired, then beeps may not be an appropriate form of communicating with the user.

When conducting usability testing with an external user, it's important to have everything set up and clear instructions available. The user will be new to the system only once; you want to gather as much information as possible from that first exposure.

Even computer-haters sometimes have to use them.

Experience Report: Usability testers on the front line

In one of my early projects as a systems analyst, I was designing a system for use by clerical people who didn't want the system. They felt that the introduction of the system threatened their jobs. Annoying though they were, this was an excellent lesson in creating a clear and clean user interface. One of the objections these people had to using the system was that it would require more knowledge and training and therefore they should be paid more. Our job was to implement a system that was so simple to use that training would be limited to how to turn on the PC. Quite a challenge—but a very interesting view into the non–computer-literate world. Anyone who has been on the leading edge of introducing a computerized system into a formerly manual environment knows that the user interface immediately comes under scrutiny by the reluctant users. As more and more people use computers, this is becoming less of a challenge, but always be prepared to find yourself leading an effort to automate a formerly manual process with resistant users.

11.4.3 Test Execution

Inspecting and Reviewing

Usability inspections and reviews are sometimes conducted by the test team, but they are generally more effective if the user (or a representative of the user) is present as well. I've worked with some truly excellent analysts over the years. In fact, I started my software career as a systems analyst, but even the best analyst won't think of everything the user will do.

Those users are full of surprises!

The analyst knows too much to act like a novice user. So do you, as a tester. So don't think you are going to be a good, representative user. Now we have a dilemma. We know the software too well to be a representative user. The user doesn't know software documentation well enough to be a good inspector. We need to work together to get the best expertise—particularly for the inspection functions.

We can put more structure around the inspection of the user interface design by conducting a heuristic evaluation. This is done by a small set of people conducting an evaluation based on a set of heuristics that are commonly recognized usability principles. The more we can involve the user in this process, the better the design will become. This is a method that is often used as part of an iterative development process where prototypes may be created and demonstrated.

It has to work for the people who have to use it.

> ### Lesson Learned: Plan up front for usable and accessible software
>
> As we've seen, good usability testing requires an overall testing approach that starts with documentation and finishes with the end product in the real user's hands. Good accessibility testing requires a strong knowledge of the accessibility requirements, regulations, and standards. Approval of the product may require passing accessibility audits and providing the appropriate testing documentation. Good planning, analysis, execution, and reporting are critical in the usability and accessibility testing world.

Doing the "Real" Testing

Performing usability tests by interacting with the software could be a simple task if we intend to just run through predefined tests. We may even combine this with other forms of functional testing, especially if usability issues are considered low risk. On the other hand, designing and executing usability tests can be a complex and highly skilled activity. We may need to take video recordings of real users working with the software, or we may need to record the number of keystrokes needed to perform tasks to get an accurate assessment of the "real" usability.

11.4.4 Reporting

In addition to actually executing the usability test cases we have designed and documenting the results as we would with any testing, usability testing frequently involves surveys and questionnaires for real users who also either execute predefined scenarios or are allowed to do some exploratory testing. The surveys are used to gather observations from the users in a usability lab environment.

There are standardized publicly available usability surveys such as Software Usability Measurement Inventory (SUMI) and Website Analysis and MeasureMent Inventory (WAMMI). By using these industry standard surveys, we can compare our results against a database of usability measurements. SUMI provides a set of measurements against which we can evaluate the usability of the software. These measurements can be used as part of the criteria specified in our test plan for entry into later test phases (for example, User Acceptance Test, or UAT) or exit from the current phase of testing.

Generalized surveys help to reduce some of the subjectivity of usability results.

SUMI provides a brief (50-question) questionnaire that is filled out by the user. These responses are then matched against a benchmark of responses that have been gathered over many projects. To each statement, the user is asked to respond "agree", "undecided", or "disagree". The statements can be as focused as "The way that system information is presented is clear and understandable" to something as generic as "Working with this software is satisfactory." Because it is used across a wide variety of software, the questions are necessarily general rather than application specific. When the user has completed the survey, the results are gathered into interpretation software that provides usability ratings in the areas of efficiency, affect, helpfulness, control (users feel they are in control), and learnability. This information can then be used to compare the product against other similar products, general usability criteria, or a previous release of the same product.

WAMMI is used to supply ongoing feedback from users regarding a website. This is done by presenting a questionnaire to the user, usually when they leave the site, asking them questions regarding their experience (you know, it's the window that pops up that you always close!). These answers are matched against a database of answers received for other websites and comparison metrics are created.

The goal of both of these survey techniques is to remove some of the subjectivity from usability assessments. Usability is always a subjective impression, but by matching survey answers to a large community of information, we are able to draw objective conclusions from the subjective data.

The usability of the software is ultimately determined by the users. Any usability defects that are reported from our user base should be used to improve our usability testing. As soon as you hear yourself say, "Why would anyone do that?" you know you have a usability issue you didn't consider. Those pesky users can certainly create significant work, but remember, without them there wouldn't be much need for our software.

> **Lesson Learned: Usability and accessibility always matter**
>
> Usability and accessibility always matter—sometimes more and sometimes less. If the user of the software is a piece of hardware, it doesn't care if the software is pretty, but it certainly cares if it gets messages in the correct format and the correct syntax and in the required time frame. If the user is a novice on an e-commerce site, the software needs to be inviting, interesting, easy to use, and learnable. Users will return to sites they have figured out. They will avoid sites that were puzzling or made them feel stupid (at least I do!). If the user is unable to access a site or to interact with it effectively due to a disability, they will go elsewhere.

11.5 Let's Be Practical

Usability and Accessibility Testing of the Marathon Application

What about Marathon? Do we care about usability and accessibility? What kind of users should we expect? It's difficult to tell since running marathons neither requires nor discourages the use of computers. In any user interface decision, you usually design for the lowest common denominator—the person with the least ability. So, this interface needs to be friendly. Does it need to be attractive? It's unlikely that people will say, "Ooh, ugly interface, I'm not entering their marathon." We don't want to repel our users, but since their use of the system will be short term, we can get away with a less-than-attractive interface.

Well that's obvious, isn't it?	What about obviousness? When determining what to do next, is it obvious to the user? Does that matter to the user? In a low-frequency-use application like this, obviousness is one of the most critical factors because the user needs to log in and do what they need to do, and that may be their only interaction with the system. Do you have software you only use occasionally? Do you log in a second time and think, "Now how did I do that?" Your ability to figure it out again is a direct indication of the obviousness of the software.

What about learnability? Do the Marathon users need to learn how to use the system and retain that knowledge? Repeat runners and sponsors, perhaps. Most likely though, they want it to be obvious with a very low learning curve since the usage will be sporadic. This is a system that needs to have good help text since that will significantly reduce the support calls we might get.

Exercise

What aspects of the Marathon application would you target for usability testing? What types of testing would you do in each area?

What types of accessibility issues would you test for in the Marathon application?

11.6 Learning

The following check lists will help you judge the knowledge you have gained from this chapter.

Terms

accessibility testing, heuristic evaluation, SUMI, usability testing, *WAMMI

Test Analyst

- Explain by examples what testing techniques are appropriate to test usability and accessibility characteristics.
- Design, specify, and execute usability tests using appropriate techniques and achieving specified test objectives, including targeting specific defects.

Technical Test Analyst

None for this section

12 Efficiency Testing

Efficiency describes the capability of the software product to provide appropriate performance relative to the amount of resources used under stated conditions.

In this chapter, two characteristics of efficiency are considered according to the ISO 9126 Quality Model [ISO 9126]:

- *Time behavior (performance)*
- *Resource behavior*

12.1 Overview

We generally associate time behavior with the performance of the system under test. We are interested in answers to the basic question, How fast? Resource behavior addresses the basic question, How much (of some resource) did we use?

We are naturally interested in answers to these two questions while the system or software under test is executing under a range of stated conditions. The specific conditions we mean here are generally represented in so-called *operational profiles*, which provide a model of our system's usage under a variety of different situations. Constructing these operational profiles is a test analysis and design activity and is covered in section 12.9.

System usage typically varies over time.

There are a number of different types of tests that may be applied in testing efficiency:

- Performance
- Load
- Stress
- Scalability
- Resource utilization

Although there are many similarities between them, the primary factor that differentiates these testing types is the testing objective they follow. In the next sections, we will consider each of the testing types, the risks they address and the testing objectives in focus.

> **Lesson Learned: Efficiency is not just performance**
>
> All too often, I've seen test analysts mistakenly use *efficiency* and *performance* interchangeably. This frequently leads to the issue of resource efficiency being at best relegated to a lower priority or, at worst, forgotten about entirely. Try to be specific. Whether you mean resource behavior or time behavior, make it clear which one you are talking about; only if you are considering both should you use the general word *efficiency*.

12.2 Performance Testing

Performance testing defined

Performance testing measures response times to user inputs or other system inputs (e.g., the receipt of a specific transaction request). Of course, we would expect a system to respond faster when it's not required to perform much processing, so we also need to consider the specific conditions under which the system provides response times. These conditions are usually modeled as an operational profile that reflects a specific load placed on the system or software under test. For these reasons, performance measurement is generally considered as a significant (but not the only) testing objective of load, stress, and scalability testing.

Creating the operational profile is covered in section 12.9, "Specification of Efficiency Tests", while the different forms of performance measurement are covered in section 12.7, "Measuring Efficiency".

12.3 Load Testing

The primary aspect that sets load testing apart from other efficiency test types is the focus on realistic anticipated loads the system or software is required to handle. While stress testing (see section 12.4) explores areas beyond this anticipated range, in load testing we are interested in how the system or software handles increasing levels of anticipated load.

What is *load*? In general, it's what causes the system to perform work. Rather like an aircraft engine when the pilot pushes the throttles forward for takeoff, load is variable throughout a given range (in this case, from idle through to maximum takeoff power). A software system typically receives load from two principal sources:

- The users, who interact with the system
- Other systems that interface with our system

Where do loads come from?

When users interact with the system, they may trigger transactions to a database or cause information to be transferred to other systems. The sum of these different transactions performed by the people currently using the system represents a load on that system and its available resources (files, databases, CPU, main memory, peripheral devices, etc.).

Similarly, loads may arise from other systems that request services from our application or system. For example, daily batch jobs may be started automatically (usually at periods of low load) and submit requests to our application by submitting a file of data records to be processed. This places a load on our system.

Testing Objectives for Load Testing

The following principal objectives are in focus:

- Ability of system components (e.g., web servers) to handle multiple users acting in parallel. Here we are interested in the system's ability to handle the sheer numbers of users (does the web server crash when the 10th person attempts to log on?)
- Ability of the system to maintain "sessions" that guarantee functional integrity for each user. Here we are interested in whether transactions from particular users get "lost" or perhaps corrupted by other users.
- Time behavior (performance) of the system (e.g., how quickly the user receives a response to a request or how many records of a given type are processed per hour from a file submitted by a batch job).
- Resource behavior of the system where the transactions generated by the users or other systems result in large volumes of information being transferred over the network (sometimes referred to as *volume testing*) or where demands for other system resources (such as buffer storage, queues, databases, or printers) are generated.

12.4 Stress Testing

The load we apply to a system or software becomes *stress* when the load applied exceeds the specified limits. Just as with load testing, stress testing is also relevant to other engineering disciplines. Here are some examples:

- An aircraft engine is stressed to beyond maximum takeoff power to ensure that a safety margin exists and that no catastrophic failures occur at, say, 130 percent power settings.
- During development, the aircraft's wing will be stressed in a specially developed laboratory until it physically breaks. We want to know what loads cause it to break and what components fail first when that happens.
- If our software system is designed to handle 100 transactions per second of a particular type, we would load-test it at between 1 and 99 transactions per second and then stress it in the range of 100 transactions and above.

Why stress a system? Why would we want to do that? Stress testing follows a number of objectives:

- We want to find out if and where the system ultimately fails when subjected to increasing stress. Knowing the "weakest link in the chain" can be very valuable information, especially for future operators of the system and system architects. They can consider failures as part of their risk management strategy and have appropriate contingency plans in place.
- We want to assess whether the system actually fails under stress or recognizes the situation and handles it in a managed way. This is what is sometimes referred to as *graceful degradation*; rather than leaving a user or another system with a failed system on their hands, we want to ensure that a minimum level of capability is always available. This "minimal level" may be stated as a certain guaranteed response time or relate to specific processing that must take place without failures (e.g., data inconsistencies).

Spike and Bounce Testing

Spike testing is a special sort of stress testing in which a sudden extreme load is placed on the system. If that spike is repeated with periods of low usage in between, we are conducting what [Splaine 01] calls *bounce tests*.

The objective of both spike and bounce tests is to determine how well the system handles sudden changes of loads and whether it's able to claim and release resources (e.g., RAM) as needed. Think of these tests as exercising the "elasticity" of your system.

Sudden load spikes can also occur on recovery from a system failure (e.g., when full message queues suddenly "flood" back into the system). Such tests are therefore often combined with a particular type of reliability tests called *failover and recovery tests* (see section 14.2.7, "Approach to Failover Testing").

Figure 12-1 illustrates the variations of stress tests.

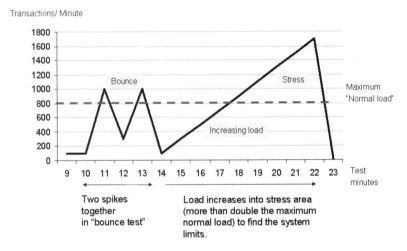

Figure 12–1

Stress conditions

> If your proposed stress testing strategy is not implemented for some reason, document the risks involved in not doing the tests and make sure the relevant stakeholders (customers, managers, and operators) are aware of them.

12.5 Scalability Testing

Scalability testing is performed when particular stakeholders such as business owners and operations departments need to know whether a system not only meets its efficiency requirements now but will continue to do so in the future.

Requirements for scalability are frequently stated for systems where growth is planned, with systems such as the following, for example:

- Systems that will be rolled out to increasingly more users (e.g., one department this year and the remaining three departments next year)
- Systems whose user bases can be only estimated at first but are expected to increase steadily as familiarity of use grows (e.g.. Internet applications)
- Systems whose user base is expected to grow (perhaps suddenly) as a result of marketing and promotional initiatives

Scalability objectives can be difficult to justify. It is important to realize that both scalability problems and new scalability requirements typically arise once a system or software application has become operative. As a result, scalability testing is often conducted on systems that are in production. So why should we care? Well, those responsible for seeing the project into production may indeed have other testing priorities, but there are stakeholders like business owners and operators who do care—or rather, they should care.

It's the job of the technical test analyst, together with the test manager, to ensure that scalability requirements are captured and agreed on and that appropriate testing measures are defined. This very often means convincing those stakeholders that scalability testing is important and possibly also requesting funding for the necessary testing. For this you need really solid justification based on both current fact and supported predictions.

Experience Report: Convincing the business owners—or not

Let's illustrate this by considering a real-life story from a travel company I once worked for. The travel industry is a highly cyclical business. It experiences peaks and troughs in business from season to season, from day to day, and even from hour to hour. The difference in the number of transactions taking place can be quite significant when one compares the lowest points with the highest (i.e., peak season, peak day, peak hour).

New systems are introduced, where possible, during periods of low transactions. This is sensible, but it's critical to ensure that the system scales to meet expected growth patterns.

Well, I talked to the business owners about their plans and made my predictions for scalability testing. Did they accept my figures as a reasonable testing goal? "Unimaginable" was their response, so tests were not performed with my predicted loads.

Later in the year at "peak-peak" time, I casually tried to book a vacation over their website. Basically, the system was available but response times were in the "minutes" range. In subsequent analysis, the business, of course, claimed to have been right all along because there had been nowhere near the number of users I had predicted (I wonder why that was?).

The lesson I learned from this is that I should have tried harder to convince them of the need for realistic scalability tests. Justifying scalability goals for testing can be an uphill struggle sometimes.

12.6 Resource Utilization Testing

Just as with performance testing, resource utilization testing is typically conducted at the same time as load, stress, and scalability testing.

Evaluation of resource behavior (e.g., usage of memory space, disk capacity, and network bandwidth) is the primary testing objective of such tests. For interconnected systems, this may typically mean testing the network's capacity to handle high data volumes (frequently the term *volume testing* is used here). For embedded systems the testing objective may be directed more toward the efficient utilization of limited memory resources.

12.7 Measuring Efficiency

There are many ways to measure efficiency. Here are some typical examples:

- User response "round-trip" times (seconds)
- Transactions per second
- Data throughput (kilobytes per second)
- CPU cycles to perform a calculation
- Memory used (bytes)

The technical test analyst will need to carefully consider the following issues according to the objectives of the test:

- Measurements to be taken
- The required precision levels
- The cost of taking those measures

Using a stop-watch only goes so far.

We need to be sure that enough measurements are taken and at sufficient levels of detail to allow analysis to take place. Take the measurement of user response time, for example. Measuring only "round-trip" time (i.e., the time between a user request and an answer being received) may be a good way to get a quick feedback on performance, but this is generally not enough to make informed decisions regarding achieved performance levels and is of little help in locating problems if performance does not meet expectations. Maybe end users would be satisfied with taking round-trip measurements, but system architects, operators of the system, and maybe even managers will want to know more. For example:

- How much time did we lose routing transactions via Server X instead of via Server Y?
- How much time was taken processing a transaction compared to its transmission over the network?
- What part of the round-trip is spent outside of the firewall?
- Is the database server slowing us down?
- Are we logging too much or too little?
- What happens if we have 10 users or 100?

Identify nodes and set monitors.

In particular for systems whose architectures consist of several components (e.g., clients, servers, databases), measurements must be taken at specific points (sometimes called *nodes*) so that we can break down the round-trip time into its individual parts. This is done by placing monitors between individual components. Such monitors may be provided by a commercial tool or you might develop your own monitors.

> **Experience Report: Performance monitors can slow the system down**
>
> While we need monitors to take efficiency-related measurements, great care is needed to limit the intrusive effects they themselves have on performance.
>
> I remember being involved in the performance testing of a three-tier client-server system way back in the days before high-quality test tools were available. We diligently put monitors directly into the code to track transactions through all the critical nodes (for example, leaving client, received by application server, processing by application [various steps], SQL sent to database, reply received from database, and so on) and started our load test with a self-made program. We couldn't easily track individual transactions, so we had to monitor and log them all as they went through the system.
>
> And the performance results (you guessed it) were appalling. We were logging about 20 individual monitor points in the system for each transaction. Each log required a message to be constructed and written to a file on disk. The system was spending so much time monitoring itself that the results afterward were meaningless. After these initial attempts (OK, we were all a bit green in those days), we resorted to highly selective monitors and small messages and eliminated excessive disk I/O by buffering data in RAM. We reckoned afterward that the refined intrusive effects of the monitoring were below 5 percent of actual system performance, which was acceptable for our testing goals.

Measurement and Precision

When measuring user response times (especially for web applications), we often find that a relatively low level of precision is sufficient, especially in the areas beyond one or two seconds. Measuring the integer number of seconds taken for a response is often more meaningful unless specific actions require "instant" responses in the sub-one-second area. If users are unable to perceive the difference between 6.3 seconds and 6.4 seconds, why measure to that level of precision?

Compare this to the high levels of precision needed when measuring the exact number of CPU cycles needed to perform a complex calculation. In this case, the actual number of CPU cycles may be the unit of measurement we are interested in, or we may wish to scale this up to a precise number of milliseconds.

Monitoring Real-Time Systems

If you are testing real-time systems, you will probably have to resort to nonintrusive monitors or the entire system behavior may be changed by your monitoring code.

Experience Report: When monitors become part of the design

I was testing a real-time application for a military aircraft in the 1970s when we moved from performing functional integration testing to system testing. Part of that move involved the deletion of all "test" software that had been inserted by development for monitoring purposes.

Did the software behave as we expected after that? No way! It was crashing everywhere (the software I mean). We had changed the timing behavior by making parts of the system execute faster than before. If this code was expecting to receive values from other parts of the software, it was now not able to pick them up until a few CPU cycles later. Unable to handle this situation (OK, bad design happens), the system would behave in an undetermined way.

This is a case where the intrusive effects of monitors inserted for performance measurement actually had a "beneficial" effect by selectively slowing down parts of the system. (I don't recommend this, but I seem to recall some of those monitors being replaced in the code by "wait" statements to ensure that the timing remained the same after the monitors were removed.)

Just as an aside, the use of debuggers to isolate defects in real-time systems may not be effective for the same reasons. Simply stepping through the code with the debugger often removes the timing problem and the code appears to function as expected (how many timing-related defect reports have been rejected as "no bug" this way, I wonder).

Monitoring in Systems of Systems

When you have a system of systems to test, it is quite likely that there will be parts of that system over which you have no control, either technically or organizationally or both. When this happens, there will be points within your end-to-end tests where it will not be possible to place monitors. You may occasionally be able to get around this by building simulations, but ultimately you may have to accept this as a gap in your system monitoring. Report this, perhaps flag it as a risk, and move on.

Measurements and Cost

Remember, there is always a cost associated with taking measurements:

- The cost of developing or purchasing the monitoring software
- The cost of storing the results
- The cost of performing the analysis

12.8 Planning of Efficiency Tests

Efficiency tests can be expensive to set up and run, but the risks associated with having software with poor efficiency characteristics are high. Problems like unacceptable user response times can endanger whole projects and result in costs that far exceed those of testing. Against this background, it is of critical importance that we recognize the need for specific types of efficiency tests, be able to set up a testing strategy that addresses those needs, and have an appreciation for both the costs and management effort involved.

In short, as technical test analysts, we don't need just technical skills, but also an appreciation of the planning issues. This includes evaluating risks, setting up testing strategies, and scheduling the various activities in the testing process (i.e., planning and controlling, analysis and design, implementation and execution, evaluating completion criteria and reporting, and test closure).

Planning skills are important.

To be able to plan for efficiency testing there are several specific issues that need to be considered. In the following paragraphs, these points are considered by using the Test Plan standard described in [IEEE 829] as a guide. The following issues are addressed:

■ Risks, more specifically, the types of defects that can be attributed to poor software efficiency
■ Different types of test objects
■ Requirements and Service Level Agreements (SLAs)
■ Approach
■ Pass/fail criteria
■ Infrastructure needs for performing the tests, including tools and environments
■ Organizational issues
■ Scheduling the tests
■ Testing deliverables

The following sections will address each of these planning issues.

12.8.1 Risks and Typical Efficiency Defects

Specific causes for poor efficiency are many and varied, but there are typical risks and associated potential defects with which we need to be familiar. These are summarized in table 12-1:

Table 12–1

Typical efficiency risks and defects

Typical risk	Type of defect that may occur
Design risk: insufficient processing capacity, poor architectural design, or an inappropriate software design	User response times too slow. The application cannot be used efficiently.
Risk that system components (e.g., web servers) are incorrectly configured or are unable to physically handle high volumes of data or transactions	Stress situations cannot be handled. System crashes when large number of users logged on. System growth limits are reached too quickly after introduction into production.
Insufficient network bandwidth (throughput)	Database queries with large-volume responses impair the system for other users.
Risk that the software implementation does not use resources efficiently	Main memory exhausted under stress loads. Databases or file capacity exceeded after a period of continuous usage.

12.8.2 Different Types of Test Objects

With efficiency tests, a variety of test objects can be identified at the planning stage. Examples of such test objects are listed below.

- Sections of the system architecture. To identify these sections, you may review the system architecture and identify specific nodes. These may be hardware (e.g., servers, routers), software (e.g., applications, business objects), and other items such as databases and firewalls. Test objects are typically defined from one node to another and over a sequence of nodes.
- The complete system. Ultimately, efficiency tests (e.g., performance) will need to be conducted with the final system as it is intended to be used in production.
- Individual time-critical elements. These are the components that must *Tool Tip* perform specified actions within a particular period of time to ensure correct functioning of the system. When planning efficiency tests for such systems, it is essential to identify those software or system components that are time critical. Conducting a risk analysis together with the developers and system architects is a good way to identify these components. Alternatively, a tool can be used to perform dynamic analysis of the system as it executes (see section 8.2 for more on dynamic analysis). This allows information to be gathered regarding actual execution times and helps highlight "hot spots" where code is executed most frequently. These would most likely cause the worst impact on overall system performance should they suffer any of the typical efficiency defects listed in section 12.8.1.

12.8.3 Requirements for Efficiency Tests

Planning for efficiency tests cannot take place without an understanding for applicable requirements and service levels. Where can we find this information?

- If we're lucky, there may be a document available that actually states the efficiency requirements in a precise, testable way. This might be a stand-alone document called, for example, a Statement of Requirements or a contractual document detailing service levels to be achieved (e.g., response times).

*Efficiency requirements
are often incomplete,
untestable, or totally absent.*

■ At a more detailed level, we may find the basis for efficiency requirements within architectural designs and technical or low-level design
specifications.

■ Frequently we will find that the information in these documents is
incomplete, untestable, or not formulated as actual requirements. For
example, architectural designs may only describe the proposed architecture for an intended audience of developers. In a similar vein, efficiency requirements may not be documented at all and exist as
"notions" in the heads of particular stakeholders like operators or
users. To address these problems, the technical test analyst needs the
material at the planning stage in order to extract the actual efficiency
requirements and specify them in a testable way. This will mean asking
questions, performing workshops, and determining the requirements
with the stakeholders (e.g., business owners, users, operators).

> **Lesson Learned: Stakeholders have different views of performance**
>
> In general, stakeholders have different views of quality (refer to
> [Evans 04] for more on this). This is often the case for performance.
> Ask a customer about performance and the answer you get will
> almost always relate to the system's response time to a particular
> user input. The technical test analyst needs to consider perform-
> ance at other levels of detail and should therefore also work closely
> with system designers and developers to obtain their views on per-
> formance and identify relevant testing goals. Only by identifying all
> measurable points of performance can the technical test analyst do
> proper testing and analysis.

If we are faced with poor, untestable requirements, we may be able to
request improvements from the test manager or perhaps a requirements
analyst specialist. However, all too often we technical test analysts are on
our own. What information do we need to gather so that we have good efficiency requirements to work with and how can we set about obtaining this
information? To illustrate an effective approach, let's consider a typical
dialogue between the technical test analyst (TTA) and a business owner of
the system to be tested.

Business owner states: "The system must be fast."

Clearly the business owner is expressing a wish here, but it's hardly a testable requirement.

TTA replies: "OK, 30 seconds then."

A good method to extract more information is to initially propose an exaggerated value for *fast*. This is usually sufficient to provoke a discussion over what the stakeholder (in this case the business owner) is willing to accept.

Business owner responds: "The system must respond to user inputs within 3 seconds."

This is better than the requirement we started with—at least we have a precise number of seconds now. But the problem with this requirement is that we have no idea what the system should be doing when this response time needs to be achieved. Are there five users logged on or five thousand, and how are they interacting with the system? The task of the technical test analyst here is to define the operational profiles under which the stated response time must be achieved. (See section 12.9, "Specification of Efficiency Tests", for further details.)

TTA asks: "Does this 3-second response time apply at all times or just in particular circumstances?"

Business owner replies: "Well, when all 100 users are logged on between 9:00 a.m. and 10:00 a.m., we need this response to all of our requests for the latest dollar currency exchange rate. For other general information requests and at other times of the day, we could accept a slower response time, but no more than 7 seconds."

Slowly we are building up the operational profiles that describe the usage of the system. This form of questioning may continue for some time until we have all the information we need. Maybe we would get the users involved at this stage to help fill in details and capture their usage patterns properly.

TTA continues: "OK, we have a good idea now of your usage patterns and the responses you are expecting. Can we now agree on your expectations on how often these requirements should be achieved? There may be a big difference in the development cost of the system if you require 100 percent achievement of requirements compared to, say, 95 percent achievement."

This is a critical issue for testing too. Allowing a certain number of response times to exceed the requirement may substantially reduce the analysis time needed to examine each and every individual response that exceeds the maximum.

Business owner replies: "No more than 5 percent of response times should exceed the values we discussed."

TTA asks: "Do your requirements also apply to users who are using the old laptops with those slow modems?"

Now we're gathering configuration data.

Business owner replies: "I guess we could relax the requirements by about 50 percent for those users. They really don't have the same equipment and it's maybe unreasonable to expect the same performance as users of the new laptops with broadband connections will get."

The discussion continues until we are confident that the efficiency requirements have been captured and are testable. If you can, go back to the stakeholders with these requirements and get their feedback on them. Maybe even a review would be helpful.

Note that this example is unlikely to be used for gathering and evaluating requirements for safety-critical applications. Here the process is much more formalized and requirements reviews are typically part of the standard to be applied (see section 17.4.8).

Summary of Requirements Issues

Just to summarize then, we must appreciate that the performance requirements needed to plan and specify our tests should contain at least the following information:

- Measurable response times (e.g., a number of seconds)
- A statement of what work the system is doing when those response times are to be achieved (represented as operational profiles)
- The percentage of times when these response times must be achieved
- The system configurations to which the response times apply

Although we have used performance testing requirements for our example, the same applies to other aspects of efficiency testing. Typical requirements here may include, for example, the following statements:

- "The installed application may not use more than 200MB of available RAM."

▓ "The web server shall permit at least 200 users to access the application in parallel."

▓ "The system shall ensure that a data transfer of at least 1GB per second is possible."

If you don't have all the information you need and it is not possible to obtain it, your only option is to make reasonable assumptions and communicate them via the project's risk management or the master test plan. Whether you then proceed with specifying and executing the tests should be something your test manager or project leader should decide.

Communicate risks if you have to make assumptions.

12.8.4 Approaches to Efficiency Tests

When planning an approach to efficiency tests, we will need to consider the following points:

▓ Tests should be based on operational profiles that represent typical system usage patterns (see section 12.9 "Specification of Efficiency Tests", for more details). As we mentioned earlier, these should have been taken into account when drafting the efficiency requirements.

▓ Performing static analysis (see section 8.1) or a code-level technical review may be a useful way to evaluate programming practices and their impact on efficiency.

▓ Where time-critical components have been identified as test objects, performance profiling may be performed with specific tools or *bench-marking* carried out against predefined criteria. CPU usage may be monitored when performing these tests.

▓ Where system architectures permit the identification of various nodes (servers, client applications, etc.), performance tests may first be carried out between individual nodes and then expanded to include several nodes. For example, initial tests may focus on the performance between a client application and an application server. This may then be expanded to include the connection between the application server and a database. Ultimately, performance tests are conducted end-to-end on the entire system.

▓ Volume tests are performed on the business processes that rely on large data transfers (e.g., information searching).

▓ In general, a manual approach to test execution is not advisable (see section 12.10, "Executing Efficiency Tests", for an explanation), and we almost always need the support of tools (see section 12.8.6 for more details).

■ It's important to note that the approach to evaluating efficiency quality characteristics is frequently analytical in nature. The task here focuses not only on conducting specific tests with pass/fail criteria (see the next section) but also on gathering and analyzing information (e.g., response times).

12.8.5 Efficiency Pass/Fail Criteria

If we have well-defined, testable requirements, the task of setting pass/fail criteria is reasonably straightforward.

Pass/fail criteria for efficiency tests in general are often less precise than those of functional tests. As we saw in the example conversation between the technical test analyst and the business owner in section 12.8.3, some degree of tolerance may be applied when deciding on the result of the test. This may be explicitly stated within the requirements (e.g., 95 percent achievement of a particular requirement) or implicitly given as a rule of thumb. One such rule, for example, is that users of an Internet application are willing to wait for no more than 7 seconds before losing interest and trying their luck somewhere else (possibly the competition!).

The subjective nature of a stakeholder's appreciation of quality (what Isabel Evans refers to in her book [Evans 04] as a *transcendant* view of quality) is particularly strong when judging whether performance is acceptable or not. If no performance requirements have been documented, this does not mean that our system is immune to rejection on performance grounds.

Finally, if the primary objective of performing efficiency tests is actually to gather data, analyze, and report, we should take care to make this absolutely clear in the master test plan. One way of doing this is to simply enter the word *none* into the chapter in our master test plan titled "Pass/ Fail Criteria."

12.8.6 Tooling for Efficiency Tests

Tool Tip   Given that it's generally not a good idea to perform meaningful and repeatable efficiency tests manually, our test planning needs to consider a number of test environment points that include required testing tools (see section 12.8.7 for further points relating to test environment planning). For tooling, the following points should be considered:

■ Simulation needs.

A tool must be able to generate the loads required for our planned tests. These may include the high loads often needed for stress testing and perhaps also scalability testing. Such loads are typically defined in terms of *virtual users* (often shortened to just VUs) that represent the real system users to be simulated by the tool. One of the most important aspects in planning our efficiency tests is to specify the number of VUs our chosen tool needs to generate. This can have a major influence on tool costs and test environment needs. Analysis of the operational profiles (see section 12.9) will enable these numbers to be estimated. The factors that can drive up the number of VUs needed are the length of time a user session is open and the number of actual transactions that take place over that period. These both affect the numbers of concurrent users to be simulated.

Estimating virtual users is an important planning task.

■ Financial considerations.

For large-scale simulations that may be complex and require many virtual users, the cost of tooling can take up a major part of the available testing budget. These costs result from either development effort, where the tool is to be developed explicitly for the system under test, or license and training costs, where the tool is a commercially available product. The license costs for products are normally based on the number of VUs to be simulated. In particular for stress testing, where large numbers of VUs are required for a relatively short time, a sensible option may be to rent *top-up* licenses. For less-complex simulations where the number of VUs required may be relatively low, freeware or shareware tools may represent a low-cost alternative.

Experience Report: Stress the software, not your budget

I was recently involved in creating a performance test strategy for an application with a huge (and I mean huge) number of users. We're talking here of tens of millions users. Even after calculating the number of VUs we would need for the required peak-load test, we knew we were in trouble. We arranged for a meeting with our friendly tools provider (he was even friendlier on that day). The scene after he announced a license cost of nearly 50 million dollars was quite memorable. Full marks to the salesman—he kept a straight and serious face throughout (as though that's the kind of deal he made every other day). We bargained on that one and got what we wanted in the end (sorry guys, I'm not telling you what the deal was).

Consider carefully before venturing into the tool writing business.

- Writing your own tool.
  This should be considered only if available performance tools cannot be used. This may be due to a technical issue (e.g., communications protocols are not supported by tools) or a financial one (i.e., can't afford the license costs). Since the development of your own performance tool will cost money, may involve a lengthy lead time, and will result in ongoing maintenance expenses, the decision to "go it alone" needs to be well planned. The technical test analyst can support the test manager in making these decisions by providing technical support and helping to choose the right tool. For more information on the build vs. buy decision, see section 18.9.

- Skills and training.
  To use a performance testing tool properly, we need technical skills like scripting, an ability to analyze results, and an understanding of communications protocols. If these skills are not available, they will need to be acquired by training or hiring staff. Requirements for skills and training should be documented in the master test plan.

12.8.7 Environments

Efficiency testing may place considerable demands upon the environment we use for testing. At the planning stage, we need to support the test manager in creating a concept for the test environments.

Load Generation

Consider renting your load generation environment.

One of the principal issues relates to the capability of the environment to generate the loads we need for testing. Assuming we are going to use a tool for load simulation, it is essential that sufficient processing power be available to create the virtual users required for the test and permit the specified operation profiles to be realistically reproduced. I was recently given a rule of thumb by a tools supplier whereby you should reckon on a high specification server for each 1,000 VUs you want to generate. Given that we may require anything from hundreds up to hundreds of thousands of VUs for a specific test, we must plan for and be able to finance the hardware required to generate the load.

Capacity Planning

The planning of load generation capacity doesn't stop with the specification of required hardware; we also need to consider our network's capacity to transport the large numbers of transactions and potentially huge data volumes. If our hardware is capable of generating the simulated load but the network has insufficient bandwidth to transport it, our network will become a bottleneck and test results will be unrealistic (typically evident in very long response times). As with hardware requirements for load generation, ensuring that sufficient bandwidth is available can be a significant load on our testing budget as well!

In particular for volume tests, some consideration must be made at the planning stage as to how the data volumes are to be made available. It may be possible to gather data from a production environment, but you must be prepared to de-personalize (or "scrub") the data prior to use to meet legal requirements. As an alternative, the data can be generated with specific tools or by developing database scripts.

Which Environment?

At the planning stage a decision has to be made regarding the system environment to be used for the actual tests. Certainly we need to plan for using the production environment at some later stage in the testing (e.g., part of operational acceptance testing) because we usually need the confidence that efficiency-relevant service levels can be achieved in production.

The problem is, we cannot assume early availability of the production environment and we certainly will not have exclusive use of it when it becomes available. Planning for a preproduction testing environment to be made available to the testing team at an early stage is also a commonly used measure to ensure that we get maximum value from our (potentially expensive) efficiency tests. Such preproduction environments generally consist of architectural components that are production-like (or indeed identical), but the environment has not yet been scaled up to full production size. By applying reduced loads to the preproduction environment, we are able to make some predictions on how the fully scaled production environment will respond to the ultimate loads we have specified in our efficiency tests.

Make use of a preproduction environment if you can.

Testing Web Applications "in the LAN"

If you are planning to deploy your system to an Internet environment, you may be fooling yourself if you carry out efficiency testing within your company's LAN. Even though testing within the LAN is a tempting option from a cost point of view, the capacity of the LAN is likely to be much higher than the capacity available via the Internet. This could well make the results of performance and volume tests look better than what you will find in the system's intended production environment.

12.8.8 Organizational Issues

The organizational aspects of planning efficiency tests may be complex and require considerable effort, especially on the part of the test manager. This may be particularly problematic where individual system components in a system of systems are not under the direct responsibility of the testing team's organization. Agreements will need to be made regarding the scheduling of the tests, the setting of specific monitors, and the responsibilities for running the tests and analyzing the results.

Using third-party test labs is sometimes less expensive than building your own environment and expertise.

Where the costs or organizational effort of setting up and running the efficiency tests are considered too high, other alternatives may be considered. This may include hiring a fully equipped test lab that can supply the required hardware, bandwidth, tools, and expertise. This third–party solution may be an attractive proposition if the testing organization is only responsible for efficiency tests in the preproduction phase. If responsibilities extend to the postproduction (maintenance) phase, the costs to the testing organization of not owning its own testing infrastructure could start to outweigh the benefits. The technical test analyst will need to support the test manager and be involved in such long-term organizational decisions.

12.8.9 Life Cycle Issues

The pros and cons of early performance testing

The scheduling of planned efficiency tests presents the test manager with a fundamental decision. Should we schedule the tests relatively early in the life cycle or wait? The technical test analyst can support this decision by providing relevant "for" and "against" information.

Consider these points in favor of scheduling efficiency tests as early as possible:

- The ability to profit from early feedback on critical design decisions, particularly relating to the overall system architecture.
- The ability to correct any faults found early. Remember, some performance- or resource-related faults can be very expensive and time consuming to correct. The result of finding such potential "showstoppers" late in the development life cycle may be needing more time and resources to fix them than we actually have. That may force us to go into production with unachieved service levels, which may result in acceptance or even financial penalties and will certainly result in long-term maintenance headaches.

There are also points in favor of scheduling efficiency tests later in the development life cycle:

- Lower commercial (project) risks. We are less likely to need repetitions of these potentially expensive tests if, for example, changes are made to the system architecture during the development life cycle.
- Lower technical (product) risks associated with the nonavailability of system components. These could be entire systems if we are testing a system of systems or a specific function of an individual system. If we test too early with an incomplete and unrepresentative system, we run the risk of making incorrect predictions on efficiency or of having to schedule too many test repetitions.
- More confidence in test results themselves because the software functionality and hardware system are likely to be more stable. Conducting performance tests early on with "buggy" code is likely to be of limited value.

> **Lesson Learned: Performance testing is frequently scheduled too late**
>
> It is a frequently held view that you can only do performance testing when the "final system" is ready for release and the production system is available. Indeed, performance tests are often scheduled and conducted as one of the last tests prior to release.
>
> While scheduling efficiency tests this late in the software development life cycle may at first appear reasonable, we are taking real risks when we do this. It's almost as if we've set ourselves a testing objective just to confirm that "everything is OK" before we go live. Is this reasonable? Not really. What would happen, for example,

if our tests show that response times are most certainly not "OK"? We'd have a major issue on our hands here that could be a potential showstopper, especially if analysis of the problem reveals a fundamental flaw in our system architecture. Given that there may well be insufficient time to fix such defects before the planned release date, we are confronted with a significant problem at a critical stage in the project.

What can be done to reduce these risks? The answer is relatively simple. Efficiency tests should be considered at all stages of the software development life cycle, even if some of the results may not be 100 percent representative of the fully scaled production environment. Take a look at the planning approaches mentioned in section 12.8.4. There is a range of approaches and measures we can take throughout the software development life cycle; we don't have to wait until it's too late. We may perform basic load testing of specific system components using simple simulators, we may conduct performance testing at the module level, and we may conduct technical reviews on the system design documents that are targeted specifically at efficiency issues.

It may be an effective approach to schedule efficiency tests in parallel with other types of testing. For example, functional tests may be performed during the execution of performance tests to detect any functional faults that may occur under high loads or stress (e.g., due to failed transactions).

Ineffective change management can mean expensive test repetitions.

A coherent testing strategy must take into account the influence that system changes may have on individual quality attributes. As we noted earlier, we should appreciate that performance may be one such attribute that is highly sensitive to changes, in particular those applied to time-critical elements (e.g., database software, middleware, modules in real-time systems) or those introduced to address other quality attributes such as system security. An effective change control process must take into account these various interrelationships in order to minimize waste of testing resources.

When scheduling efficiency testing tasks, remember that many of the planning issues discussed in previous sections rely on gathering information about operational profiles before important decisions (e.g., regarding tool licensing and test environments) can be made. To this extent, the specification of operational profiles needs to take place as soon as practically feasible and where possible in parallel to the test planning.

12.9 Specification of Efficiency Tests

As technical test analysts, we need know how to develop test cases that generate the loads needed to investigate the various objectives of load testing, stress testing, scalability testing, and resource utilization testing.

The task of specifying the test cases is essentially a modeling activity. How do we construct realistic models of the anticipated real world? How realistic do these models actually need to be? These are the principal questions the technical test analyst has to solve in order to create good, cost-effective test cases that address the efficiency objectives.

To construct models of the real world in an efficiency testing sense, we need to develop operational profiles that represent a distinct form of user behavior when interacting with an application. Sometimes a single activity can represent an application's principal use, but we are more likely to be confronted with systems to test that are used in a number of different ways and by several different groups of users. To cope with these complexities, we need to consider a collection of different operational profiles that we can later combine to create the load needed for a specific test (sometimes referred to as the *load profile* or *workload*).

Figuring out what "real" people do in the "real" world.

Getting started at creating operational profiles means asking a lot of questions and, where available, analyzing data. The stakeholders we typically ask and the kind of information they can give us are shown in table 12-2:

Stakeholder	Information provided
Business owners and marketing	Principal services (functions) the system must provide. Numbers of users expected to use the system's functions (perhaps also including plans for future expansion).
End users	Details concerning the system's use or intended use. Usage patterns (e.g., peak times when particular activities are performed).
Operators	Current system usage gathered from monitoring. The "current system" here does not have to be the system under test; it could also be the system that is to be replaced or even one that is broadly similar. Service Level Agreements relating, for example, to the number of parallel users to be handled by the system, data volumes to be handled, and response times to specific transactions performed by various categories of user.
Developers and analysts	Design documentation. Requirements specifications.

Table 12–2

Principal stakeholders as suppliers of efficiency information

By way of example, let's consider an application that enables vacations to be chosen and booked via the Internet. After talking to the users or analyzing the system specification, we might define operational profiles for the following application users:

- Browsers, who are "just looking" at basic vacation information
- Choosers, who select details of specific vacations currently offered
- Bookers, who book a specific vacation and pay for it
- Modifiers, who change or cancel their booked vacations

Table 12-3 describes some typical workloads we could build from these operational profiles.

Table 12–3

*Typical load profiles for an
Internet vacation booking
application*

Name of workload and brief description	Typical duration of test	Usage patterns / operational profiles making up the workload
Peak Browsing: Most people have no vacation plans or only a general notion of the vacation they want. They spend a lot of time browsing the site to gather ideas. Some go into further detail (choosers). Significant peaks take place around midday and especially in the evenings. See figure 12-2.	24 hours	20000 browsers, 1,000 choosers, 250 bookers
Peak Choosing: People have focused on a particular type of vacation now and are gathering offers and details. Some book spontaneously. See figure 12-3.	5 hours	1,000 browsers, 6,000 choosers, 1,200 bookers
Peak Booking: People have made up their minds. This is the most intensive booking time (e.g., the first weekend in January between 10:00 a.m. and 11:00 a.m.) with also considerable modification to bookings taking place. See figure 12-4.	3 hours	550 browsers, 1,300 choosers, 3,100 bookers

We may still need to add a considerable amount of specific detail to finalize the operational profiles and workloads for our tests. In particular, the distribution of users over the time period set for the test may vary considerably, as we would expect for the vacation system described earlier.

Numbers of users, types of users, and activities may vary considerably over time.

Figures 12-2, 12-3, and 12-4 show how the operational profiles could appear once a time distribution has been added. Note that a maximum normal load of 2,500 users has been chosen so that stress conditions can be shown.

All load profiles feature step changes in user numbers at the hour boundaries rather than smooth transitions. Decisions like these are made by the technical test analyst according to the need for realism and specific test objectives. Step changes, for example, may be preferred if we want to trigger possible resource allocation problems.

The Peak Browsing load profile shown in figure 12-2 illustrates the typical peaks and troughs in user numbers experienced by the web server at a time of year when we're gathering ideas for our next vacation.

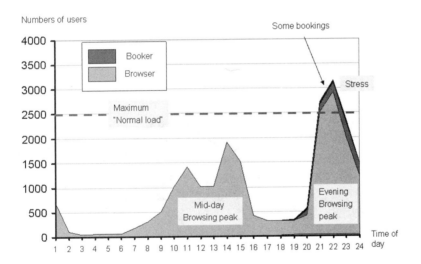

Figure 12–2

Load profile for Peak Browsing

The Peak Choosing load profile shown in figure 12-3 would be a good candidate for volume testing since the operational profile for a chooser calls for a number of database searches, which can be specified to generate high data loads.

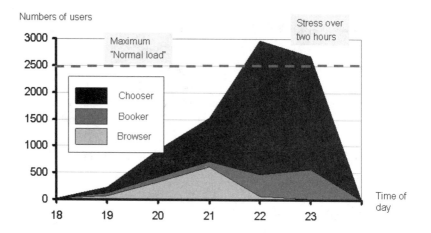

Figure 12–3

Load profile for Peak Choosing

The Peak Booking load profile shown in figure 12-4 illustrates a slow ramp-up and ramp-down of user numbers either side of the three-hour test period.

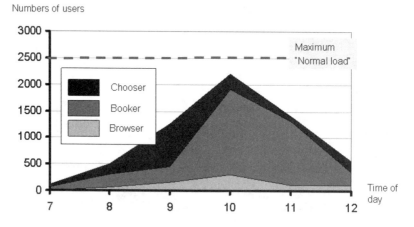

Figure 12–4

Load profile for Peak Booking

Tool Tip Once the descriptions of our operational profiles have been completed, they are normally implemented as executable scripts using a performance test tool. The tool then allows us to combine the individual operational profiles in the specified quantities to create the workloads needed (refer to section 12.8.6, "Tooling for Efficiency Tests", for further details).

The level of detail we choose to implement in our operational profiles is a trade-off between realism and simplicity. For example, the amount of time a user waits between individual steps ("think time") may need to be modeled, or it may be necessary to specify particular browser settings. These issues are well described in [Splaine 01].

Note that the example used earlier represents a typical web-based application with the user as the prime source of load. This will not be the case for all applications though, and it's important that we recognize other sources of system load, such as external devices, batch processes, and other applications that may be cohosted on our environment.

12.10 Executing Efficiency Tests

By the time you get to test execution, your planning has been implemented and you're ready to go. Your test environment is ready, your workloads have been defined and implemented, the entire infrastructure you need to generate the load is ready, monitors are in place, your performance test team is in place, and all the organizational preconditions for test execution have been completed. (The list can be so long that it may be useful to construct a check list to go through in advance with your test manager.)

It would be too easy to think of test execution as just a "click" in your performance test tool to call up and start the appropriate scripts. Mostly we are involved in a whole range of activities during the test execution, as in the following examples:

- Monitoring the load generation infrastructure to ensure that the load we specified is actually being generated. This is especially important with new or modified scripts or after introducing changes to the load generation infrastructure. It's quite common to need some form of tuning or configuration of scripts or infrastructure before conducting our first "real" test runs. This needs to be planned for and often means having experts on hand to do the tuning and troubleshoot any problems.

- Online monitoring and analysis of the system response to our generated loads. Especially where significant problems are evident at the start of the test, it may be wise to break off the test and investigate the problem instead of pressing on with a potentially lengthy test. Similarly, if we are running stress tests (remember, we may be trying to force a system crash), we will need to monitor system parameters carefully and may need to stop the test quickly if a component fails. This could be to prevent physical damage from occurring to our test system or to stop possible corruption of (production) data.

Performance test execution: a busy time for the technical test analyst. We recommend wearing running shoes.

■ As mentioned earlier, the objective of performance testing may be more investigative and analytical in nature than focused on pure fault finding or the verification of service levels. If this is the case, the execution of performance tests may take on a more hands-on iterative style with repeated "what if" adjustments being made to the system or the load-generating scripts.

■ Results will need to be captured during the performance test to support postexecution analysis and reporting. These tasks are normally supported by performance test tools (see section 12.12).

12.11 Reporting Efficiency Tests

Reporting of results and defects from efficiency tests needs to be related to the testing goals. This may sound obvious, but especially with efficiency-related testing there is so much information we *could* put into our reports that the danger exists of simply swamping the reader with too much non-relevant information. The commercial performance tools provide us with excellent facilities for reporting results; we as technical test analysts must ensure that those results relate directly to our testing goals (requirements) and support the stakeholder in gaining an overview of results and of making correct decisions relating to the quality of the software.

The results were hard to gather, so they should be hard to read!

The task of reporting efficiency test results focuses primarily on selecting the information that is really relevant and presenting it in an easy to understand manner. This generally involves creating diagrams. Of course, if our efficiency requirements have been poorly stated or are even untestable, this is where we really feel the consequences. What should we report? What should we be highlighting as a problem? How much or how little detail? Without good testing goals, the default approach is invariably to cram the report with as much detail as possible in the hope that the reader will find what they are looking for somewhere or other. Should we then complain if our reports don't get read or acted on? Remember, you have probably invested a lot of work in getting these results. What a shame it is if nobody takes notice of them.

A criticism often heard from stakeholders about reports is that the content provided contains only limited information regarding its actual significance. This may be a general problem for reporting, but it surfaces frequently in reporting efficiency-related results. Don't just paste "wonderful" colorful charts and graphs into your reports; add value to them by telling the reader what the information provided actually means and what we might have to do now (Will we achieve our service levels? Will our system scale?) In section 12.13, we consider the Marathon system as a practical example for efficiency testing and show the types of test reports we might produce.

Defect Reporting for Efficiency Issues

Raising defect reports for efficiency-related issues requires careful consideration. If the results show clearly that our system is not achieving expected efficiency goals or if failures occur, then a defect report must be issued (see chapter 19).

However, the decision of whether we have an actual defect is often not so clear-cut. In particular, we need to take care when raising defect reports based on extrapolations of data or where the results do not relate to production-identical system configurations. Defect reports like this can too easily be dismissed as "not a problem" and forgotten. If you are absolutely convinced that there really is a problem and a defect report is necessary, be ready to justify your report with facts and stand your ground. Depending on your project culture, it may be a better solution to report your findings as potential problems (i.e., risks) and then discuss the consequences with the relevant stakeholders. This in no way reduces the importance of your results and may contribute to a positive project atmosphere.

Report risks and decide on next steps.

12.12 Tools for Efficiency Testing

Several of the sections in this efficiency testing chapter have considered the use of tools. This section summarizes some of the points made in those sections.

Section 12.7, "Measuring Efficiency", lists a number of parameters that may be measured by tools.

In section 12.8, "Planning of Efficiency Tests". you learned that there are several tools-related issues that need to be considered early on at the planning stage:

- Estimating simulation needs (numbers of virtual users)
- Considering the financial implications of these simulation needs

■ Deciding whether to write your own tool or purchase a commercial product

■ Assessing available skills and scheduling any necessary training

Tool Tip Section 12.9, "Specification of Efficiency Tests", explains the steps taken to define operational profiles, combine them into load profiles, and use a tool to create executable scripts from them. These executable scripts are first captured by the tool for a single specific operational profile and represent a user's interaction with the system at a communications protocol level (not the graphical user interface). The tool allows individual scripts to be mixed and parameterized to create a specific load profile. Section 12.10, "Executing Efficiency Tests", describes how tools are used during test execution for monitoring and analysis.

Section 12.11, "Reporting Efficiency Tests", notes that tools provide us with a wealth of information that we need to carefully relate to our testing objectives.

12.13 Let's Be Practical

Efficiency Testing of the Marathon Application

Let's go through the steps of recognizing efficiency requirements, specifying appropriate test cases, and planning the efficiency test of the Marathon application. Just for reference purposes, here's the Marathon system overview (figure 12-5).

Planning: Test Objectives for Marathon

One of the basic aspects of planning is to define test objectives based on requirements. First, consider the general requirements described in section 2.2. Are there any aspects that give us answers or hints to questions like How fast?, With what resources?, and Under what conditions? These are the aspects we need to identify in order to plan and specify our efficiency testing. Remember, as technical test analysts, we try not to rely just on what's stated in the specifications.

The following statements from the requirements are significant for efficiency:

Marathon has several efficiency requirements, but we need to find them

■ "The Marathon application is designed to provide timely and accurate information to runners and the media." While this doesn't give us any

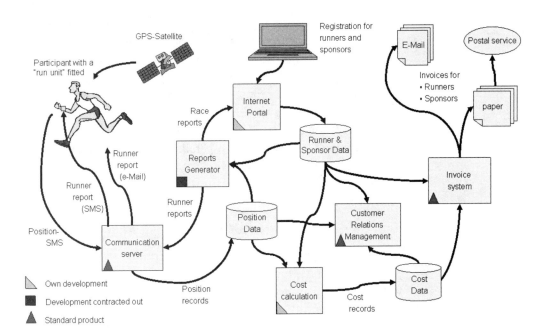

GPS-Satellite

Participant with a "run unit" fitted

Registration for runners and sponsors

E-Mail

Postal service

Invoices for
• Runners
• Sponsors

paper

Internet Portal

Race reports

Runner & Sponsor Data

Runner report (e-Mail)

Reports Generator

Invoice system

Runner report (SMS)

Runner reports

Position Data

Customer Relations Management

Position-SMS

Communication server

Own development

Development contracted out

Standard product

Position records

Cost calculation

Cost records

Cost Data

specific information, it is a typical indication that performance is regarded as an important quality characteristic for this system.

- "The system needs to be capable of handling up to 100,000 runners and 10,000 sponsors for a given race without failing." This gives us some specific values regarding volumes, but we still need to find out what lies behind that word *handling*. How are runners and sponsors using the system and in what time periods? This is the information we need so we can construct our operational profiles.

- "Registration starts four weeks before the race commences and lasts for one week. As soon as the registration week starts, a runner may register for the race using an Internet application." This narrows down the time period (i.e., one week), but are there any peaks and troughs in usage during that week? For example, will most people register on the weekend?

- "Anyone can register for the race, but the maximum number of participants (100,000) may not be exceeded. A first come, first served policy is used." In other words, when the registration window opens, the "flood gates" open. This is the peak in load we were looking for! The specification of this peak load is considered in more detail later.

Figure 12–5
The Marathon system

- "Response time for the registering runners and sponsors must never exceed eight seconds from the time the Submit button is pushed to the time the confirmation screen is displayed." This is a fairly resonable requirement on an Internet-based part of the application. It may still be tough meeting these response times at peak load.
- "It must be possible to handle up to five races each year." This could have a major impact on the loads the system needs to handle if those races are allowed to take place in parallel. This is a huge *if*, which we need to clarify with stakeholders (e.g., business owners) before defining our loads. For the time being, we will assume that races do not take place in parallel.

Other planning aspects for Marathon:

- Exclusive use of a production-identical environment is required for a period of six hours for the test execution (we will need to specify the test environment as well).
- To generate the run unit load, a simulator will be developed that can construct and submit the peak load of 1,666 unique SMS messages per second.
- To generate loads on the Internet portal, a commercial tool will be purchased that can simulate 5,000 virtual users. A training course will be scheduled for staff using this tool.
- Two high-range servers will be required to generate the load. One of these will be purchased new and has a delivery time of six months.
- Monitoring will be established to ensure that the communications server can process the SMS messages and write position records to the position database.
- A commercial tool will be used to monitor loads placed on the Internet portal. Test data for these loads will be held in a separate database and generated with a script.
- The run unit test will be performed three months before the first live race is performed.
- All tests scheduled on the Internet portal will be performed as soon as the portal is available (six months before race begin).

Test Specification for Marathon

- The requirement to handle the load created by run units without failing can be specified as follows:

- We are dealing here with a system interaction generated by an external device (the run unit) rather than a human user. The actual operational profile is quite simply stated: "The Run Unit sends an SMS once per minute to a predefined telephone number."

- The workload we define consists of three distinct race phases: start, peak, and end.

- Start: Assuming an even distribution of runners pass the starting line and 5,000 runners per minute is considered achievable, the load will ramp up to a maximum after 20 minutes.

  Defining the load at each stage of the race

- Peak: The maximum load is placed on the system after completion of the start phase. The communications server must process an average of 100,000/60 = 1,666 SMS records per second. Note that this is just an average; it's quite possible that several individual records could arrive within the same second, causing a short-lived spike.

- End: Peak load starts to reduce after one hour as some runners drop out of the race. After three hours, the first runners pass the finishing line. After that we assume that the reduction is shaped like an S-curve. This calls for a gradual reduction as the fastest runners finish followed by increasingly more finishers up to six hours after the race began and then a further gradual reduction as the slower runners finish. We assume that runners switch off their run units when they are no longer in the race.

  What if our assumption is wrong and people leave the run units on?

Figure 12-6 shows the load profile with the three distinct phases mentioned earlier. The simulator will be configured to generate this load profile and perform the necessary monitoring.

As a further example for test specification, the peak load to be placed on the Internet portal will be considered.

Loading the Internet portal

- To recap on the requirement, 100,000 runners have a week in which to register.

- Operational profiles will be defined for the user type Registering Runner and Browser. The Registering Runner profile consists of a candidate runner making a standard request for registration, completing the registration form online, submitting the application, and receiving an acknowledgement with acceptance or rejection. The Browser profile consists of a series of requests for information regarding the race (route, organization, fees, important dates, etc.).

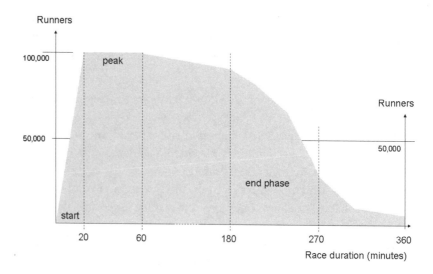

Figure 12–6

*Load profile of runners for a
typical marathon race*

- The commercial tool we purchased is used to capture single Registering Runner and Browser operational profiles as scripts.
- To specify the load profile, we need to determine how many in the Registering Runner and Browser user types will use the system and how they are distributed over time. For those in the Registering Runner user type, the "first come, first served" requirement inevitably means there will be a major peak in usage as soon as the registration week commences (at 4:00 p.m. EST on a Saturday). Since this is the first time the system has been used in operation, we will have to make some assumptions about these numbers. Let's say 50,000 runners try to register within the first 24 hours and 20,000 of those are within the first hour. Immediately after the system is opened, a spike of 5,000 users tries to log on and register. For the people in the Browser user type, we can assume that there will be a similar surge of interest at first that declines after the first day to a steady level. For the sake of simplicity, we assume that the number of people of user type Browser is 50 percent more than the number of user type Registering Runner and that the same proportions apply.
- The tool is now used to construct the load profile. The script is parameterised to generate the numbers and distribution of people in the Registering Runner and Browser user types as described earlier. The script is configured to access the runner data (names, addresses, etc.)

generated by the database script. Figure 12-7 represents the load profile for "peak registration".

Numbers of users

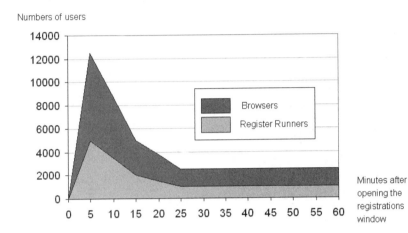

Figure 12–7

Load profile for Marathon "peak registration"

Test Execution for Marathon

For the communications server load test:

- The simulator is started and the system is monitored closely for at least the first hour. By this time the load has ramped up to the maximum 100,000 simulated runners and the system has operated at maximum required capacity for a further 40 minutes.
- A decision should be made one hour after starting the tests regarding its continuation. If the system has not failed, the test is continued until the load test has been completed (six hours after starting the test).

For the peak load test on the Internet portal:

- The tool is now used to construct the load profile described earlier and shown in figure 12-7. The script created with the tool is configured to access the runner data generated by the database script.

Reporting the Marathon Test Results

Reporting will feature diagrams of the monitored data and a statement relating these results to the requirements. For the peak load test on the

Internet portal, the diagram of load vs. response times in figure 12-8 shows a typical example.

Figure 12–8

Response times when executing the peak registration load

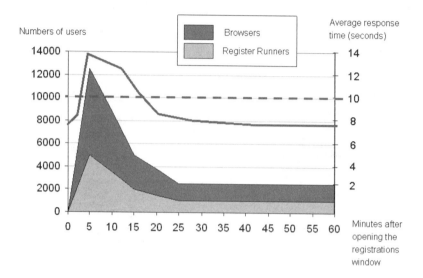

- We could include the following statements in a report regarding these results:

- The response time requirement of 10 seconds will not be achieved in the first 20 minutes after opening the registration.
- At other times, the response time is below 8 seconds

Exercises

The vacation example described in table 12-3 defines operational profiles for Browsers, Choosers, and Bookers. Define at least one more type of usage for this application and suggest the operational profile that would expect for the "peak booking" scenario shown in figure 12-4.

Did we cover all efficiency aspects for the Marathon application? Take a look at the functional specification describing what the system should do during the race itself and consider the following questions:

- Identify at least one further efficiency-related requirement from the description and specify an appropriate operational profile. Pay attention to any trends in system usage, types of usage, and test duration.

- Are there any particular aspects that need to be planned to execute the test?
- If a tool is already available that is capable of simulating 5,000 users, will this be sufficient for the tests you have specified?

12.14 Learning Check

The following check lists will help you judge the knowledge you have gained from this chapter.

Terms

efficiency testing, load profile, load testing, operational profile, performance profiling, performance testing, scalability testing, stress testing, volume testing

Technical Test Analyst

- Understand the types of faults found.
- Recognize and distinguish between the quality attributes relating to efficiency described in ISO 9126.
- Be able to identify and break down an efficiency requirement into a test specification.
- Understand and explain the stages in an application's life cycle where efficiency tests may be applied.
- Propose risk-based approaches for efficiency testing.
- Be able to schedule performance tests.
- Be able to specify an operational profile.
- Describe the preconditions for test execution, including testware, test environments, and monitors.
- Report on whether efficiency criteria have been fulfilled.
- Understand the different types of performance test tools.

Test Analyst

- Recognize the types of quality attributes relating to efficiency.
- Understand the types of faults found.
- Understand and explain the reasons for including efficiency tests in the overall testing strategy.

13 Security Testing

This book divides security testing activities into functional security testing, which is typically performed by the test analyst (see section 10.5, "Functional Security Testing"), and technical security testing, which is performed by the technical test analyst (this chapter).

Generally speaking, the functional security testing performed by the test analyst looks at aspects of penetration testing, making sure access to data and functionality is granted to those with the correct rights and denied to those without those rights. All other types of security tests, however, require specific technical expertise and are therefore best performed by the technical test analyst. This is what we cover in this chapter.

13.1 Overview of Security Testing

In common with the testing of other quality attributes, the basic steps in the fundamental test process can also be applied to security testing. Within this framework, however, several security-specific risks need to be addressed at the planning stage. These risks, which are outlined in section 13.3, "Planning Security Tests", often require that a different approach be taken when compared to other forms of testing (see section 13.4, "Security Test Analysis and Design").

The material presented in this chapter draws partly on the concept of software security *attacks* described by James Whittaker. Anyone wishing to specialize in the field of security testing should read his book [Whittaker 04].

Security testing requires knowledge and creativity.

13.2 Defining Security

To provide consistency, the definitions provided in ISO 9126 are used throughout this book. In this standard, the following high-level definition of security is provided:

> Security describes software characteristics which relate to the ability of the software to prevent unauthorized access to a program or its data, independent of whether this takes place deliberately or by accident.

Note that ISO 9126 also categorizes security as being a functional quality characteristic.

13.3 Planning Security Tests

Planning security tests is first and foremost about appreciating the types of security *threats* (risks) that can affect software systems and then assessing your particular system's vulnerability to these threats. Once the level and type of vulnerability has been established, a decision can be made regarding the approach to specifying and executing the security tests to be performed.

In common with the planning of all other types of quality attributes, the planning of security tests must also take into account specific security requirements placed on the system (including those contained in applicable standards), organizational considerations, and life cycle issues.

13.4 Typical Security Threats

Planning for security testing is often hampered by the vague notion that it is a fundamentally unnecessary activity (i.e., "no one would get the idea to do that"). Unfortunately, experience tells us that this is a flawed approach; hackers do exist, companies do lose millions through security breaches, and, yes, technical test analysts themselves often need to improve their awareness of security threats.

Know your enemy.   Perhaps more than with any other type of testing, the security tester's motto is characterized by the statement "Know your enemy." The fundamental security threat facing an application is the loss of valuable information (credit card details, user privileges, etc.) to an unauthorized person. Within the context of this general threat there exists a wide range of possibilities to compromise a system's security, the most common of which are outlined below. An awareness of these potential threats is essential when planning the security testing needed for a given application.

Please be aware that this list cannot be considered to be complete; there are simply too many variations on the basic types of security threats mentioned to make that an achievable goal. The list does, however, provide an insight into the principal types of security threats and makes us better prepared to approach security testing properly. For further details, please refer to the books published by [Whittaker 04] and [Chess&West 07], both of which give detailed insight into the complex and constantly evolving world of security testing. Data on specific security issues can also be obtained from the following sources:

- Common Vulnerabilities and Exposures (CVE). This is a dictionary of common names (i.e., CVE Identifiers) for publicly known information security vulnerabilities [URL: CVE].
- Open Web Application Security Project [URL: OWASP].

Before we get into the details of the principal security threats, the following list provides an overview. Many of these threats have specific names (security testing is full of them), which will be explained later. For now, a jargon-free description will help set the scene. Here are the main security threats we need to think of:

- Exceeding the permitted entry length of an input field
- Side effects when conducting permitted functions
- Unauthorized copying or deletion of data or applications
- Unauthorized access to an application (deliberate or not)
- Violation of user rights
- Blocking the application to permitted users
- Listening in on communications
- Cracking security encryptions
- Code that has a deliberately negative impact on an application or its data
- Using Web applications to transmit a security attack
- Luring Web users to an insecure site

The following sections now turn to considering each of the principal security threats in this list.

Security threat: Exceeding the permitted entry length of an input field (input buffer overflow)

Buffer overflows—
Number 1 threat?

Even though this security threat is perhaps the most well known of them all, the number of input buffer overflow attacks reported since 2000 has not fallen significantly. Many of the worst security violations recorded have resulted from buffer overflow. Let's take a closer look at this particular threat.

If you have ever been involved in testing GUI applications, you may have tried entering an excessively large text string into input fields to check that the software constrains the input to a maximum specified length. This could be one of the standard types of test we design systematically using equivalence partitioning (i.e., entering a value in a negative equivalence partition), using a check list (as is commonly the case with manual GUI testing), or as part of an exploratory testing approach.

It's a small conceptual step from this type of GUI testing to understanding the security threat posed by input buffer overflow. Just as with the GUI test, we are interested in whether inputs to a system are constrained properly. There is a significant difference in the two scenarios though, and that lies in the intention behind the excessively long input made when attemting to force an input buffer overflow. In the GUI test, the tester focuses on whether the input is constrained properly (perhaps we are looking for a particular message being issued to the user), but with the security threat, the intention originates not from a tester, but from a malicious person who is attempting to exploit any unconstrained inputs in order to compromise the system's security. An example from [Chess&West 07] shows how this can happen.

Consider the pseudocode for the following simple function called **trouble**. It declares two local variables and uses the standard function **gets** to read text into a fixed-length character array **stack_buffer**.

```
trouble {
    integer        a = 32
    character      stack_buffer[128]
    gets(stack_buffer) }
```

If we now examine the computer's stack frame (part of its main memory) prior to execution (1 in figure 13-1), during an *unexploited* execution (2) and then during an *exploited* execution (3), it will become apparent why the function was named "trouble".

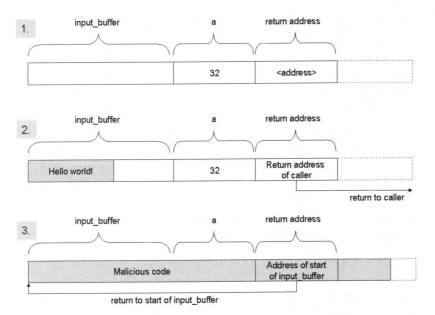

Figure 13–1

Stack frame states with buffer overflow

In situation 2, the function **trouble** behaves in a normal way. It reads the input text "Hello world!" into the input buffer but does not need to use all characters available. The return address of the calling function is used to return to the caller on completion of the code in function **trouble**.

In situation 3, an attacker has exploited the buffer overflow vulnerability caused by the unconstrained input of text into the input buffer. In the example, some malicious code (perhaps a script) has been entered. This text is long enough to fill not only the input buffer but also the space allocated for integer "a" and, critically, the return address of the calling function. After reading in the malicious text (sometimes referred to as *the exploit*), the function does not return normally to the calling function but instead returns to the start of the input buffer and executes the malicious code. What happens next depends on what the malicious code actually contains. One thing is certain though, the system's security has been breached.

We've been exploited!

Security threat: Side effects when conducting permitted functions

When planning functional tests, we typically have a particular objective in mind. We want to show, for example, that a function **xy** performs as specified when executing particular test conditions we have designed. Our focus is primarily on the function under test. What we often find in security testing is that the main focus isn't so much concerned with the actions the system should do (e.g., performing a particular function) but rather on those "other" things that the system might do while performing those actions. For example, when a hotel information system is used by a guest in a "permitted" way, the system may store sensitive information in a local file. If a subsequent guest manages to gain access to the application's file system (yes, some guests might try this too!), all details of previous users can be read from the individual files the system should have protected or deleted.

Security threat: Unauthorized copying or deletion of data or applications

Unchecked inputs strike again.

There are a number of ways in which stored data or applications can be manipulated, deleted, or copied by unauthorized people. Perhaps the most well known, known as SQL-Injection, has similarities with the input buffer overflow threat described earlier. The similarity in both threats is that both involve specific user inputs that have been crafted by a malevolent user to exploit particular security vulnerabilities. With input buffer overflow, unconstrained user input can overwrite critical parts of memory and allow the user to take over control of the system (e.g., with a script). With SQL-Injection, the user input is crafted so that the system performs database manipulations not thought about by the system designer or programmer.

The classic example of SQL-Injection involves a GUI dialog that requests from the user data that is then used to search a database. For example, an insurance system may accepts a user's name in order to perform a variety of actions on that user's policies held in the database. The system creates a database command from the input provided by the user and submits it to the database for execution. No problem, except that if the user chooses to enter their name as "delete all records in policies table", sometimes very undesirable things might then happen to the policies data. Even though this example is, of course, simplistic in nature and programs are rarely as naïve as portrayed here, highly sophisticated measures can still be taken by malevolent users to bypass a program's security checks. In planning security tests, we therefore need to be especially aware of any aspect in a system where user input is taken to query a database.

Security threat: Unauthorized access to an application

This threat is perhaps the most well known of all. It's the classic hacker domain where passwords are cracked and unauthorized access is gained to applications or data. The sources of such threats are quite varied though:

- Access may be gained using special programs developed by the hacker.
- Computer viruses may be spread (e.g., via e-mail) and reside on a user's machine and send sensitive information like passwords back to a location controlled by the hacker.
- Passwords are acquired from users via other nonelectronic means that are often the result of carelessness on the part of the password's owner.

Don't leave your password on a sticky note stuck on the wall of your office.

Security threat: Violation of user rights

Many applications permit certain operations only for users who belong to a specific group with individual rights. For example, a user in the Standard group may only have rights to read data, those in the Special group may be entitled to modify or delete data, and those in the Admin group can perform all operations, including the registration of users and allocation of rights. Security threats exist wherever rights can become incorrectly allocated or acquired, whether deliberately or resulting from defective software.

As you saw in section 10.5, functional security testing will be aimed at finding defects in the system for allocating user access rights and seeking out incorrect implementations of rights in the application (e.g., functions available to people in the wrong user group).

Technical security testing focuses on finding exploitable vulnerabilities that would give a malicious person rights other than those allocated to them (which may include, of course, no rights at all). For example, an unauthorized person may obtain access to system configuration files that enable that person to access user rights data or even assume the role of someone with extensive privileges (typically administrator rights are the "prize" here).

It's important to recognize that many security violations result from design or programming defects. A typical software defect, for example, might result in user rights being allocated to all members of a particular group when it was intended that just an individual in that group should be reassigned. As a result, all members of the group acquire new privileges instead of one person.

Many security violations result from design or programming defects.

Security threat: Blocking the application to permitted users

More commonly known as denial of service, or just plain DOS, this security threat prevents users from accessing or interacting with an application. For example, scripts spread via computer virus can cause huge volumes of "nuisance" transactions to be set off; they are intended to load a web server so heavily that system responses for real users becomes effectively blocked. Ultimately, the affected web server may fail under the load. Launches of new web-based applications are favorite targets for this kind of attack, although this has more to do with the impact a successful DOS has in the media than for any technical reasons.

Security threat: Listening in on communications

Certain communications protocols such as HTTP transfer information over the Internet in text form. This means the contents of the messages can be easily read by any unauthorized person gaining access to them as a result of a successful security attack. Web communications that involve the transfer of sensitive data should therefore use a secure communications protocol such as HTTPS.

Security threat: "Cracking" security encryptions

Even though our communications can be "scrambled" using an encryption mechanism, we should be aware that even these security measures have the potential to be deciphered using dedicated programs.

Homegrown encryptions are easily cracked.

In particular, the use of *homegrown* security encryptions can often be trivial for a skilled hacker to decipher and should be discouraged.

Security threat: Code that has a deliberately negative impact on an application or its data

Even "funny" Easter eggs aren't really that cool.

Malicious code does not always have to be received from some external source, as we have seen with input buffer overflow and SQL-Injection. It can also be entered directly into the code by accident or as a deliberate act of sabotage. These security threats are often referred to as *Easter eggs* or *logic bombs* and remain dormant in the code until triggered by a specific event such as a date (e.g., the programmer's birthday) or a counter reaching a specific value. Even though many Easter eggs are frequently the result of harmless pranks by programmers, they may cause substantial damage to applications and data if they are inserted as an act of revenge.

Security threat: Using Web applications to transmit a security attack

This common form of security threat is usually referred to as *cross-site scripting (XSS)* and is applied when a vulnerable application is exploited by attackers in order to then direct a security attack at their intended victims. The exploited application effectively operates as the *middleman* for the attacker.

In common with the input buffer overflow threat mentioned earlier, a cross-site scripting vulnerability is exploited by receiving data from a source such as a user or a database and not validating that input for potential malicious content. With XSS, this information (*the exploit*) is then passed on to victims by including it in the responses sent out to other Web users when they contact the infected application. When the user's browser receives the response it unpacks the content and executes the exploit. This can result in almost any kind of security problem, but it often involves the transmission of private data to the attacker.

Security threat: Luring Web users to an insecure site

If Web users can be lured to an insecure website, it may be possible for the malicious person controlling that site to gain access to their personal information. This is sometimes referred to as *phishing*. Victims are typically lured to the site with e-mail messages that appear to have originated from an authentic organization. The message requests users to visit the site to perform some kind of apparently legitimate activity (e.g., registering for a free prize or verifying credit card details) that exposes the user's data. A number of strategies exist for luring a victim to a fake website (see [Chess&West 07]) for further details).

Phishing for the unsuspecting

Summary of Security Threats

Table 13-1 summarizes the threats, the terms commonly used to describe them, and the general applicability of these threats to testing done by test analysts or technical test analysts.

Threat description	Commonly used terms	Technical test analyst	Test analyst
Exceeding the permitted entry length of an input field	Input buffer overflow	X	X (via user interface)
Side effects when conducting "permitted" functions		X	X (limited to functional issues)
Unauthorized copy or deletion of data or applications	SQL-Injection	X	
Unauthorized access to an application	Hacking	X	X
Violation of user rights			X
Blocking the application to permitted users	Denial of service	X	
Listening in on communications		X	
Deciphering security encryptions	Cracking	X	
Code that has a deliberately negative impact on an application or its data	Easter eggs, logic bombs	X	
Using Web applications to transm it a security attack	Cross-site scripting (XSS)	X	
Luring Web users to an insecure site	Phishing	X	

Security testing is not hacking.

13.4.1 Approach to Security Testing

It would be incorrect to think of security testing as being equivalent to a *hacking* operation. A good approach to security testing involves a well-balanced selection of different static and dynamic testing elements, which can include the following:

- Technical reviews of documents
- Static analysis of code
- Dynamic analysis during code execution
- Performing planned attacks on identified security vulnerabilities

Technical Reviews and Security

Technical reviews are directed primarily at the code and at documents that implement a system's security policy. These are typically architectural documents, although any other document can be reviewed provided it contains sufficient technical detail to make a security review possible.

The following aspects can be reviewed to identify fundamental security problems in such documents:

Basic check list for security reviews

- Communications protocols to be used
- Encryption methods to be used
- Specific hardware elements in the architecture (e.g., routers, firewalls, servers), especially those that are outside of our own control
- Measures to be adopted for administering user privileges and issuing passwords and IDs (e.g., PINs for credit cards)
- Measures to be adopted for implementing configurations (e.g., of application servers and web clients)
- Measures to be used for ensuring protection against viruses
- Physical security issues (e.g., ensuring restricted entry to data centers)
- Policies to be adopted to ensure that national or company security standards are applied

Technical reviews of code can be a useful approach for detecting certain security violations, although the use of specialized tools is likely to be a more effective and cost-efficient solution (provided, of course, that a tool is available for the programming language used). Some security vulnerabilities such as Easter eggs can often be readily detected by a skilled reviewer focusing on such issues.

Formal reviews may be required in order to demonstrate compliance with the specific security policy required by a customer (e.g., a government agency). The security policy may have been developed by the customer itself or may refer to an existing recognized standard like the ones defined by the National Institute of Standards and Technology [URL: NIST] or the International Organization for Standardization (ISO) as in "the code of practice for information security management" (ISO/IEC17799). These reviews are often performed by an external organization nominated by the customer and could take the form of an official security audit.

Static Analysis and Security

Tool Tip   Static analysis of code is an effective approach for locating potential security vulnerabilities and actual security violations. If tools can be used for
this task, a large number of security threats can be evaluated and both the
effectiveness and efficiency aspects of the analysis are improved. A major
advantage to using static analysis tools is that the companies who develop
them have a group of security experts who are constantly updating the
tools to check for the latest security threats. Given the risks posed by undetected security vulnerabilities, it is hard to imagine a serious approach to
security testing without the use of such tools.

Security Attacks

Performing planned attacks on identified security vulnerabilities is an
interactive, defect-based strategy for detecting security violations. The
approach recommended by [Whittaker 04] involves the development of
attack plans, which represent the testing actions to be performed when

Experience Report: Electronic health application

Electronic health cards permit the owner and their doctors to
quickly access their health cases and allow medicines to be prescribed and delivered in a timely manner. This represents a big step
forward in patient care but poses significant security risks regarding
patient data.

In one such project, (in which I developed the testing concept),
security issues had a significant influence on both development and
testing. A few of the lessons learned on this project are discussed
here (dear reader, I'm sure you will understand why I can't be too
specific!):

The effort required to test the application's use cases was less
than the effort spent on technical and functional security issues.

Creating representative test data was a major challenge. Data
held on the cards of test patients still had to be encrypted and put
onto those cards using the prescribed procedures. This involved
trust centers, card production facilities, and external organizations.
Our ability to apply exploratory approaches was severely limited by
these factors; we simply could not respond quickly to testing situations as they occurred and had to wait days while new "patients"
were created for exploratory purposes.

attempting to compromise a particular aspect of system security. Attacks are considered in more detail in section 13.4, "Security Test Analysis and Design".

13.4.2 Organizational Issues

It's not unusual to find security testing in the hands of a group of skilled specialists who may be independent of both the development organization and the testing team. This in part is due to the very nature of security; we want to keep information about security issues confined to a small group of people.

13.4.3 Life Cycle Issues

As mentioned in section 13.3.2 "Approach to Security Testing", a number of measures can be defined to detect security vulnerabilities or actual violations at different stages in the software development life cycle. The actual measures adopted vary according to risk and the availability of items such as documents and code. Table 13-2 provides some guidance on when it may be appropriate to conduct security tests.

Security testing applies throughout the life cycle.

Stage in life cycle	Security testing measures
Security requirements available	Technical review of security policy
System architecture available	Technical review of architecture
Code written	Static analysis (with tool) Code review
System implemented	Dynamic analysis (with tool) Dedicated attacks
System productive	Any of the above measures

Table 13–2
When to perform security testing

When scheduling security tests, it is important to recognize that our systems are generally not exposed to attempted violations until they have entered productive use. Since potential sources of security violations (in particular, those transmitted via the Internet) may then occur at any time, it is essential that our security testing approach considers the operational phase of our system's life cycle. Monitoring measures, maintenance testing strategies, and change procedures all need to consider new or changing security vulnerabilities.

13.5 Security Test Analysis and Design

13.5.1 Software Attacks

Three steps in developing attacks

As mentioned in section 13.3.2, "Approach to Security Testing", a number of options are available for creating a well-balanced approach to security testing, one of which includes the application of attacks to the system under test. Three principal steps are identified by [Whittaker 04] concerning the development of security attacks:

- Initial gathering of security-relevant information
- Performing a vulnerability scan
- Developing the security attacks themselves

Initial gathering of information typically involves obtaining data about networks used (such as IP numbers) and the version numbers or identities of hardware and software used. Tools can assist in this task or documents may be available that contain relevant information.

Tool tip

The vulnerability scan then helps to identify areas in our system that may be good candidates for security attacks. An understanding of the types of security threats that typically occur (see section 13.3.1, "Typical Security Threats") will help us to identify where the vulnerabilities need to be addressed in our own specific application. Static analysis tools with security specializations can be of considerable assistance here, or we can apply check lists and security defect taxonomies to either code or design documents (refer to [URL: TestingStandards] for a check list example).

Examples of the security threats and their sources are shown in table 13-3.

13.5.2 Other Design Techniques for Security Tests

Combine systematic and nonsystematic techniques.

Security attacks may utilize a number of systematic and nonsystematic testing techniques to achieve their overall objectives.

Exploratory approaches are particularly appropriate for performing certain security attacks. Consider, for example, the security threat described in section 13.3.1 as "Side effects when conducting permitted functions". We want to show that a function does "other things" when performing its intended task correctly. Detecting those "other things" is intrinsically an exploratory testing activity where we use our knowledge of the system, our testing skills, and heuristics to exploit security vulnerabilities (see section 7.4).

Source	Typical threat
User interface (UI)	Unauthorized access Malicious inputs (e.g., input buffer overflow, SQL-Injection)
File system	Access to sensitive data stored in files or repositories
Operating system	Crashing the operating system through malicious inputs may expose sensitive information held in memory.
External software	Packets or messages exchanged at network level may include malicious input similar to those entered via the user interface. A software component on which an application relies may itself not be secure and could affect the "user" application's own security.

Table 13–3
Typical sources of security threats

Other kinds of security defects can be uncovered by using systematic testing techniques. The allocation of user rights, for example, is often governed by a set of logical rules that can be tested using the cause-effect graphing technique (see section 4.2.3) to cover all possible combinations of inputs (causes) and outputs (effects). Similarly, equivalence partitioning may be a useful systematic technique to apply when designing tests for input buffer overflows (negative partitions).

Generally speaking, we need to consider a combination of both systematic and nonsystematic techniques to design good dynamic security tests. If we adopt an approach that combines this with an appropriate balance of reviews and analysis techniques, we will be making the most of the resources available for testing software security.

13.6 Execution of Security Tests

Before executing attacks it may be necessary to create any specific test data and exploits required (e.g., malicious SQL statements or scripts for attempted insertion via the user interface). It goes (hopefully) without saying that extreme care should be exercised when conducting security tests, even under test conditions. Before execution, ensure that the environment in which the test is conducted can be returned to its previous state.

Security tests can be destructive—be careful if you value your data!

Security attacks are a planned activity and provide a framework for test execution that is frequently exploratory in nature (see chapter 7). The testers performing these activities require considerable skill to execute security attacks in this way. Notes taken during execution should be carefully stored for use in reporting.

Experience Report: Hotel information system

I once attended a class in exploratory testing given by a well-known disciple of the exploratory school. While we were waiting in the hotel foyer one evening, the online hotel information system naturally became the target for a spot of exploring by said expert. It didn't take that long before the input of some meta characters had exposed the hotel's file system for all to see. A brief look revealed that files had been created for each person that had used the system for anything other than browsing.

I learned two really important lessons there, the first one of which was that a skilled tester really can compromise systems like this with comparative ease. The most important lesson, however, concerned ethics. We as testers are not hackers out to do damage or compromise other people's privacy. We are professionals who know when to say "stop" and pass the relevant information on to those who can act on it.

In this case, it would have been too easy to open files and examine private data, but instead the session was terminated and the hotel manager informed of the security vulnerability. Of course, the manager didn't really understand and was somewhat annoyed at having had his system "hacked", but the exercise was a good one and should be remembered by all of us.

13.7 Reporting Security Tests

Security reporting must show traceability between the specific security vulnerabilities identified for the system under test, the actual tests performed, and the test results obtained.

The highly sensitive nature of security testing generally calls for special precautions to be taken when reporting results. It is common for the following measures to be taken:

- Creation of security-specific reports, which are distributed to a restricted number of recipients
- Use of a separate defect tracking system for security-related defects
- Use of encryption when reporting security-related test results or defects using electronic media (e.g., e-mail, FTP)

The test manager is responsible for making decisions related to these issues and communicating them to all those engaged in security testing.

13.8 Tools for Security Testing

Tools used for security testing support analysis and conducting attacks.

Tool Tip

Static analysis tools for security testing work to the same principle as any other static analysis tools; they analyze code according to predefined rules of good programming practice. In this case, the rules relate specifically to several of the security threats identified in section 13.3.1. The thoroughness and efficiency with which these tools operate make them an attractive option for any security testing strategy. An example of such a tool is Fortify Source Code Analysis [URL: Fortify]. A list of tools is included in [Chess&West 07].

Conducting attacks can be supported by a variety of individual tools, each with its own speciality. Free tools are available that, for example, permit very long strings to be constructed for use in detecting input buffer overflows. Tools also exist that can simulate exception conditions raised by operating systems that might otherwise be difficult to create. An example of such a tool is Holodeck [URL: Holodeck].

13.9   Let's Be Practical

Security of the Marathon Application

The Marathon application has a number of features that could exhibit security vulnerabilities, some examples of which are discussed in the following sections:

Marathon User Groups

The Internet portal offers different functions to race participants and sponsors. The race organizers wish to prevent participants from also being sponsors and have designated separate user groups. In addition, each race has an organizer who can allocate privileges to the two groups using a configuration file.

Potential vulnerabilities:

- The separation of functions according to user groups may not be correctly implemented.
- It may be possible for nonadministrators to access the configuration file and change the privileges.

Marathon Public Information System

The Internet portal offers a variety of information to the general public concerning race details, how to enter, how to sponsor, and (after the race) the results. Registering to become either a participant or a sponsor requires filling out a form online and submitting it to the race organizer.

Potential vulnerabilities:

- Denial of service attacks by those wishing to stop the race from taking place.

- Registration forms may be vulnerable to input buffer overflow or cross-site scripting threats.

- Lack of control around the issuing of passwords to participants and sponsors

Upon completion of an application form, the system uses a strict set of conditions to decide whether a Marathon participant has been successful or whether a sponsor can be accepted. In either case, the system allocates a username and password that is then communicated by e-mail.

Potential vulnerabilities:

- A successful cross-site scripting attack could result in the password and username also being sent to an address or website controlled by the exploiter.
- An Easter Egg may have been inserted into the code to make sure a particular Marathon participant (maybe a friend of the programmer) is accepted.

The list of vulnerabilities goes on and on.

Marathon: Password-Protected Areas for Participants and Sponsors

Registered Marathon runners and sponsors use their login data to access a protected area of the Internet portal. In the participant area, registered runners can view and change certain items of master data or withdraw from the race. In the sponsors' area, master data can also be changed and runners selected for sponsorship.

Potential vulnerabilities:

- The login and password data for sponsors or runners could be "cracked" by a hacker, who is then able to access sensitive master data, such as credit card details used for invoicing sponsors.
- A malicious person may be able to avoid the system's checks and obtain registration as a runner or sponsor. This enables the person to access exploitable input fields.

Marathon: Storage of Invoicing Information

The cost database holds all data needed to prepare invoices for sponsors after completion of the race. The data is then archived on the server for one year.

Potential vulnerabilities:

- The file system may present an exploitable vulnerability that could result in access to all stored cost records.

13.10 Learning Check

The following check lists will help you judge the knowledge you have gained from this chapter.

Terms

input buffer overflow, software attack, *Easter Eggs, *pfishing, *denial of service, *SQL injection, *vulnerability scan, *cross-site scripting

Exercises

The reports generator system in the Marathon application creates individual reports for each runner and sends them to the communications server for onward communication via e-mail to runners. Can you identify any potential security vulnerabilities associated with this functionality? (Remember, development of the reports generator has been contracted out to a third party).

Technical Test Analyst and Test Analyst

The following list applies to both test analysts and technical test analysts. Some of the specific threats and techniques on this list apply more to one than the other depending on whether they are fundamentally functional or technical in nature (the summary table at the end of section 13.3.1, "Typical Security Threats", provides a guideline on which aspects are relevant to which type of test analyst).

- Understand types of security threats and their potential impact on a system.
- Propose a risk-based approach for testing security using appropriate techniques.
- Understand and explain the stages in an application's life cycle where security tests may be applied.
- Be able to identify the basic elements of security attacks and relate them to a system's security vulnerabilities.
- Describe the preconditions for security test execution.
- Understand the different types of security testing tools.

14 Reliability Testing

Reliability testing is designed to determine if the software will work in the expected environment for an acceptable amount of time without degradation. Reliability testing is difficult to do effectively and is frequently made more difficult due to the lack of clear requirements. Everyone expects the software to "work", but no one wants to define what "work" means. That's one of the challenges the technical test analyst faces when planning and executing reliability tests.

14.1 Overview

It's important before we start talking about reliability in detail to get a proper grasp of its meaning, especially since reliability is often not so well understood when compared to other quality attributes like functionality, performance, and security. Just like other quality attributes, there are a number of different aspects of reliability, which are introduced in this section.

The software will just work, won't it?

Generally speaking, reliability describes the ability of the software product to perform its required functions under stated conditions for a specified period of time or for a specified number of operations (see ISO 9126 and the ISTQB Glossary). When we talk about reliability, we therefore always need to think of the two factors "doing what?" (stated conditions) and "for how long?" (time or operations).

Reliability is normally measured by a specific failure intensity metric, such as the mean time between failures (MTBF) (see section 14.2.2, "Setting Reliability Objectives", for details). Software that fails on average once a week is considered less reliable than software that fails once a month. When we make statements like this, we shouldn't forget to differentiate between the severities of those failures and the conditions under which the software was operating (the "doing what?" element of our reliability definition).

Software reliability can be improved by programming practices that "catch" error conditions as they occur and handle them in a defined manner (e.g., issue an error message, perform an alternative action, use default values if calculated values are in some way considered to be incorrect). This ability of the software to maintain a specified level of performance and not to break when a failure or an unexpected event takes place is referred to as *fault tolerance*. The word *robustness* is also used in this context.

Planning for disasters   An important aspect of reliability relates to the software's ability to reestablish a specified level of performance and recover any data directly affected by the failure. The "recoverability" of our software can be considered under the following two aspects:

■ Failover capability: Ability to maintain continuous system operations even in the event of failure. In this case, the re-establishing of a specified level of performance may actually take place seamlessly and without the users of our software (e.g., end users or other systems) noticing. For more information on failover testing, see [URL: Testing Standards].

■ Restore capability: Ability to minimize the effects of a failure on the system's data.

If the recovery should take place as a result of some catastrophic event (e.g., fire, earthquake), it is common to call this *disaster recovery*.

14.2 Reliability Test Planning

Test planning needs to consider all of the reliability attributes mentioned earlier within the context of the specific software or system under test. This means performing the following primary activities:

■ Assessment of risks associated with reliability
■ Definition of an appropriate testing approach to address those risks
■ Setting reliability goals
■ Scheduling the tests

14.2.1 Assessing the Risk

Reliability risks can affect a wide range of system types and industries. The examples in table 14-1 demonstrate this by considering just a sample of applications where high reliability levels can be expected.

Type of Application	Consequence of Poor Reliability
Control software for chemical processes that need to run continuously	Exposure to the risk of uncontrolled chemical reactions taking place
Software for military surveillance radars	Risk to a country's defenses
Online systems with worldwide user bases (e.g., eBay, Amazon)	Considerable financial loss and damage to their corporate images
Check-in software for airlines	Delays to passengers and loss of market share
Service Oriented Architectures (SOA) in which web-based business services offer general services for use by other applications	Loss of functionality for any application using this service

Table 14–1

The effects of poor reliability on particular types of application

When considering the recoverability aspects of reliability, we need to understand the impact of a failure or disruption:

- The criticality of system failures
- The consequences of interruptions in normal operations (whether planned or not)
- The implications of any data losses resulting from failures

The applications shown in table 14-2 are examples of where poor software recoverability can pose significant risks.

Type of Application	Consequence of Poor Recoverability
Safety-critical software that must not fail while in operation (e.g., flight control software).	Exposure to safety risk (e.g., aircraft crash).
Business applications that, for example, make use of external systems and must provide at least basic standby functionality despite failure in those external systems. For example, an online theatre reservation system may rely on an external application for credit card validation. If this fails, the system must still be able to accept reservations for later confirmation.	Basic standby functionality cannot be provided. In the example, the online theatre reservation system cannot accept unconfirmed reservations and will cause its business owner loss of revenue.

Table 14–2

The effects of poor recoverability on particular types of application

Table continues

Table 14-2

continued

Type of Application	Consequence of Poor Recoverability
Any application where downtimes must be minimized and could even be regulated by Service Level Agreements (SLAs). For example, a system for automatically collecting money from users of a rail network.	System takes too much time to restore to an agreed-upon level of service following failure or planned downtime. In the example, the system may not have recovered after scheduled night-time maintenance by the time the rush hour starts. The system owner loses money, the operator may be fined for breach of SLA, and the users pay nothing (hey, not all consequences have to be negative).
Any application where data backups are considered a necessity. For example, an application used by a sales force may need to regularly back up its customer database.	Data loss as a result of scheduled or unplanned application downtime. In the example, the sales force may actually lose customer data (with a variety of consequences according to what data was lost for which customer).

Lesson Learned: Know your reliability risks

Testing budgets for fault tolerance and failover testing suffer from the same kind of "that would never happen here" syndrome that can also affect security testing. An important aspect of being a technical test analyst is being aware of the risks and being able to communicate them to other stakeholders.

Lessons Learned from Major Failures

It seems to be a feature of real headline-grabbing failures that they could have been avoided with better fault tolerance and failover testing. Two examples spring to mind here:

1. The failure of entire sections of the U.S. telecommunications system resulting from an unhandled failure in a switching station.

2. Half of Europe went dark one Saturday night in 2006 when a single power cable was cut by a passing ship's mast on a waterway in northern Germany.

Both major failures resulted from systems that did not handle the local failure correctly and propagated the problem throughout an extensive and highly interdependent system.

These types of failures are not easy to predict in advance, often because the risks are simply not recognized. Reliability testing can help identify and mitigate these risks, but we need good analysis skills to do it effectively.

14.2.2 Setting Reliability Objectives

Reliability isn't a software quality characteristic that just happens—it grows. At the planning stage, we need to set out the reliability objectives to be achieved and state how their achievement will be measured. As we will see in section 14.3, "Reliability Test Specification", this involves not only setting the end objective, but also considering how we expect reliability to gradually improve over time.

Reliability grows over time.

A commonly used time-based measure for reliability is the mean time between failures (MTBF), which is made up of the following two components:

- The mean time to failure (MTTF), representing the actual time elapsed (in hours) between observed failures

- The mean time to repair (MTTR), representing the number of hours needed by a developer to fix the problem

Ilene Burnstein [Burnstein 03] reminds us that we should be precise in our measurements and that CPU execution time is often a more appropriate measure than simple elapsed "wall clock" time. This enables planned downtimes and other disturbances to be taken into account and removes the possibility of calculating overly pessimistic values of reliability.

In Ilene Burnstein's book, a measure for reliability (R) is also mentioned, which is based on MTBF and takes a value between 0 (totally unreliable) and 1 (completely reliable). The calculation of R is simply MTBF divided by (1 + MTBF). Clearly, the larger the value of MTBF (i.e., failures occur further apart), the closer R approaches (but, significantly, never reaches) 1.

If recoverability tests are included in our approach to reliability testing, it may be appropriate to define testing objectives as follows:

Typical recoverability testing objectives

Failover

- Test objectives are to create failure modes that require failover measures to be taken (possibly also associated with a time constraint within which this must happen).

Backup

- ■ Test objectives are to verify that different types of backup (e.g., full, incremental, image) can be completed, possibly within a given time period.
- ■ Objectives may also relate to service levels for guaranteed data backup (e.g., master data no more than 4 days old, noncritical transaction data no more than 48 hours old, critical transaction data no older than 10 minutes).

Restore

- ■ Test objectives are to verify that a specified level of functionality (e.g., emergency, partial, full) can be achieved, possibly within a given time period.
- ■ An objective may also be to measure the time taken to recognize whether any data losses or corruptions have occurred after a failure and restore the lost or corrupted data (possibly differentiated by the types of data backed up, as mentioned earlier).

It is not uncommon for one of more of the objectives discussed in this section to be carried over into production and monitored as Service Level Agreements.

14.2.3 Life Cycle Issues

Several test repetitions are necessary to measure reliability levels.

Tests to measure reliability levels are mostly conducted during the system test or (operational) acceptance test levels. This is primarily because these test levels present more opportunity for executing the test cycle repetitions necessary to measure reliability levels accurately. The repetitious nature of these reliability tests also makes them good candidates for conducting dynamic analysis in parallel, especially regarding memory leaks (see section 8.2.3).

Tests aimed at measuring reliability levels can also be conducted in a highly controlled manner with a large number of test cases. If this approach is taken, it may be necessary to plan for a number of days for their execution and possibly the exclusive use of a testing environment with a stable software configuration over that time frame.

It may be efficient to schedule tests of fault tolerance (robustness) at the same time as failover tests or even certain security tests since the required test inputs (e.g., exception conditions raised by the operating system) may be common.

The operational acceptance test (OAT) level is typically where procedural tests for backup and restoration are conducted. These tests are best scheduled together with the staff that will be responsible for actually performing the specified procedures in production.

Finally, the scheduling of any reliability tests (but in particular, failover tests) for a system of systems can present a technical and managerial challenge that should not be underestimated, especially if one or more components are outside of our direct control.

14.2.4 Approaches to Reliability Testing

Our approach to reliability testing in the context of a specific project is governed by a number of factors:

- Identified risks, in particular those relating to safety-critical systems
- Applicable standards
- Available resources (as ever)

The following sections discuss possible approaches that can be taken for the different types of reliability testing should your project context demand them.

When planning an approach to reliability tests it is worth bearing in mind that some tests will be defined with one aspect of reliability in focus but which might also be applicable to other reliability aspects. If we decide, for example, to evaluate the recoverability of a system, we may first need to cause that system to fail. The very act of defining these tests (i.e., getting the system to fail) may give us insights into the fault tolerance of our system.

14.2.5 Approach for Measuring Reliability Levels

A systematic approach to demonstrating achieved levels of reliability is to submit functional test cases to successive versions of the software at regular intervals, measure the number of failures that occur, and compare this failure rate to a model of predicted reliability. The possible sources of the test cases and details regarding reliability growth models are described in section 14.3, "Reliability Test Specification".

14.2.6 Approach for Establishing Fault Tolerance

It's good to be negative when looking for fault tolerance. To establish fault tolerance, *negative* tests are designed to generate or simulate specific conditions to be handled by the application or system. Fault tolerance testing should be considered at several testing levels:

- At the unit test level, the testing approach focuses on the unit's handling of exceptions, in particular those relating to its interface parameters. Incorrect inputs may include values out of range, use of incorrect formats, and semantically incorrect values.
- Functional integration testing may focus on incorrect inputs submitted to the software via the user interface, from files, or from databases. These tests apply the same kind of incorrect inputs as described above for unit tests, although more focus may be applied to semantically incorrect inputs. The tests can effectively be combined with usability tests (see chapter 11), which evaluate the relevance and understandability of error messages presented to users.
- System testing is more appropriate for applying incorrect inputs that originate from an external source such as the operating system or another system. Since especially these external sources of failure can be difficult to simulate, a tool-based approach using commercial products or self-developed simulators or emulators may be appropriate.

Specification-based testing techniques (e.g., boundary value analysis) are generally used as an approach to designing tests for fault tolerance, although it may be advisable to supplement this approach with nonsystematic techniques such as software attacks and exploratory testing.

intending to show coverage of error-handling code in our testing, we should also be aware of this to avoid underestimating the size of the task.

14.2.7 Approach to Failover Testing

Failover testing should be considered as an essential component in our test planning when the risks associated with the failure of an application or system are assessed as unacceptably high.

Planning to fail...over

Ensuring that failover mechanisms are implemented that address the risks is primarily the concern of system architects. An important element of our testing approach should therefore include technical reviews of the architectural documents that describe the proposed failover measures to be taken. The technical reviews should focus on how the hardware and the software architecture ensure that alternative system components are used if a particular component fails. Technical test analysts should have an understanding of these measures so that architectural faults can be detected early and in order to assess the impact of the failover measures on testing. The following measures are possible:

- Use of redundant hardware devices (e.g., servers, processors, disks), which are arranged such that one component immediately takes over from another should it fail. Disks, for example, can be included in the architecture as a RAID element (Redundant Array of Inexpensive Disks).
- Redundant software implementation, in which more than one independent instance of a software system is implemented (perhaps by independent teams) using the same set of requirements. These so-called *redundant dissimilar systems* are expensive to implement but provide a level of risk coverage against external events (e.g., defective inputs) that are less likely to be handled in the same way and therefore less likely to cause software failures.
- Use of multiple levels of redundancy, which can be applied to both software and hardware to effectively add additional "safety nets" should a component fail. These systems are called duplex, triplex, or quadruplex systems, depending on how many independent instances (2, 3, or 4 respectively) of the software or hardware are implemented.
- Use of detection and switching mechanisms for determining whether a failure in the software or hardware has occurred and whether to switch

(failover) to an alternative. Sometimes these decisions are relatively simple; software has crashed or hardware has failed and a failover needs to be enacted. In other circumstances, the decision may not be that simple. A hardware component may be physically available but supplying incorrect data due to some malfunction. Mechanisms need to be implemented that enable these untrustworthy data sources to be identified and trustworthy ones used instead. In software, these mechanisms are often referred to as *voting* systems because they are constantly monitoring and conducting a vote on which of the redundant data sources to trust. Ultimately these systems may shut down hardware components deemed to be no longer trustworthy (i.e., failed).

Voting software for redundant systems requires rigorous testing. Depending on the type of redundancy implemented (duplex, triplex, etc.), voting systems can be highly complex and are often among the most critical components in the software. For these reasons, it is advisable to include thorough structural and specification-based testing of this software in the testing approach. Since voting software is highly rule and state based, the adoption of decision table testing or state transitions testing techniques may be appropriate.

Dynamic testing of the failover mechanisms of complete applications or systems of systems is an essential element of a reliability testing approach. The value of these tests arises from our ability to realistically describe the failure modes to be handled and simulate them in a controlled and fully representative environment.

14.2.8 Approach to Backup and Restore Testing

The approach to testing the backup and restore capability of systems focuses principally on procedure testing and on specification-based dynamic testing techniques.

Have the operations staff walk though the procedures. Procedural testing is used to statically validate the backup and restore procedures to be followed by the organization responsible for operating the system. At an informal level, the procedures may be subjected to a structured walkthrough with the operations staff. It can be quite useful here to ask staff to walk through their own part of the procedure and explain each step. Of course, other review types such as technical reviews may also be proposed in your testing approach and may, for example, focus in detail specifically on critical or frequently used paths through the procedures.

Especially for complex systems, the backup and restore procedures can themselves be viewed as manually executed "programs" with many of the associated programming constructs (sequences of operations, decisions, loops, etc.). The use of structural testing techniques such as decision coverage may be a valuable approach to adopt here. These techniques can provide reviews with coverage data or be used to design test cases for dynamic tests.

Use structural testing techniques.

Backup and restore procedures should be subjected to dynamic testing as part of the system testing or operational acceptance tests (OATs). Tests are designed that exercise specific aspects of the backup and restore procedures in various time-dependent scenarios.

14.3 Reliability Test Specification

14.3.1 Test Specification for Reliability Growth

Specifying tests to establish reliability levels involves the following three principal steps:

- Establishing an *operational profile*
- Selecting a *reliability growth model*
- Designing or selecting the test cases to be used

Establishing an Operational Profile

It is essential that representative patterns of usage are used when collecting reliability data. These patterns of usage are referred to as operational profiles and can be gathered from the functional requirements or from stakeholders such as business owners or end users. Similar operational profiles may have been defined for performance testing (see section 12.9, "Specification of Efficiency Tests"), in which case they can be reused for reliability testing if appropriate.

Selecting a Reliability Growth Model

Before commencing with reliability testing, the levels of acceptable reliability are set (see section 14.2.2, "Setting Reliability Objectives") together with the rate at which the measured reliability level is expected to improve from test run to test run. In this case, *test run* means the repeated execution of several defined test cases that represent the given operational profile. A test run can be representative of many hours of operational use. A reliability growth model is effectively nothing more than a prediction of failures to be expected over time (remember, CPU time is better).

The big questions now are What form of reliability growth model is appropriate for my particular application/system? and What use is this going to be to me anyway? Ilene Burnstein [Burnstein 03] provides some good insights into these aspects of reliability testing that can help us answer these questions.

Three useful types of reliability growth models

To answer the first question, we first need to know what forms of growth model exist and are likely to be useful. Many studies have been conducted into this subject (see Burnstein's book for references to these studies), but three types stand out as most useful:

- Static growth models.
  These are used where everything is expected to stay as it is—no software changes and no changes to operational profiles. They may be appropriate for stable, standard software components that are already productive.

- Basic growth models (also known as *continuous*).
  These are more appropriate for software development projects where failures are expected. We expect the interval between failures to increase steadily over time as the software matures (i.e., becomes more reliable). The rate of increase we have to decide by ourselves though. The diagram in figure 14-1 shows test results compared to a basic reliability growth model. In the example, reliability is currently lower than we would expect. Between failures 249 and 250, we would expect to need approximately 14 CPU hours of testing, but instead the interval is at 9 CPU hours.

- Logarithmic Poisson models (also known as *exponential*)
  These are particularly useful if we assume that improvements to reliability increase exponentially as corrections are made to any failures discovered. Parameters defining the growth model need to be carefully defined.

Figure 14-2 shows an example of an exponential reliability growth curve. In this example, the reliability objectives have not been defined in terms of CPU hours between failures (as in the preceding example) but in terms of failures found per test run (remember, a test run can consist of many test

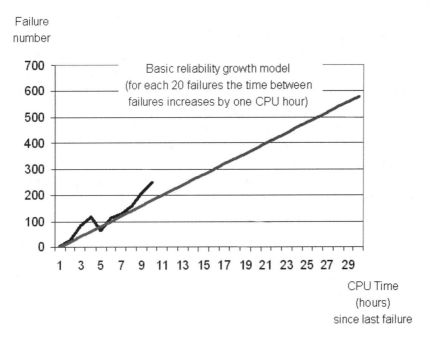

Failure
number

Basic reliability growth model
(for each 20 failures the time between
failures increases by one CPU hour)

CPU Time
(hours)
since last failure

Figure 14–1
Continuous growth model

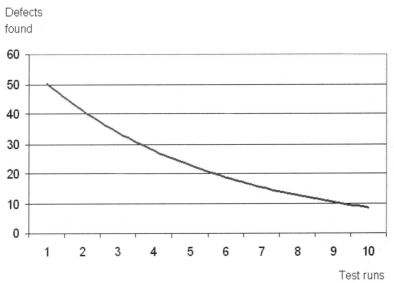

Defects
found

Test runs

Figure 14–2
Defect removal curve

cases performed on a given software configuration). A possible reliability objective may be defined at 10 defects found per test run. In that case, we would expect to perform nine test runs.

As you may imagine, the task of selecting a reliability growth model is not always a simple one. If testing is being carried out as part of a software development project, it may be best to start with a basic model and refine as experience develops and better information becomes available. Tools can also help to track failure data to determine the most appropriate reliability growth curve for our project. Whatever growth model we use, we should be able to justify our choice. After that we should realize that our model is really just a model; uncertainties will arise, inconsistencies might appear during our testing, and perhaps revisions will have to be made.

Where's the benefit?   This would seem like a good time to return to the second of our original two questions: What benefit do we have from reliability growth models?

- We can make predictions regarding how much testing time would be needed to detect the next failure or achieve reliability objectives. This provides helpful input in balancing out the cost of quality (which includes testing) with the cost of failure and communicating this to stakeholders.
- We can judge whether our software's reliability is growing as expected and make appropriate management decisions to correct discrepancies.
- We can measure reliability objectives that can be used as exit criteria for testing.

To summarize, reliability growth models are an important part of reliability testing and provide a beneficial instrument primarily to the test manager.

Designing or Selecting the Test Cases to Be Used

Test cases for measuring reliability testing levels can come from a number of different sources:

- If test cases are already available, it may be acceptable to identify a subset to be executed in the regular reliability test runs. The selection can be performed manually with the intention of achieving a good balance across different functional aspects of the system or, alternatively, can be made according to risk criteria. More formal approaches may randomly select test cases from a pool (database).
- More formal reliability testing strategies may generate sets of test data for the test cases. This can be done either randomly or according to some predefined statistical distribution or model.

■ In some circumstances, the test cases and associated data are designed specifically for the purpose of reliability testing. This may be the case where particular types of defects are targeted (e.g., memory leaks, defective logic in complex algorithms, incorrect state transitions, timing problems).

14.3.2 Test Specification for Fault Tolerance

The most important task for specifying test cases for the fault tolerance aspects of reliability is the analysis that leads to a list of specific negative events the system should be able to handle in a defined way. These test conditions can initially be obtained from analysis of requirements and architectural design documents (if they are available), but they should be supplemented with the results from brainstorming sessions and workshops conducted together with developers, software architects, and operations staff. Defect taxonomies may be used to support this activity (see section 6.2).

Here are some typical events of interest to fault tolerance testing:

■ Process or interface not available (especially relevant for systems of systems)
■ Network connection down
■ Link not found (for web-based systems)
■ Various hardware and software failures raised by the operating system, such as "disk full" when attempting to write a record to a database or insufficient memory available for operation

The network went down???

Once the list of negative events is available, test cases can be documented according to [IEEE 829], attacks can be defined (see sections 7.5 and 13.4.1), or the list used to support exploratory testing (see section 7.4). If security testing is to be performed for this application, the list should be made known to those responsible so that synergies can be generated where possible.

Negative tests that are specified as part of the unit or functional testing are generally designed using specification-based techniques such as equivalence partitioning or state transition testing. These tests may also have been specified by developers, business specialists, or test analysts without direct responsibility for reliability tests.

14.3.3 Test Specification for Failover

In contrast to fault tolerance testing, the test design for failover testing is primarily concerned with identifying different hardware and software conditions that could cause the system to actually fail. If a Failure Mode and Effect Analysis (FMEA) or a Software Common Cause Failure Analysis (SCCFA) has been performed for the system under test, a valuable source of failover conditions may be available. Otherwise, failure conditions must be identified in the same manner as conditions for fault tolerance tests.

Test cases are designed for system tests that typically consist of the following elements:

- Simulation of the failure conditions (or specific combinations of conditions)
- Evaluation of whether the failure condition was correctly detected and the required failover mechanisms activated (possibly also within a maximum time period)
- Verification that functionality and data are consistent with the pre-failover state

Test cases may also be developed explicitly to test the software responsible for identifying failures and initiating the failover mechanisms. These tests are generally designed to the highest level of rigor where safety-critical systems are involved.

> **Experience Report: Flight control system**
>
> For 18 months I participated in the testing of a safety-critical component of the flight control system for a multinational fighter aircraft. The aircraft was designed to be aerodynamically unstable to improve maneuverability in flight, but this made it totally dependent on its systems to stay in the air (this is about as safety-critical as it gets folks). The entire flight control system (hardware and software) was designed as a quadruplex redundant system (everything four times), and naturally the failover testing was a major component of the testing approach.
>
> Here are some of the aspects of this testing that stood out:
>
> 1. A formal Failure Mode and Effect Analysis (FMEA) was conducted and provided a valuable source of information for test design.
>
> 2. Formal inspections were performed on the *voting* software, which decided on the trustworthiness of inputs received from each of the

four separate systems (we called them lanes). This included inspection of documents and code, all of which were developed to strict project standards.
3. Performing failover tests with production-identical equipment is essential. Simulations are rarely identical with the "real thing".

14.3.4 Test Specification for Backup and Restore

For systems where failures are permitted to occasionally happen but the consequences of such failures must be minimized, backup and restore procedures and mechanisms are implemented. The test cases that are developed to evaluate a system's backup and restore implementation typically consist of the following basic steps:

You have to back it up before you can restore it.

- Perform backup.
- Enact a system failure.
- Perform restoration of backed-up data.
- Assess whether any essential data has been lost and, if so, whether it can been identified.
- Verify that the system returns to an agreed-upon level of service.

The test cases are designed to explore variations on these basic steps:

- Different types of backup may be taken (full, partial).
- We may choose to cause or simulate a system failure just after a backup or just before one is about to be taken. This will influence, for example, the amounts and possibly also the types of data that may have been lost, and will complicate the task of detecting any inconsistencies in existing data.
- The restoration activities may be started at different time periods following failure. This will influence, for example, the volumes of buffered data to be processed once the recovery procedure is started.

A decisive element of backup and restore test cases is the simulation of any online interfaces to the system under test during the period in which it is in a failed state or otherwise unavailable (e.g., due to emergency fixes being implemented or backups being taken). These interfaces will continue to be active during the period of failure and may be supplying data that is not being processed.

Don't forget activities that may occur while the system is incapacitated.

Test cases should in particular focus on the following aspects:

- Evaluating whether information supplied from "live" external systems is lost when the receiving system is unavailable.
- If message queues (buffers) are used to store data and requests submitted by these external interfaces, then the tests should assess whether they are large enough to handle the volumes that may build up during downtime.
- Examining how well and how quickly the system recovers to an agreed-upon level of service when the source of failure is removed, recovery procedures are started, and the sudden peak load of message queues is released onto the system (the equivalent of "opening the flood gates" on our system).
- Evaluating the mechanisms (such as database scripts) used for identifying and possibly also correcting any data inconsistencies that may have occurred during the period of failure and could not be recovered from backed-up data.

Experience Report: Billing system

Back in 2001 I was involved in a major project for the automatic billing of users of a transport system. Service Level Agreements regarding the restoration of services after failure were very strict since even short downtimes could cost the customer millions in lost revenues. The following features of the testing stood out in this project:

1. The challenge for the test team was not so much in the test design, but rather in the detailed analysis of system states, message queue "fill" levels, and response times once system restoration had been initiated. Analysis showed that message queue levels tended to cause problems by setting off a ripple effect through the system. This required a system change to be implemented so that particular interfaces downstream of the failure were disabled on detection of the failure and reinstated in a controlled sequence on recovery. The change prevented the newly recovered system from being swamped with requests.

2. Tests were repeated many times in support of the development team to provide them with analysis data. Repeatable test cases were absolutely essential here. An exploratory approach to this kind of testing would not have been appropriate.

3. The risks associated with defective system recoverability were high enough to justify having a separate team for performing the various recoverability testing tasks. The experience gained by this team was particularly useful when conducting operational acceptance tests together with the customer.

As mentioned in section 14.2.8, "Approach to Backup and Restore Testing", procedure testing plays an important role in addition to the type of test cases described earlier. If the risks associated with incorrect procedures justify a formal approach with verifiable coverage levels, specific test cases may be designed for backup and recovery procedures using, for example, structural techniques such as decision coverage testing or specification-based techniques such as use case testing.

14.4 Reliability Test Execution

Executing Tests for Reliability Growth

Executing reliability tests involves repeating the test cases for the defined operational profiles. The tests are executed when specific events occur, such as major software releases, the completion of a time-box, or simply at regular time intervals (e.g., weekly). The test cases may already be fully specified or the required test data may be generated dynamically prior to execution (e.g., using a statistical model). For efficiency, thought should be given to implementing tests intended for repeated execution as automatically executable tests using an appropriate test execution tool. The conditions for the test (e.g., test environment, test data) should remain constant during the test to enable subsequent comparisons between execution cycles to be made.

Tool Tip

Executing Other Types of Reliability Tests

Other types of reliability tests are executed as planned and specified. Particular tests (e.g., backup and recovery tests) may require a considerable amount of organizational "orchestration" for successful execution, especially if external organizations are involved.

Following the execution of recoverability tests (failover, backup and recovery), the results and monitored data may require detailed analysis in order to establish the presence of defects or the achievement of required service levels. For example, the fill levels of message queues may be analyzed after executing a system recovery to establish the adequacy of queue sizes.

14.5 Reporting Reliability Tests

Achieved levels of reliability are reported after each test cycle. The information provided in the report reflects the parameters established for measuring testing objectives, such as MTBF (refer to section 14.2.2, "Setting Reliability Objectives", for further details).

Compare actual with expected reliability levels.   Results of reliability tests are best compared graphically with the reliability growth model in use, after which the following information may be included in the report:

- Achieved level of reliability (e.g., expressed as a value between 0 and 1 or as the number of defects found in the latest cycle of reliability tests)
- Differences between achieved levels and those expected from the growth model
- Predictions of when required reliability levels may be achieved and the effort still required

Reporting the results of other types of reliability tests is highly specific to the test cases. This list includes some of the most commonly reported information:

- Time and effort required to perform different types of backup (e.g., full or incremental)
- Time and effort required to restore normal operations to a defined level after a failure
- The operational readiness of procedures for backup and recovery (expressed either in terms of coverage achieved or a simple qualitative statement)
- The achievement of agreed-upon service levels relating to reliability
- (Remaining) risks associated with reliability

14.6 Tools for Reliability Testing

Tests relating to reliability growth can benefit from the following tools:

▨ Test management tools for easily identifying and selecting a set of functional test cases for use in reliability testing.

▨ Tools for test data generation, perhaps incorporating a statistical model to be applied.   *Tool Tip*

▨ Test execution tools.

▨ Some unit testing tools are able to automatically execute tests that test the error handling mechanisms relating to a unit's interface parameters (an example of such a tool can be found at [URL: JTest]).

▨ Code coverage tools can be useful in fault tolerance testing if formal coverage of error handling code needs to be demonstrated. The tools help identify the areas of the code not yet exercised after performing functional tests, which are often the areas associated with error-handling code. Note that this use of tools focuses on the fault tolerance measures already implemented and should not be considered a substitute for designing test cases that attempt to find unhandled error conditions.

14.7 Let's Be Practical

Reliability Testing for the Marathon Application

Let's sketch out a possible reliability testing approach for the Marathon application. We'll often be referring to the Marathon system when doing this, so an overview will help.

If we first consider the requirements for reliability given in the overview (see section 2.2), a first indication that high reliability is required can be identified:

"The system needs to be capable of handling up to 100,000 runners and 10,000 sponsors for a given race without failing."

This is typical of general reliability statements for applications that are not safety critical; they are frequently overstated and need some further analysis to extract more useful, affordable requirements. Looking back on our definition of reliability, the technical test analyst would be searching for things that can be measured and assessed, such as, "What is the application doing?, For how long?, What are the fundamental reliability risks? and What can I measure?"

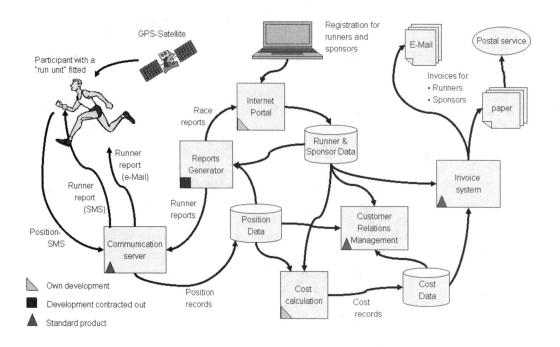

GPS-Satellite

Participant with a "run unit" fitted

Registration for runners and sponsors

E-Mail

Postal service

Race reports

Internet Portal

Invoices for
• Runners
• Sponsors

paper

Runner report (e-Mail)

Reports Generator

Runner & Sponsor Data

Invoice system

Runner report (SMS)

Runner reports

Position Data

Customer Relations Management

Position-SMS

Communication server

Cost calculation

Cost Data

Position records

Cost records

Own development

Development contracted out

Standard product

Figure 14-3

The Marathon system

If we take a closer look at how the application will be used (see section 2.3), we can extract some details to help answer these questions. Marathon itself provides functionality for three distinct phases:

■ During the registration period prior to the race
■ During the race itself
■ After the race

Sometimes the expectations become the requirements.

We can use these project phases as a basic structure for gaining a more precise view of reliability requirements, risks, and expectations. Some of our expectations would then need to be discussed with stakeholders before being considered as actual requirements. For the purpose of our example though, we will treat our expectations as actual requirements.

Marathon: Reliability Issues Prior to the Race

Starting with the runner registration week, the functional specification indicates that this is a period where the Marathon Internet portal will be used intensively, in particular once the week is officially opened and the rush for registration (also from international runners) begins. In this period the project risks of failures are relatively high (bad press, complaints, etc.) so we would expect the Internet portal to demonstrate high levels of reliability (we'll define *high* a little later).

The intensity with which the Internet portal is used during the three weeks of sponsor registration that follow the runner registration week will be lower. If the system becomes unavailable due to failure, then sponsors (who are likely to be more tolerant of such occurrences than, say, casual browsers) will likely return at another time. There is a project risk if this continues however; the potential sponsors may ultimately lose interest and sponsorship money will be lost.

All transactions initiated by the Internet portal that involve capture, storage, or manipulation of data in the runners and sponsors database should be particularly robust and capable of handling incorrect or unexpected inputs from the users (e.g., language-specific characters in names). Due to the high risks associated with losing or corrupting any of this data, we would expect at least a daily backup of the entire database to be taken with an hourly partial backup of accepted registrations. During the runner registration week, we would expect a rapid recovery of this data if a failure should occur. Recovery times can be relaxed during the sponsor registration weeks. Procedures for backup and recovery are expected to be relatively simple.

Get stakeholder input when determining risk.

The reliability of the invoicing system does not have to be as high as the reliability of the Internet portal. The financial risk of failures in this area is assessed as relatively low; the worst that can happen is that the invoices to runners are issued late (invoices to sponsors are issued after the race is over).

Due to the international nature of the races supported by the Marathon application, it is expected that the help-desk/customer relations system should be available at all times and function with high levels of reliability.

Marathon: Reliability Issues During the Race

The run unit carried by each runner to transmit position information must be able to perform reliably without failure for at least the maximum duration of a race (assumed six hours).

Failure of the communications server hardware represents one of the highest risks for the Marathon application, and it is reasonable to expect a guarantee that the server runs without failure for at least six hours. As technical test analysts, we would expect some form of failover mechanism to be included in the system's architectural design and that this mechanism has been correctly implemented.

The reports generator does not represent a high-risk component. Low reliability levels may result in sporadic information flow, but this is not considered critical to the overall success of the race.

Marathon: Reliability Issues After the Race

After race day, all data must be available to the help-desk/customer relations system between 08:00 and 20:00 local time for a further week, after which all invoice data and master data relating to runners and sponsors must be archived for at least two years.

The reliability of the invoicing application is not considered a high risk. It is assumed that functional tests will adequately test the business logic involved.

Marathon: Proposal for a Reliability Testing Approach for Marathon

Now propose an approach according to risks and requirements.

The following testing approach is a first (nonexhaustive) proposal for addressing the risks and requirements established earlier. Individual reliability testing objectives and approaches are proposed for components of the Marathon system.

Reliability Testing Approach for the Internet Portal

Testing approach for demonstrating reliability:

- Establish operational profiles for runners, sponsors, and casual browsers.
- Choose an exponential growth model that assumes defects found per test run falls from 45 to 3 over eight test runs. Establish separate release criteria for the final test run of 3 defects for the runner registration week and 10 defects for the sponsor registration weeks.
- Select 50 functional test cases each (from an existing test case database) for the runner and sponsor operational profiles.
- Choose 30 test cases at random from the test case database for the casual browser operational profile.
- Perform test runs at the beginning and at the end of each of four planned software releases.

▧ Measure test results against the growth model and report results after each test run to the test manager. Revise overall testing approach if reliability levels are less than half the values expected after completion of test run 4.

Testing approach for finding robustness (fault tolerance) defects:

▧ Perform technical reviews of code to ensure that developers have implemented error handling in accordance with project coding guidelines. Purchase license for static analysis tool if the amount of code to be reviewed warrants it.

▧ Design negative tests in cooperation with test analysts. Try to get end users from different countries involved in this testing.

▧ After delivery of each software release, perform exploratory testing that is focused on finding defects in the handling of incorrect or unexpected inputs from the users. Increase the amount of exploratory testing if many defects are found.

Testing approach for backup and recovery:

▧ Perform a technical review of documented procedures with the operations staff. Procedures will also be evaluated for backing up and archiving all relevant data before closing down the application one week after the race.

▧ Verify that procedures for taking daily full backups of the runners and sponsors database function correctly and do not take more than one hour to perform.

▧ Verify that a full backup can be restored within one hour of failure and that a partial backup can be restored within 30 minutes.

▧ Design test cases that simulate failures at different intervals over the 24-hour period since taking a full backup.

▧ Execute test cases and verify that all data inconsistencies can be fully identified.

Reliability Testing Approach for the Invoicing System and Help-Desk/Customer Relations System

▧ Both of these system components are to be purchased as standard products. The guaranteed levels of reliability should be compared to those required and any deviations reported to the test manager.

Standard products are not necessarily more reliable.

Reliability Testing Approach for the Run Units

Testing approach for demonstrating reliability:

- Reliability levels shall be agreed upon by the project manager and the suppliers of the units, who are responsible for guaranteeing failure-free operation of both hardware and software for six hours continuous use. No other specific reliability testing will take place, although functional integration testing of the run units and the communications server will include fault tolerance testing relating to the specified interfaces.

Reliability Testing Approach for the Communications Server

Testing approach for demonstrating failover capability:

- Failure modes will be evaluated with the development and operations staff.
- A technical review will be performed on the system architecture documentation to ensure that a failover mechanism is defined for communications server hardware.
- A run unit emulator or an equivalent software simulator will be required to generate a load for failover testing purposes. The performance testing team should be approached to assist with this part of the testing.
- Test cases will be designed to simulate failure modes.
- Monitors (e.g., of processor parameters) will be established prior to test execution (assuming the technical review revealed that a failover mechanism has actually been considered!).
- Tests will be executed in cooperation with operations staff and the performance testing team.
- Test results and data will be monitored to ensure that a maximum of 10 SMS messages are lost as a result of the failover. Information received by the communications server from the reports generator must not be lost as a result of the failover.

Exercises

In the Marathon system, the cost calculation system (developed in-house) reads data from two databases for performing its calculations and then writes calculated costs to the cost database.

Describe at least two reliability risks that could be associated with this element of the system and propose an appropriate testing approach to mitigate them, stating your assumptions.

14.8 Learning Check

The following check lists will help you judge the knowledge you have gained from this chapter.

Terms

*failover testing, fault tolerance, *MTBF, *MTTF, *MTTR, operational acceptance test (OAT), operational profile, procedure testing, recoverability testing, *redundant systems, reliability growth model, reliability testing, robustness

Technical Test Analyst

- Understand reliability risks and their potential impact on a system.
- Understand and compare the different types of reliability tests.
- Understand and explain the stages in an application's life cycle where reliability tests may be applied and where synergies with other types of testing can be achieved.
- Propose a risk-based approach for testing reliability.
- Understand types of failover mechanisms.
- Be able to specify different types of reliability tests.
- Understand the different types of tools that can support reliability testing.

Test Analyst

- Understand the stages in an application's life cycle where reliability tests may be applied.

15 Maintainability Testing

Poor old maintainability, always relegated toward the end of the list of software characteristics, often neglected entirely in master test plans, and frequently not even recognized as the root cause when we later get bitten by symptoms of poor maintainability. You would think that more attention would be paid to this aspect of software quality, wouldn't you? After all, there is evidence that maintenance-related tasks can account for up to 80 percent of the effort spent on an application, measured over its entire life cycle. This chapter tries to redress the imbalance and make the technical test analyst more aware of maintainability issues in terms of both maintenance (after release) and maintainability (before release) testing.

15.1 Overview

15.1.1 What Is Maintenance Testing?

Maintenance testing is about testing the changes to an operational system or the impact of a changed environment to an operational system. In other words, it's about keeping (maintaining) the achieved levels of quality across the entire life cycle of the software application. *Quality* here can mean one or more of the quality attributes discussed in this book and in standards such as [ISO 9126].

If maintenance costs can be 80 percent of a project, shouldn't we test for maintainability?

Isabel Evans [Evans 04] notes that as postdelivery changes are introduced to an existing application, each change could be considered to start a new Software Development Life Cycle (SDLC), More accurately, the project is now in a Software Maintenance Life Cycle (SMLC). Many projects spend most of their time in a post-delivery SMLC rather than the pre-delivery SDLC.

Maintenance testing is an activity performed in the SMLC and can be described in terms of the following principal activities (see the following sections for details):

■ Dynamic maintenance
■ Corrective maintenance
■ Adaptive maintenance

In general, the task of performing maintenance testing is made more efficient when the software has good maintainability (see the discussion on maintainability attributes later in this chapter).

15.1.2 What Is Maintainability?

Rather like reliability, *maintainability* is a word we all know in testing but sometimes have difficulty explaining. It's generally regarded as something we would like to have in our software, but it's hard putting our finger on what maintainability actually is. The ISO 9126 Quality Model [ISO 9126] is quite helpful here; it defines maintainability as "the ease with which a software product can be modified to correct defects, modified to meet new requirements, modified to make future maintenance easier or adapted to a changed environment."

According to ISO 9126, maintainability can be described in terms of four subattributes, each of which will be discussed later:

■ Analyzability
■ Changeability
■ Stability
■ Testability

Let's try to clarify these attributes right from the start.

Have you ever raised a fairly innocent looking, well-defined defect report and found that either it takes a long time before a fix comes back from the developers or the status gets set to "not reproducible"? If you make inquiries with the developers about this, you may get a feel for analyzability and changeability issues. Analyzability relates to the effort required (usually by the developers) to diagnose defects or to identify parts of the software system requiring change. Changeability relates to the effort required to actually fix defects or make improvements. Even a simple-looking defect report can mean considerable amounts of effort to analyze, localize, and fix the defect, especially if the software exhibits poor analyzability and changeability quality attributes. I'm not saying it's a good thing in these circumstances to set the status to "not reproducible", but at least we should understand why this can happen and, incidentally, I have not yet seen a defect management process that includes the status "takes too much effort to analyze (or fix)".

Stability is the likelihood that unexpected side effects occur as a result of making changes to the software. It's what we have in mind when we sometimes say that the software is *brittle*.

Testability describes the effort required for testing changed software. This is one of the principal software quality attributes that directly affects our work.

Experience Report: "Testing without test data"

In a recent project, a maintainability issue arose that affects many systems with strict requirements regarding the security of data. The health system was developed to give patients better access to their medical records, but it also needed to stop unauthorized people from being able to access the data. Meeting the very strict requirements was a technological challenge, but the developers managed to do so successfully. The problem was that the very mechanisms that protected the data made the testability of the system extremely poor (especially at the system level); we had virtually no access points to the data. We could only view the data in encrypted form and it was not permitted to provide special facilities for testing purposes because this would represent a security vulnerability. We could therefore work only with "test" patients, but the effort to have specific test data put onto electronically readable cards for virtually every distinct test case was high.

The lesson leaned from this experience was that systems with high levels of data security may by design have low testability. As technical test analysts, we should understand that the testing effort can be high, even though it's perhaps unfair to talk here of "poor quality" software regarding testability.

When considering the various attributes of maintainability, two common factors seem to stand out: we nearly all experience the effects of poor software maintainability (directly or indirectly), and they are all significant drivers of effort and cost.

*Maintainable software
comes from mature software
development processes.*

Good software maintainability is the product of a mature software development process. This applies to both initial software development and any changes introduced during an application's life cycle. Integral parts of that process include the design and programming practices used and the conduct of specific tests to ensure maintainability. It can be risky and expensive to attempt a kind of "catch-up" strategy once software with poor maintainability characteristics has already entered productive use (Isabel Evans [Evans 04] describes this catch-up approach as *perfective maintenance*).

15.1.3 Why Is Maintainability Underrepresented?

There are a number of interrelated factors working against a better representation of software maintainability in our software development and testing. It might help the technical test analyst to be aware of these issues when asked to contribute to an overall testing strategy.

From my experience and observations, these limiting factors can be categorized as follows:

- Low perceptions of maintenance risks
- Lack of ownership for maintainability as a quality attribute
- Lack of a life cycle view on investment in maintainability
- Contractual restrictions
- Lack of awareness regarding maintenance issues

Let's briefly look at each of these points.

Low Levels of Risk Perception

In teaching the ISTQB Advanced Level Test Manager module, I conduct a practical session with experienced testers where we consider a prepared description of a project for 10 minutes or so and brainstorm the risks. How often do you think the term *poor maintainability* has crossed the lips of a participant? You guessed it—not once. I have observed that when faced with other (perhaps more obvious) risks, participants simply don't come up with maintainability as an issue at all. When the brainstorming session is over, I ask why no one thought of poor maintainability as a risk, especially since the project described in the exercise is a definite candidate for this. The replies nearly always fit one of the five factors listed earlier. If I had to choose though, I would put "I see no risk" high on the list of the most common replies. Low perceptions of risk regarding poor maintainability invariably result in no maintainability testing being performed. The reasons for these low perceptions of risk are varied, but lack of ownership and poor awareness are major contributors. Sections 15.2.1 and 15.2.2 will help raise awareness by highlighting some fundamental maintainability risks and root causes.

Lack of Ownership

Who "owns" maintainability as a quality attribute? Who is responsible for ensuring that the software we develop is maintainable? In the introductory notes to this chapter, it was noted that maintenance-related tasks can account for up to 80 percent of the effort spent on an application, measured over its entire life cycle. The majority of this effort comes after the software enters production, which can lead to the general perception that maintenance is only a postproduction issue. In a self-serving way, those who own the software preproduction are concerned about shipping on time. As a result, it's difficult to find an "owner" for maintainability as a quality attribute in the preproduction development phase of the software development life cycle. The owners of the software postproduction are the ones that care about maintainability, but it's too late to build it in then.

Maintainability? Someone else is responsible for that.

Lack of a Life Cycle View

The payback for maintainable software often comes years after the software has entered production, making it necessary to take a long-term life cycle view. Some development models make it hard to take this long-term view. They are focused on the next time-box or iteration and encourage a flexible but short-term view to be taken, which does not adequately reward long-term investments in maintainability.

Contractual Restrictions

Contractual restrictions can cause a barrier to achieving maintainable software. Software development and operations are often separately contracted to different organizations, making for a low return on investment to the development organization for developing maintainable software.

Lack of Awareness

Lack of awareness regarding maintainability issues is an area where training and publications can help. Many books on the subject of testing hardly touch on maintainability, except to mention that it exists as a quality attribute. Apart from the content of this particular chapter, [Evans 04] and [URL: Testing Standards] also cover aspects of maintainability at a reasonable level of detail.

15.2 Planning Issues in Maintenance

To test the maintainability attributes of software, we need an appreciation of certain planning issues (remember, planning includes more than just scheduling). If our software application is in a preproduction stage of its life cycle, the results of these planning activities may be documented in a master test plan. In a postproduction stage, however, the documentation may take another form, such as a release test plan or even a collection of less formal documents.

These principal planning issues covered in the following sections:

- Identifying risks
- Establishing an approach
- Scheduling the tests

15.2.1 Fundamental Maintainability Risks

In section 15.1.3, we posed the question, Why is maintainability underrepresented? and one of the factors listed was a generally low appreciation and awareness of maintainability risks. Table 15-1 shows some fundamental maintainability risks. Taken together with the causes for poor maintainability listed in section 15.2.2, this information will raise our awareness levels and (hopefully) prevent some of the consequences of poor maintainability shown in the table from becoming reality in our projects.

15.2.2 The Causes of Poor Maintainability

We frequently experience the symptoms of poor software maintainability without appreciating the root causes.

We frequently experience the symptoms of poor software maintainability without appreciating the root causes. In this section, we expand on reasons for poor maintainability introduced in section 15.1.3 and look in more detail at some of the potential problem areas for each of the four maintainability attributes (remember, these are analyzability, changeability, stability, and testability). As we will see, some problem areas can have an influence on more than one specific aspect of maintainability.

Fundamental Risks	Consequence of Poor Maintainability
Effort required for fixing defects and implementing changes may be more than planned.	If the size of the maintenance team performing these tasks is fixed (a common situation), this will also translate into longer time scales.
Time taken for maintenance tasks exceeds the fixed-length maintenance windows.	Production could be negatively affected (e.g., staff arriving for work find that an application server is unavailable due to the scheduled nightly mainte-nance window slipping). Maintainers may be forced to take shortcuts to keep within agreed-upon maintenance periods They may need to make assumptions regarding the implemen-tation of required changes (perhaps due to poor documentation). Penalties may be imposed if Service Level Agree-ments apply.
Long-term buildup of poor maintainability resulting from the cumulative effects of bad software development practices.	Reliability levels slowly reduce. The number of functional defects introduced by changes (regressions) increases. Defects take longer to fix. Maintenance staff are put under steadily more pressure, which may even result in a further worsening of the situation.

Table 15–1

Fundamental maintainability risks

Problem Areas Affecting Software Analyzability

Just to recap, analyzability relates to the effort required to diagnose defects or to identify parts of the software system requiring change or affected by the change.

What can lead to poor analyzability?

- Business logic that is not implemented in an understandable way can hide the intention of the code and can make traceability to a specific requirement difficult to identify. The consequences of making changes are difficult to analyze.
- Software that is not built in a modular style makes the localization of defects more time intensive. Large monolithic segments of code are generally more difficult and time consuming to analyze than shorter, modular code implementations.
- If an application is developed using an object-oriented methodology, the object-oriented analysis (OOA) may result in the definition of several layers of abstraction. The benefits of abstraction (e.g., less actual

Too much abstraction can actually make it more difficult to analyze code.

code, more reusability, easier adaptation of code) must be balanced against the levels of effort required to analyze the code and localize defects. For example, developers are often faced with the problem of finding out whether a reported defect lies in a specific instance of a class (module) or in parts of the class inherited from other, more abstract classes. Depending on the skills of the developer, the availability of supporting tools, and, of course, the nature of the defect itself, the task of localizing defects and assessing the impact of changes can be high for object-oriented systems using multiple layers of abstraction. (Remember, just as the lower levels inherit from the upper-level classes, so the change that is made may be inherited by a lower-level class, resulting in unexpected changes to that class).

■ If the documentation available to those responsible for maintaining an application is insufficient, inaccurate, or outdated, we can expect the effort needed for localizing defects or assessing changes to be higher than if good documentation is available. The cost of writing and maintaining good documentation must always be balanced against the need for that documentation and the projected life of the software in question, but the negative effects of poor documentation on analyzability (and maintainability in general) are often not recognized. Software development models that promote a documentation-light approach may be particularly vulnerable to these maintainability risks.

■ Poor coding style is a major contributor to poor maintainability in general. Particular aspects that impact analyzability include the use of good, understandable comments, the issue of meaningful error messages (e.g., to log files), and the avoidance of overly complex code structure (e.g., multiple levels of nesting). If coding guidelines have been established for a project, the general failure to apply these guidelines may be considered as a factor contributing to poor code analyzability.

Problem Areas Affecting Software Changeability

The ability to change software easily relies on good development practices

Changeability relates to the effort required to perform improvements or to fix defects. There are many individual factors that can explicitly influence changeability, most of which relate to design and coding practices. Some examples are provided in the following lists.

Changeability problems caused by aspects of software design:

- Coupling between software modules results when they have some form of mutual dependency (e.g., semantic or data dependencies). This means that a change to one of the modules will likely necessitate a change to others. Modules that are strongly coupled generally result in more development and testing effort being expended when software changes are implemented.

- Software cohesion is a desirable design attribute relating to the principle that a given module should implement one (and only one) piece of functionality. Software modules with poor cohesion tend to collect various fragments of functionality together (we can often identify such modules by their "multipurpose" or "collection of" names). If a functional change needs to be made, the effort required to make that change will be less if the module design ensures strong cohesion.

- Generally speaking, the problems of high module coupling and low cohesion tend to be less dominant when using object-oriented design techniques, although much of this lies in the hands of the analyst.

Changeability problems caused by poor coding practices:

- Code that uses global variables represents perhaps one of the best known maintenance problems. A *global* variable is one that is shared between more than one module. Some modules may change the variable, some may just use its value. Global variables create strong coupling between the modules that share them and can result in the maintainability problems described earlier. A change made to a global variable in one module can cause unforeseen effects in other modules that use that variable and can increase the effort needed to make the changes and test them.

- Hard-coded values are bad news for changeability. If our program contains a logical statement that goes something like "if (exchange_rate > 1.4) then", we might have had a working program at the time when 1.4 was a sensible value to use. What happens three years later when we want to raise the threshold value to a more appropriate value of, say, 2.3? Do we really want to search all our code for occurrences of 1.4 and change them to 2.3? Nearly every programmer knows not to use hard-coded values like this, and yet in pressure situations, corners do get cut. (Normally the programmer's conscience is eased by a promise to go back and do the coding properly after the dust has settled, maybe).

  Coding should be planned to handle future changes.

- Explicit use of software details that are dependent on specific versions of system software (e.g., operating systems, database software, and communications software) can result in considerable rework effort if new versions of that system software are introduced. A combination of good design and coding practices should ensure that we have to make system software changes once only in common modules instead of having to first locate specific system calls throughout the code and then changing each instance explicitly. (We will come across this problem again when considering software adaptability in section 16.1).

Code complexity often increases postproduction.

- Generally high levels of semantic or structural software complexity can increase the effort required to make changes. This may become more noticeable postproduction as numerous changes are made to the software and a tendency develops for code to become more complex.

- Applications that enter production with many defects can be particularly prone to decreasing levels of changeability. As failures occur in production, emergency situations may arise where it is necessary to provide solutions as quickly as possible by developing software *patches* or so-called *hotfixes*. These situations encourage a "do something" rather than a "do something right" approach. In my experience, changes like this are frequently implemented at the expense of the software's long-term maintainability (changeability being one of the subattributes primarily affected, together with analyzability).

- The effort required to change software may increase due to lack of detailed knowledge about the software. As Isabel Evans [Evans 04] points out, the "supporters" who implement postproduction changes are often not the people who understand why the software is structured the way it is. The following experience report describes the consequences this had on a project I was involved in.

Experience Report: "Guiding satellites with spaghetti"

As a project leader for a satellite project, I inherited some code for controlling the orientation of the spacecraft. The code was written before the days of structured programming techniques and contained lots of "goto" statements. The code functioned correctly, had almost no comments, and was no doubt considered in its day by its creator to have been "clever" code. In fact, one critical module ended with a sequence of 13 consecutive decisions with their associated "goto" statements, making the maintainability of this code poor, to say the least. Changes had to be made to this code, its author was long gone, and we rapidly realized that we could not fathom what to change or where. The analyzability characteristics of the code were low and the changeability lower. Fortunately one of the Oxford, U.K. universities had developed a tool to manage this kind of problem; it was called a *spaghetti code unscrambler*. It basically took unstructured code and made it structured. I bought the tool and, guess what, it worked wonderfully well. We ran tests to ensure that the code still worked and inserted comments at the start of each decision point. Then we could make the changes needed without needing huge amounts of development and testing effort.

These days it's less common to come across code as bad as this (thanks to lessons learned by the development community), but it still serves as a lesson to developers and testers alike. If you write "clever" code that conforms to the requirements of the day but cannot be maintained because only you can understand it, you are actually creating poor-quality software. The people maintaining the code will have to pick up the tab for you.

Experience Report: "Let sleeping monsters lie"

When I was consulting at a bank, I helped the maintenance staff assess the changeability of a large legacy system written in Cobol. A number of failures had occurred in production as a result of changes they had introduced and the aim was to identify software modules that might be especially prone to such risks. As a first step, we listed the modules in a section of the application that was causing them particular pain (as I recall, it was around 100 modules), and we evaluated each module according to a catalog of potential maintainability problems (complexity, coherence, coupling, levels of commenting, etc.). There were around 15 criteria in our catalog, so it took some time gathering the information. At the end of the exercise, one module stood head and shoulders above the rest as *the* maintenance risk that just had to be attended to.

A strange thing happened when I discussed this with the team; a mixture of wry smiles, hollow laughter, and cries of despair would best describe the response. I had put my finger right on the module that had developed over the years to be almost a "no go" area.

was a monster of a module with over 10,000 (yes) lines of code, hardly any comments, a structure that resembled a patchwork quilt, global variables scattered around; in short, it was a maintenance nightmare. The strange thing was, though, it worked (hence the wry smiles).

What did I learn from this? After a brief assessment of the situation, it became clear that the risks of making this module more maintainable, (sometimes the term *perfective maintenance* is used in this sense) were far higher than the potential benefits to be gained from better maintainability. It's best to introduce maintainability quality during development rather than by re-engineering a working system. We left the module in peace and it's probably still growing happily to this day. We were able to introduce a number of design and coding practices to avoid such problems in future developments, and we did actually change some code in other modules to improve maintainability (but only where there was low risk).

Other issues affecting changeability:

■ One fairly obvious but sometimes overlooked issue that can influence the changeability characteristics of systems is the capability to physically change the code of some aspects of that system. Issues such as ownership and licensing may mean that we are unable to change code even if we want to. Does this mean poor code quality? Maybe not, but it certainly may impact your ability to maintain the system properly.

■ Beware of code generators. If the tool is inflexible, poorly configured, or just plain dumb, we may end up being able to generate tons of unmaintainable code at the press of a button.

Problem Areas Affecting Software Stability

Brittle software often results from badly implemented software changes.

Stability as a quality attribute relates to the likelihood that unexpected side effects occur as a result of making changes to the software. Many of the factors that influence analyzability and changeability can also affect stability.

The following list describes just some of these factors:

■ Poorly understood requirements. Changes made to one requirement have unexpected side effects on others.

- High nesting levels in code structure (i.e., multiple levels of decision logic). Changes at a particular level of nesting can have unexpected consequences on code within lower nesting levels.
- Use of global variables in code. Changes to a global variable in one module can introduce defects in one or more modules that also use it. (Thankfully, the use of global variables is generally accepted as bad programming practice now.)
- Poorly documented system interfaces. Apparently minor changes to data structures passed between systems can have unexpected consequences regarding, for example, the use of that data for controlling business logic.
- Extreme sensitivity to timing changes. Modifications to real-time systems can result in timing changes that lead to failures, especially where those systems are already operating near to their processing limits.

Problem Areas Affecting Software Testability

Testability relates to the effort required to test changed software. Some of the factors that can explicitly increase the effort are listed here:

- Poor or unavailable documents result in additional effort being required to obtain the information with which to design test cases using specification-based techniques (exploratory testing techniques are not affected by this lack of documentation).
- Documentation may have been available prior to entry into production, but successive postproduction software changes have not been reflected in the documentation. As the documentation steadily grows more and more out of touch with the software, the testability of the software (and perhaps also other maintainability attributes) declines. This is perhaps one of the most common problem areas affecting maintainability.

Bad documentation: perhaps the most common cause of poor maintainability

- Complex interrelationships and dependencies between application data can make the creation of realistic test input data and expected results expensive.
- Systems that are implemented using uncommon programming languages, communications protocols, or platforms can limit the availability of testing tools and testers with required experience levels. Both of these issues can negatively influence the testability of such systems.

- Certain object-oriented programming languages, such as C++, include the ability to define "private" data types which are more difficult to access for testing purposes.
- Some applications use data encryption and other security measures to protect data and variables from unauthorized access. These measures also increase the effort required to test the application.

15.2.3   Establishing a Test Approach

The list of risks and potential sources of maintainability problems just outlined is relatively lengthy; there are many factors to be considered. Unless the software under development is intended to be used for only a short period of time or if postproduction changes and defect fixes are unlikely (a rare occurrence), establishing a testing approach for maintainability aspects should be considered an essential part of test planning.

In establishing the approach, two interrelated aspects are considered:

- How to evaluate the achieved levels of quality for each attribute of maintainability
- How to approach maintenance testing as an activity

Evaluating Achieved Levels of Maintainability

The possible sources of maintainability problems listed in section 15.2.2 illustrate the significance of good practices in the design and implementation of software.

Maintainability has to be measured.

An important aspect of any testing approach for maintainability is gathering information about the maintainability levels achieved in design and implementation. We can deliver two principal kinds of information regarding maintainability:

- Effort required to perform specific maintenance tasks
- Metrics derived from static analysis

Our approach to gathering statistics on maintenance effort and times should be agreed upon in advance with the test manager to ensure that we are able to capture all the data we need. Otherwise, it's very unlikely that we will be permitted to gather this sensitive data. The test manager can explain the intended use to the maintenance testing staff and help avoid dysfunctional situations.

Metrics obtained from static analysis or code reviews will provide information on the sources of maintainability problems. Here are a few examples of useful metrics for assessing maintainability:

Static analysis and reviews provide maintainability data.

- Levels of structural complexity, such as the McCabe Cyclomatic Complexity metric
- Nesting (indentation) levels of code
- Depth of inheritance trees (object-oriented systems)
- Number of methods in a class (object-oriented systems)
- Size of a class or unit (lines of code)
- Number of comments per 100 lines of executable code (perhaps also related to the structural complexity of the code)

Once maintainability information has been gathered, violations of agreed-upon service levels, requirements or required coding, and design practices can be determined.

At the test planning stage, a careful consideration of maintainability requirements is needed to ensure that meaningful levels of effort or time are established before testing commences. The factors that influence maintenance effort should be taken into account when setting these levels (e.g., the size of the change expressed in lines of code or function points).

Measuring stability is not as straightforward as taking measurements of effort or time. We have to identify any "knock-on" defects resulting from a software change and that's usually not easy. Just like a stone dropped into water, changes to software can cause ripples to go through the software that are seen as "knock-on" defects. Perhaps the most practical approach to gathering this type of information is to ensure that thorough root cause analysis takes place on reported defects. If one of the causes considered in the analysis is "knock-on effect from changed software", a measure for system stability can be obtained and compared to a required value (e.g., number of defects introduced per one hundred lines of executable code changed should not exceed 2).

Identifying "knock-on" defects requires thorough root cause analysis.

Approaches to Maintenance Testing as an Activity

Three principal types of maintenance testing are identified in the ISTQB Advanced syllabus.

Dynamic, corrective, and adaptive

- Dynamic maintenance testing
- Corrective maintenance testing
- Adaptive maintenance testing

Dynamic Maintenance Testing

The discussion earlier regarding the testing of maintainability attributes considered two ways of doing this: statically and dynamically. Static approaches involve the use of tools and reviews to gather information, mostly about code. Dynamic maintenance testing is when documented procedures that have been developed for maintenance purposes are evaluated by (dynamically) executing tests and assessing the ability of those procedures to meet maintainability requirements or uphold agreed-upon service levels.

To apply dynamic maintenance testing, we define specific maintenance scenarios (e.g., implement and test a minor change to a particular part of the application) and execute them using the prescribed procedures. Measurements of effort are taken while performing these tests to evaluate analyzability, changeability, and testability. These measurements may highlight deficiencies in maintenance procedures and would typically be performed as part of the operational acceptance test (OAT).

Dynamic maintenance testing should be considered in our approach when the maintenance procedures to be used are technically or organizationally complex.

Corrective Maintenance Testing

This type of maintenance testing focuses on the time taken or effort used to diagnose and fix defects (i.e., analyzability and changeability). We can often use data gathered from other testing levels (e.g., system testing) for these evaluations.

Adaptive Maintenance Testing

This form of maintenance testing measures the effort required to adapt a system to a new or changed environment. Adaptive changes might include, for example, new hardware platforms, changes to operating systems, upgrades to database software, or changes to browser software. This form of maintainability testing combines measurements of analyzability, changeability, and testability, as described earlier in this section.

Individual adaptations can be measured or a systematic series of changes carried out from which an average can be taken. The size of changes should, where possible, be quantifiable (lines of code, number of function points), especially if the measurements are to be used for predicting effort or for comparison against a specified requirement or service level.

15.3 Let's Be Practical

Maintainability Testing for the Marathon Application

After talking to the business owner, we learned that the Marathon application is not expected to be in use for much of the year and there should therefore be sufficient time to perform routine changes and upgrades. The project leader has ensured us that maintenance contracts are in place with suppliers of system components, so an appropriate approach to maintainability testing may feature the following three elements:

- Dynamic maintenance testing for the reports generator component, for which we might expect to receive a number of changes during Marathon's life cycle (e.g., new reports, changed formats, more languages supported). The maintenance procedures will be evaluated to ensure that the changes required to implement a new report can be introduced with no more than 20 hours of effort, including regression testing.
- From our risk analysis of reliability issues, we already identified failures in the communications server as a major risk. Corrective maintenance testing will therefore be performed to ensure that emergency changes can be introduced within an average time of 15 minutes of notification. Several types of failure will be simulated and the mean time to repair (MTTR) calculated.
- Static analysis of the communications server code shall be conducted to provide information on the analyzability of the code. The analysis will determine whether minimum levels of code comments have been included and that complexity levels are not exceeded (a value of 7 for the McCabe Complexity Metric shall be used as a maximum value). A technical review of the code will be performed to ensure that the comments included are semantically correct and understandable by maintenance staff.

Exercise

Metrics can give insights into the code's maintainability. Consider the code metrics in table 15-2 and state which ones you would find most useful in assessing the analyzability, changeability, and testability of code. Use a scale of 0 (irrelevant) to 5 (highly relevant).

Metric	Relevance for assessing analyzability (0–5)	Relevance for assessing changeability (0–5)	Relevance for assessing testability (0–5)
Structural complexity			
Nesting (indentation) levels of code			
Depth of inheritance tree (object-oriented systems)			
Number of comments per 100 lines of code			
Size of a class or module (lines of code)			

15.4 Learning Check

The following check lists will help you judge the knowledge you have gained from this chapter.

Terms

analyzability, changeability, maintainability testing, maintenance testing, root cause, root cause analysis, stability, *testability

Technical Test Analyst

■ Recognize the different types of maintainability quality attributes according to [ISO 9126].

■ Understand the sources of maintainability risks and the particular maintainability attributes they influence.

■ Understand and compare the different approaches that can be taken to maintainability testing.

■ Explain the stages in an application's life cycle where maintainability tests may be applied and why a life cycle approach is needed for maintainability testing.

Test Analyst

■ Understand the stages in an application's life cycle where maintainability tests may be applied.

16 Portability Testing

*ISO 9126 defines portability as relating to the ease with which soft-
ware can be transferred into its intended environment, either initially
or from an existing environment.*

*Portability quality characteristics are grouped by the ISO 9126
Quality Model [ISO 9126] into the following subattributes:*

- *Adaptability*
- *Installability*
- *Replaceability*
- *Co-existence*

*In the sections that follow, each of these subattributes of portability
is examined. Particular emphasis is placed on risks associated with
poor software portability and effective testing strategies.*

16.1 Adaptability

The environment in which a software application operates can be made up
of the hardware platform and a variety of different types of software. This
can include the operating system, network software, database software,
browsers, and middleware (i.e., the software "glue" with which systems
communicate with each other).

Sometimes we develop a software application for a given environment
and that's it; the adaptability of the software simply isn't an issue. This
could be the case for specialized or embedded applications (e.g., military
systems), where we can be quite sure that the software will "stay put" for
its entire life cycle. These days it's more common for software applications
to be targeted for many environments. Think of standard software pack-
ages, computer games, and practically any software intended to operate via
the Internet. This software needs flexibility to be commercially successful

*Environment flexibility often
equals marketability.*

for its producer. In addition to the flexibility issue, those who invest in software applications frequently assume that a return on that investment takes place over several years. Can we be sure that the environment in which the application operates is going to remain constant for that whole period? Almost certainly not. Something is going to change, and when it does we want to be sure that our software is adaptable.

Interoperability and adaptability are closely related but subtly different.

Remember when we talked about interoperability in section 10.4? We described interoperability as belonging to the family of quality attributes called *functionality* and mentioned that testing in different environmental configurations was a principal feature of interoperability testing. In this sense, interoperability and adaptability are closely related to each other; they are both concerned with different types and configurations of environments in which the software application needs to operate. They are subtly different though. Interoperability testing checks whether the required functions of the software are available when the software is operated in different environments, but adaptability testing assesses how easy it is to actually make the transfer into those target environments. That's why adaptability is considered part of the family of quality attributes called *portability*.

16.1.1 Reasons for Poor Adaptability Characteristics

If we currently propose to run our application in different environments, or even if that isn't yet planned but we intend to operate our application for a number of years, we ought to think about adaptability issues.

Many of the causes for poor adaptability lie in the specific technical details of the system architecture and code. These are issues primarily for architects and developers, but the technical test analyst should have an awareness of some of these issues. Here are some of the typical causes for poor adaptability. This will give you a feel for the types of issues to watch out for.

Environment-Specific Implementation

System-specific code reduces the ability to adapt to new environments.

If the code or architecture has been designed or implemented from the outset with only the initial operational environment in mind, it will be difficult to adapt to a new one. Classic examples of this are using file names with environment-specific extensions (will the documents we need to open always have the .doc suffix?), making calls to system routines with specific names (will we always want to open a file using the sys$file_open routine?). Any experienced developer will tell you that issues like these call for measures such as parameterization or the use of function libraries. If your database system changes, you swap the function library or change a parameter file rather than pick your way through the code making individual changes.

Software Not Configurable

Software can be adapted to a new environment more efficiently if it is parameterized and a mechanism exists to elegantly change the values to those used by the new environment. Sometimes this parameterization is static (maybe we compile software using specific parameter values) or dynamic, where the system interrogates its environment at runtime and configures itself accordingly.

No Procedures for Adapting the Software

OK, I know it sounds obvious, but you would normally need some kind of written procedure to tell you how to efficiently adapt your application to its new environment (it rarely happens by magic). If you don't have this documentation, there could be a lot of head scratching and trial and error going on before the adaptation process has been completed satisfactorily.

16.1.2 Adaptability Testing

When considering a testing strategy for adaptability, many of the points we discussed in section 10.4 that relate to interoperability testing are also relevant. Here is just a summary of the main points:

- We need to identify combinations of different hardware and software system configurations that represent potential target environments for the software application under consideration.
- If the number of potential environments identified is too large to be practically tested, it may be necessary to reduce the number considered. This can be achieved by adopting the all-pairs technique (see section 4.2.5) or simply by identifying only those environments that are most likely to come into question.
- The tests can be combined with any planned installation tests.

Installation tests often find adaptability problems.

The principal test objectives of adaptability testing start with the fundamental question, Is it possible to adapt to a particular environment using the prescribed procedure? Once this question has been positively answered, the objective turns to measuring the actual effort and time required to do this and whether this meets any specified requirements. Functional testing may also be performed to locate defects that may have been introduced by adapting to the new platform. Static analysis or even simple search routines can be applied to detect coding practices that are detrimental to adaptability.

16.2 Replaceability

Good replaceability helps keep our systems flexible.

Replaceability describes the ability of software systems to function correctly with different alternative software components. Modern software architectures frequently incorporate elements that are designed to be replaced at a later date. Maybe new, improved versions of software components will become available in the future or perhaps complete systems with which the application interacts will need to be exchanged. Even if the replacement of software components is not planned at the moment, software stakeholders (especially business owners and operators) may demand the option to be flexible if new opportunities arise over the life cycle of the application. In this sense, the motivation for requiring good software replaceability characteristics is similar to those discussed earlier when considering adaptability.

16.2.1 Replaceability Considerations

Systems that incorporate replaceable components such as commercial off-the-shelf software (COTS) or that make use of service-oriented architectures (SOA) are typical examples of systems for which software replaceability is important. If replaceability was not on the agenda during development, we may need so much effort to replace software components later on that the twin benefits of flexibility and responsiveness to market needs may be completely eroded.

Poor replaceability characteristics do not necessarily mean we have poor-quality software.

The design of our application's architecture is a principal factor in determining replaceability. Technical test analysts should have an awareness of some of the issues affecting replaceability and be able to discuss them with system architects. Don't forget though, poor replaceability characteristics do not necessarily mean we have poor quality software from our stakeholders' point of view. In common with other portability attributes, it all depends on what those stakeholders want from their system. The following discussion covers some of the typical causes for poor replaceability and will give you an idea of what to look out for.

Component Interdependence

If the interfaces between individual software components are not designed with replaceability in mind, we may end up with tight coupling (inter-dependence) between those components. This is particularly common where the business logic is not designed with the required amount of modularization. A typical indicator for issues like these is where control parameters are passed from one software component to another. The receiving component does not know how to process the received data without first interpreting some of the parameters passed to it (e.g., the value of an integer variable or Boolean data type). These control parameters create interdependencies that reduce the replaceability of software components. We could not easily use a different software component without first ensuring that it "understood" the meanings of all the control parameters passed to it. Software components (e.g., COTS) that are designed to be easily inserted into existing systems generally have simple interfaces that do not presume any knowledge about the software component that is calling it. A "clean" interface design will ensure that we can make use of these standard components easily and avoid having to redesign major parts of our application when a component is swapped.

Clean interfaces facilitate the ability to swap components.

Supplier Dependencies

This is a tricky subject and one that goes beyond purely technical issues. Put quite simply, if we design our applications with high levels of replace-ability by incorporating COTS or technologies like SOA, we run the risk of becoming overdependent on the suppliers or providers of the software we rely on. This could expose us to one or more of the following project risks:

Good technical test analysts advise on supplier dependencies but stay out of the politics!

- New versions of the standard software may be imposed on us by the supplier. Of course, this is all part of progress, and the new versions will undoubtedly offer some advantages. The fact is, though, that we will sooner or later have to go with the upgrade or suffer the maintenance problems of unsupported software. For some software applications with low replaceability levels, this can have major cost implications. Don't forget the lesson we learned from maintainability testing here (chapter 15); our software may have started out with good replaceability characteristics, but this may have eroded over time as a result of changes made to the application.

■ If we decide to incorporate COTS into our software application, the supplier of that software may not always be able to provide support; they may simply go out of business or withdraw their product from the market. Decisions on which supplier to choose should be made only after weighing these risks carefully.

■ If service-oriented architectures are being used to gain benefits from replaceable software components, some monitors and guarantees need to be available to ensure that these services stay available. We don't own these services, we are users. A proper system of management (sometimes called SOA governance) needs to be in place to prevent our applications from being exposed to such risks.

As technical test analysts, we should point out these issues if we are invited to a technical review for a system that is explicitly designed for high levels of replaceability quality by using COTS or SOA. The stakeholders may be grateful for this ("Hey, these testing guys don't just pick holes in our software; they give us good advice too").

16.2.2 Replaceability Testing

Actually evaluating the effort required to replace software components in our applications by performing dynamic testing can be technically quite simple. During integration or system testing, alternative software components are used to build different versions of the same application. How can we assess replaceability?

■ We can simply answer the question, Is it possible?
■ We can measure the time or effort required to replace software components using defined procedures.
■ We can execute a number of available test cases (e.g., a regression test suite) to ensure that functionality is consistently available from version to version.

Replaceability testing usually is technically easy but organizationally difficult. The technical simplicity of these tests has to be balanced against the possible organizational difficulties of staging them. Is the software we plan to use in the future actually available? Can we build different versions of the application without having to obtain potentially expensive licenses?

As with adaptability testing, technical reviews and inspections can also be performed to identify issues that may affect replaceability. Interface definitions should receive particular emphasis in these reviews.

16.3 Installability

Installability describes the ability of the software to be made ready for use in its intended target environment. Just as with other portability quality attributes, we need to carefully consider whether installability is a characteristic we need to evaluate by testing. Some software applications are developed in a stable environment where required software components like operating systems, databases, and communications software can be considered as "given". Often it is not our responsibility to ensure that these standard components are installed, and we can frequently assume for the purpose of our testing strategy that they are available when our software application is installed. Given this situation, we might rate installability as a low-risk issue. Compare this with the risk factors discussed in the next section and we might think again. In fact, installability failures represent perhaps one of the highest risks we can have for an application. If we can't install the software on its target environment, then we simply have no application.

If you think installability is a low-risk attribute, think again.

16.3.1 Risk Factors for Installability

Here's a short check list to help you judge whether installability is a risk area in your project. A test strategy for installability should be established if one or more of the following applies.

1. **People who are installing the application do not belong to the developing organization.**
   This could mean your customer, the operating organization, or you as a consumer of software products. (Calling all parents: Remember the good old days when we would spend joyful hours in the days after Christmas wrestling with stacks of diskettes in an effort to get junior's present installed on the computer? Could we honestly say that the level of software quality regarding installability was good, regardless of how cool the graphics were?)

2. **The installation is procedurally complex.**
   If there are many steps to be performed with multiple options, parameter setups, activities that must be performed in a particular sequence,

and dependencies on other software systems or organizations, then the installation procedures (including any documented script examples) have to be tested.

3. **The installation itself is supported by a dedicated software application.**

Leading on from points 1 and 2, if the installation is complex or the installation will be performed by others, then a dedicated software installation application may be created to support the installation. We can argue whether testing this application counts as installation testing or not, but since it directly affects the installability of the software as a quality attribute, I think there are good reasons for considering it as installability testing.

4. **Software has to be installed from scratch.**

Installing from scratch can be an exciting adventure.

Sometimes all we have to start with is a hardware environment. Every single piece of software we need to get our application functioning properly has to be installed onto that hardware: operating system, communications software, the lot. Embedded software systems generally fall into this category, but other types of systems may also be affected. The recovery procedures for nonembedded systems may also require that the entire system be reinstalled from scratch. In this case, the testing often has the added objective of measuring the time and effort taken to reinstall the system up to a specified level of functionality (see section 14.2.8, "Approach to Backup and Restore Testing").

5. **The target environment is significantly different from the development environment.**

There are many reasons we develop our software on environments that are not the target environment itself. It may be too costly or too impractical, or the target environment may simply not be available yet. Think of the radar system for a military aircraft; do we really want a live radar device in our test lab? Do we want to pay out millions to procure one, and do we really want to wait the six months until a unit is available? Probably not. So we develop and test our software in another environment (using a radar simulator perhaps) and perform operation tests with the real target environment at a later date. If those tests do not include installation, we may be in for a surprise.

6. **Software uninstallation is required.**

Now that you got the software installed, uninstall it!

Remember the discussion on adaptability (section 16.1) and replaceability (section 16.2)? At some stage in our application's life cycle, we may need to adapt to a new environment or replace some software components with others. Both of these activities may require that the existing application (or parts of it) first be uninstalled. If the procedures for doing this are poor or nonexistent, then the software uninstallation may not be "clean". We may end up deleting software (e.g., shared DLLs) needed for other applications or failing to remove redundant software.

7. **Software reinstallation is required.**
   Reinstallation relates to the risks of failed installations. Can we go back to what we had before (i.e., reinstall the software) or are we left with nothing if the installation fails?

Lesson Learned: Les Hatton and the new television

Les Hatton, professor at Kingston University, U.K., recounted an experience at a recent testing conference where he highlighted the installation problems we can have with everyday consumer articles—in this case a new television. After proudly unpacking his new purchase and switching it on, he reports that a message appeared, "Do you want to download new software?" Being experienced in these things, he reached for the remote control in order to enter No but was unfortunately beaten to the draw; Yes was selected instead. The download commenced, and after a few seconds the installation broke off with an error message. For this equipment, the installation procedure did not save the original installed software before the installation of the new, presumably better software started. It couldn't therefore be reinstalled after the failure occurred. The television had "functioned" for less than one minute before it had to be packed up and returned to the shop. On arriving at the shop, Les was apparently greeted by a salesman with a tired smile who instructed him to put it in the corner with all the others. What do we learn from this (apart from the fact that Les Hatton tells a great story to back up his presentations on software engineering practices)? Well, maybe we should try to find out how the installation procedure works before we start it (if it's even documented, that is). Perhaps it's even more important that we ensure that our software installs and de-installs before we release it to the general public, especially if we are developing embedded software for general distribution. It can save a lot of recalls and expensive guarantee claims.

8.   **Software installation is time constrained.**

Maintenance testing is often time constrained (see chapter 15). We may need to install an emergency fix, perform routine upgrades, or restore the entire system within an agreed-upon time frame. The installability of our software is one of the decisive factors in keeping within these time constraints. If installation takes excessively long, we may delay operational use of the application.

Installation defects can result in complete project failure.

The impact of the risks mentioned is highly dependent on project context and the severity of any defect that may arise. Severity levels can range from minor irritation for the person performing the installation (e.g., parents' blood pressure rises short term) to complete project failure. It's this latter point that should make us always put installability on our agenda when proposing a testing strategy.

16.3.2 Installability Testing

In risk-based approaches to testing, we consider the risk factors and apply testing measures to mitigate the risks. Some of the risk factors for installability were outlined earlier. This section describes some of the measures we can define in a test strategy.

Test of Installation Mechanisms

Software installations can employ a variety of mechanisms:

- Internet download
- CD
- Use of specific software applications for coordinated installation schemes (e.g., in a large organization) and automatic software installations

The focus of our testing strategy will include verifying that the mechanism actually works as expected and that functionality is maintained after (and possibly also during) the installation.

Test of Error Handling

Installations can be prone to a range of specific error conditions beyond those covered in section 14.2.6, "Approach for Establishing Fault Tolerance". The applicability of each error condition should be assessed for the application in question and appropriate tests developed. There are some typical installation error conditions:

- Installation interrupted by user (e.g., if download takes too long and the user decides to cancel)
- Installation interrupted by system (e.g., time frame expired in an automatic installation)
- Installation failed (at various stages in the procedure)
- Target hardware not switched on or incompatible (e.g., automatic installation cannot be performed)
- Operating system not compatible
- Incompatible software upgrade paths

Functional tests should always be performed after the simulated error condition has been applied to ensure that this has been correctly dealt with by the installation software and that the system is never left in an undefined state (e.g., partially installed software). Where applicable, reinstallation procedures should also be exercised.

Always check that you can go back.

Procedure Testing

The quality of installation procedures is decisive for ensuring successful installations. Testing involves designing tests to provide coverage of at least the principal paths through the procedures for performing installations with varying configurable options (e.g., full or partial installations or de-installations). In section 14.2.8, "Approach to Backup and Restore Testing", we considered testing the procedures for backup and restore by asking the people who will be responsible for performing the tasks to actually execute them. The same principle applies to testing installation procedures. The time taken to perform the tasks may be measured and compared against any installation requirements or specified service levels.

Other Tests Combined with Installation Testing

Installation tests are the focus point for many different forms of testing. During installation tests, one or more of the following quality attributes may also be considered:

Installation testing can often be combined with other tests.

- Usability tests: The usability and flexibility of procedures and any software applications (e.g., scripts or wizards) used to support the installation will be evaluated (refer to chapter 11 for details).

■ Security tests: As we mentioned in chapter 13, installation routines can present a security vulnerability, especially if administrator rights are allocated as part of the installation.

■ Functionality tests: Basic functional tests (*smoke tests*) may be carried out directly after the installation or de-installation to check for incorrect or incomplete (de-) installations.

Physical Testing

For embedded systems, the physical environment into which the software will be installed may play a significant role in the testing strategy. Physical issues such as heat, humidity, and vibration can all influence the ability of the system to be made ready for use in its intended target environment. System or operational acceptance tests may all involve this form of testing.

16.4 Co-Existence

Co-existence describes the ability of an application to share an environment with other applications without experiencing or causing negative effects.

Co-existence defects can be hard on your reputation (and your employment opportunities).

I've only experienced the negative impact of co-existence problems once in a project, but I can tell you, it's one of the most frustrating and potentially damaging faults you can have. Frustrating because you just put your application through all of its tests (OK, maybe you missed the co-existence tests), the test criteria have been achieved, the installation goes fine, and then on production day the application runs like you've never tested it at all. It's damaging not only because this is now happening in production, with all the consequences that can bring, but also because your testing reputation just took a nose dive. How can these problems arise?

After some analysis of the failures that are happening, you will probably start to see patterns (possibly in more ways than one):

■ There seems to be competition for scarce resources going on. Someone else's application has the nerve to grab CPU, RAM, printers from the pool, file handles, and other parts of the environment that now have to be shared among resident applications. When I demand those resources for my application, I seem to be getting exceptions, which my code isn't handling properly (e.g., resubmitting requests, issuing message to user).

■ Performance seems to suffer when other applications run parts of their functionality that create high levels of network traffic. Maybe users spend the first hour of the day using other applications to search databases for customer records, or maybe a regular batch program is started at a particular time of day to synchronize databases.

If you're aware of what can go wrong, these kinds of failures and the underlying reasons for them can be readily identified. A particularly awkward problem can occur long after entering production when we are in the maintenance phase. New, resource-hungry applications may be installed in the environment or maintenance changes (e.g., operating system or database upgrades) may be introduced for the benefit of one application but adversely affect others.

Co-existence problems often arise in the maintenance phase.

16.4.1 Co-Existence Testing

If you know in advance that your application will share its production environment with others, co-existence risks should be assessed and appropriate tests (functional and non-functional) planned. Any co-existence tests to be conducted will probably require considerable coordination with the operators of co-existing applications so that peaks in requests for resources can be created.

The design of functional test cases for identifying co-existence problems will also require some orchestration. Which steps should be executed in which application in which sequence? Which actions do we need to perform simultaneously to create resource shortages?

Co-existence also needs to be taken into account when designing load profiles for performance testing (see section 12.9, "Specification of Efficiency Tests"). The technique in this case is essentially the same as for an individual application; we simply have to overlay the load profiles from other applications to give a representative load for co-existing applications.

Co-existence testing is normally performed when user acceptance tests have been successfully completed. The need for coordinated testing, potentially across several organizations, generally requires that the testing takes place in a relatively short time frame.

Co-existence tests often require considerable coordination.

Since changes made to one application can cause problems for co-existing applications, our maintenance testing strategies should also consider the risks mentioned earlier.

16.5 Let's Be Practical

Portability Testing of the Marathon Application

The description of the Marathon application indicates that changes are already planned, in particular regarding the interface between runners (or, more precisely, the run units they carry) and the communications server, which handles the messaging to and from the run units. Let's take a look at the overview diagram again (figure 16-1); there are sure to be other portability issues to be discovered.

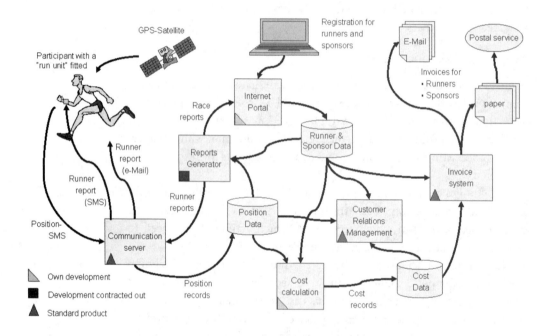

Figure 16–1
The Marathon system

Now what do those upright triangles in the boxes representing system components mean? Standard products! It seems our system architects have designed a system of systems with replaceability in mind. The three system components that use the standard products (communications server, invoice system, and Customer Relations Management system) ought to function equally well with other interchangeable products delivering similar or better services. It's time to talk with the stakeholders about portability issues.

After a meeting with the business owner and the future operators of the system, the following details emerged about portability:

- The Customer Relations Management (CRM) system and the invoicing system are produced by different suppliers. The intention is to reduce to one supplier within the next year, but a choice has not yet been made.
- When the communications server was selected, support for a wide range of communications protocols was a requirement. The planned extensions to the run units will therefore not require replacing this system component.
- The business owners are hopeful of selling the system to other countries, and maybe even for the Olympic Games. This would mean having to adapt to the systems used by the organizations in those countries and being able to install the entire system from scratch. There are no time restrictions placed on this, just as long as the system is installed and ready for operational acceptance tests two months before the system goes into operation (start of runner registration). To keep prices down, local operations staff should be able to perform the installation.
- At present, the Marathon application is installed on its own environment, which is not shared with other applications.

How could we set up a test strategy for Marathon given these requirements? The following list outlines the principal risks that we might want to address with various portability tests.

Adaptability

Risks:

- If the Marathon system is to be sold worldwide, there is a high probability that other target environments will be used. If the system cannot be adapted, we may lose a valuable contract.

Strategy:

- Ask marketing what platforms the Marathon system will be made available for.
- Perform operational acceptance tests and alpha tests for each specified platform. We may choose not to test all possible combinations (these will be excluded from the list of supported environments).

Replaceability

Risks:

- CRM and the invoicing system may not be easily replaced with alternative standard software from a competitor's product range. There is a medium risk that we will either be stuck with current software for several years or be forced to remodel the databases.

Strategy:

- Perform a technical review with the system architects and make sure there is also someone with database expertise available. Concentrate on any possible interdependencies between suppliers of data to the cost database and the runner and sponsor database and the CRM and invoicing systems.
- Ask the supplier of the CRM system to demonstrate its invoicing products and conduct functional end-to-end tests to ensure functionality of essential business processes. Repeat the procedure for the supplier of the invoicing system, assuming it has a CRM product in its range

Installability

Risks:

- Installation must be performed by people external to our organization. It is highly probable that some procedures require knowledge that is not documented (members of our operations staff have a lot of know-how, but much of it is in their heads). This could lead to a large number of calls to our support staff or even lead to incorrect installations.
- Installation must be possible from scratch. This has never been done before for Marathon. There is a risk that the installation sequence requires some steps to be performed before others, but this isn't known. There should be time to rectify any problems that may arise so the risk is not considered critical.
- We always use the same configurations for installing the system. If we sell to other organizations, they may select other options that we have not yet used. There is a high risk that some of these configurations may not work properly. This could have a severe impact on the correct functioning of the installed system.
- Installation staff may not speak English. There is a risk that they don't understand parts of our installation procedures.

Strategy:

- Have procedures reviewed by testing and operations staff.
- Perform workshops to detect any paths through the installation not yet documented.
- Discuss target countries with marketing staff and have all procedures translated into appropriate languages. Invite foreign information technology students from a local university to dry-run the procedures and evaluate their usability.
- Use structure-based techniques to design tests that would ensure 100 percent decision coverage through the procedures. Conduct different installations according to the test cases and ensure that de-installation procedures are used between each installation run (assuming those de-installation procedures have already been independently tested).

Co-existence

Risks:

- None identified

Strategy:

- No testing planned at present.
- Monitor in maintenance phase.

16.6 Learning Check

The following check lists will help you judge the knowledge you have gained from this chapter.

Terms

adaptability, co-existence, installability, portability, replaceability

Technical Test Analyst

- Recognize the different types of portability quality attributes according to [ISO 9126].
- Understand the sources of portability risks.
- Understand different approaches that can be taken for portability testing.

Test Analyst

■ Understand the stages in an application's life cycle where portability tests may be applied.

17 Reviews

According to the ISTQB Advanced syllabus, reviews are the single biggest and most cost-effective contributor to overall delivered quality when done properly.

In this chapter, we will expand on our Foundation Level knowledge of reviews to look at various other forms of reviews and a number of issues that can help make the review sessions and our participation more effective.

17.1 Introduction

So how can we make our reviews effective? We need to make sure we are doing the following:

- We are reviewing the right work products.
- We are conducting the review at the right time in the project.
- We are conducting an effective review based on the type selected.
- We have the right people.
- We have a team that is trained and receptive to the review process.
- We act on the defects found in the reviews and track them to resolution.

Whose responsibility is this? The test manager is responsible for coordinating the training and the process involved in implementing and sustaining an effective review program. Test analysts and technical test analysts are prime contributors to the reviews and must be able to participate in all types and levels of reviews as their skills and organizations allow. So, while this chapter discusses reviews overall, it's important to remember that the manager coordinates and provides training and planning. It's up to the test analysts and technical test analysts to actively participate and seek opportunities to expand the review process and make it work.

17.2 What Types of Work Products Can We Review?

If we can read it, we can review it.

Are you ready for some good news? We already know that reviews are very cost effective and can locate large numbers of defects. Even better, the list of the work items we can review is very large. Reviews are a form of static testing, static meaning that we don't execute the software but rather we look at it in a *static* state—it's not doing anything but being examined by us. In fact, if you can read it, you can review it. How cool is that? This opens up the horizon for review opportunities to requirements documents (marketing, customer generated, product), specifications (functional, design, database), models, diagrams, mock-ups, use cases, code, unit tests, test plans, test cases, test automation design docs, test automation code … the list goes on and on. Different organizations produce different documents. Sometimes documentation is different between projects within an organization. Regardless of what is produced, anything you can read should be subject to a review.

You probably noticed that test documentation is also included in this list. Test cases and test automation code should receive the same scrutiny as the product design documents and code. We don't want to waste testing time executing invalid cases or looking for situations that can't occur. It saves everyone time to review these documents before we begin implementation or execution based on them

17.3 When Should We Do the Reviews?

It's best to conduct a review as soon as we have the relevant source documents that describe the project requirements. We also need clear definitions of any standards to which we must adhere. Only in this way can we be sure that the work item being reviewed conforms to the stated requirements. During the review, we also want to check for inconsistencies between documents and identify and resolve any that are discovered. If we look only at an isolated use case, we can discover only problems within that use case. If we look at the use case within the entire set of use cases and with the functional specifications, we can discover conflicts, inconsistencies, and gaps.

Should we do a review of an incomplete document? Maybe. Sometimes it is good to get an early look at a work product while it is still in progress. This is frequently done in code reviews where parts may be reviewed individually before the review of the entire program. Requirements documents sometimes lend themselves to a staged review. Regardless of how many partial reviews we do, we have to be sure to do one final review of the entire work item to verify internal and external consistency. When you review only parts, it's easy to say, "Oh, that must be covered in another section that hasn't been written yet." Only when you get the entire item can you verify that everything is there (or isn't!).

17.4 What Type of Review Should We Do?

The ISTQB Foundation syllabus refers to the IEEE 1028, Standard for Software Reviews. This document provides guidelines for the various types of defined reviews.

The following is the high-level outline of that specification.

- Overview—purpose, scope, conformance, organization, application
- References
- Definitions
- Management reviews—responsibilities, inputs/outputs, entry/exit criteria, procedures
- Technical reviews—responsibilities, inputs/outputs, entry/exit criteria, procedures
- Inspections—responsibilities, inputs/outputs, entry/exit criteria, procedures, metrics, process improvement
- Walkthroughs—responsibilities, inputs/outputs, entry/exit criteria, procedures, metrics, process improvement
- Audits—responsibilities, inputs/outputs, entry/exit criteria, procedures

As you can see, there are a number of different review types. The Advanced syllabus expands on those already covered in the Foundation syllabus. Some of the review types are general classifications based on the formality and the participants. Some are classifications that are based on the type of item being reviewed or the phase of the project in which the review will occur. All vary in formality, number of attendees, type of work item, contractual requirements, and goal. It's important to remember that it may be most effective to use more than one type of review, even on a single product. For the best success, match the review type to the work item, the phase of the project, the skills of the team, and the goals of the review. Let's look at each of these individually, including those covered in the Foundation syllabus.

17.4.1 Informal Reviews

Informal doesn't mean ineffective.

The informal review is conducted informally, hence the clever name. The informal review and the walkthrough are the most commonly used review forms in the industry. They are effective and fast and have low overhead. On the downside, they rarely gather metrics and don't necessarily contribute significantly to process improvement efforts.

The informal review is conducted by the author of the product and a selected set of reviewers. Together they go through the document and provide input for changes and improvements. The author takes notes and is responsible for making the suggested changes. Informal reviews can take the form of peer reviews in which a group of peers, often developers, sit down and go through a section of code or a group of testers review test cases.

17.4.2 Walkthroughs

Walkthroughs are very similar to the informal reviews. The main difference is that in the walkthrough, the author is expected to "walk through" the work item—basically leading the discussion and going through the item section by section, explaining as he goes. As with the informal review, the author is responsible for taking notes and making the agreed-upon changes. Metrics may be tracked but usually aren't.

17.4.3 Technical Reviews

Technical reviews are conducted by technically oriented reviewers (rather than business reviewers) who are analyzing the work product. This is a more formal review type that may include a moderator who is responsible for guiding the meeting and ensuring that everyone is given an opportunity to speak. Technical reviews often occur between peers on the same project or include experts in the subject area, but they may involve a larger group depending on the formality required and the knowledge of the participants.

17.4.4 Inspections

Inspections are generally the most formal type of internal reviews. A moderator is responsible for running the review session and keeping the discussion on track. The author of the work item is there but does not present the work item, rather the moderator (sometimes called the inspection leader) guides the discussion. The reviewers arrive at the meeting having prepared by carefully reviewing the work item. They then present their comments and suggestions. A scribe records the notes (this should be the person with the best handwriting!). A reader is sometimes involved in an inspection. The reader's job is to paraphrase sections of the work product during the meeting as a precursor to the discussion of that section. In some inspections, reviewers may be assigned a type of defect to look for in the work item. For example, one person might be the security reviewer and another might be the performance reviewer.

I never get to be the scribe.

Inspections differ from the other types of reviews in their formality and dedication to tracking metrics. Only in the inspection are metrics mandatory. These metrics track such things as the number of defects found, types of defects, and issues to be considered for process improvement.

17.4.5 Management Reviews

Management reviews have a different orientation than the review types discussed in the previous sections. Rather than reviewing a particular work item, management reviews are used to review the project or parts of the project to assess progress, get the status, verify any deviations from plans, validate the management procedures in use, and make decisions regarding future actions. These reviews are usually conducted by or for the managers who have direct responsibility for the projects. In some cases, stakeholders or upper management may also conduct these reviews, but in these cases there is normally also participation by the responsible manager as well. Management reviews often include a review of the project risks and mitigation plans and gather additions and changes to those risk items.

As with any review, a management review produces a list of action items and issues that are to be resolved as well as a record of any decisions made during the review process. A management review can be conducted for any part of a project—for example, the development manager might have a management review to assess development progress and the team's adherence to the defined process at any time in the project. Similarly, the test manager should consider having management reviews of the testing process and the progress toward the published goals.

17.4.6 Audits

Audits are the most formal of the review types and the least effective at finding defects. Audits are often conducted by an independent group or individual whose job is to determine conformance to standards, processes, contractual requirements, or some other set of published expectations. There is generally a lead auditor who has the overall responsibility for the audit and acts as the moderator in review meetings. Through interviews, observation, and document examination, the auditing team determines compliance (or noncompliance) with the specified expectations. The audit results in recommendations for change and a list of corrective actions and generally includes an overall pass/fail assessment.

Audits are usually the product of an external engagement or commitment rather than initiated internally. For example, an audit may be conducted as part of an assessment that is being conducted for a process improvement effort. An audit is not the appropriate mechanism to use to review code in an effort to detect defects prior to dynamic testing.

17.4.7 Contractual Reviews

Contractual reviews are generally associated with a particular contract milestone and are conducted to verify adherence to the contract criteria. These usually include a management review of the project and often involve managers, customers, and the technical staff working on the project. Contractual reviews are frequently used on large systems or safety-critical systems where substantial functionality has been "contracted out" to a vendor or set of vendors. These reviews are used to assess the vendor's progress and to determine any risks that should be addressed.

Contractual review frequency and criteria are often specified within the contract itself and become a requirement for compliance. The depth and formality of these reviews depend upon the contractor/customer relationship, criticality of the project, and schedule.

17.4.8 Requirements Reviews

Requirements reviews are among the most frequently used reviews and provide one of the highest returns on investment. A requirements review may be an informal walkthrough, a technical review, or a formal inspection, depending on the criticality of the product and the experience of the reviewing team. Requirements reviews cover the functional and non-functional requirements and also consider other aspects of the product, such as dependability and safety issues. Participants in the requirements review should include all the project stakeholders, both customer focused and technically focused. The wider the viewpoints captured in this review process, the better the resultant product.

17.4.9 Design Reviews

Design reviews are usually technical reviews between peers or formal inspections. Depending on the technical level of the design, customers and other stakeholders may also be included. As with requirements reviews, the wider the viewpoints, the better, but unlike with requirements reviews, the reviewers must have the required technical knowledge to participate effectively. Design reviews are sometimes broken down into two parts, preliminary design reviews and critical design reviews. Preliminary design reviews are used to propose the initial approach to the technical design and tests. The critical design review investigates all the proposed design solutions, including the test cases and procedures that will be employed.

Problems can sneak in between the requirements and the design.

In practice, design reviews vary widely in depth, reviewers, and effectiveness. A well-run design review will yield a number of issues that should be resolved before work progresses further on implementation of the proposed product. It is important that the design review also ensure that the design fulfills the requirements as agreed upon in the requirements review sessions. In some cases, there will be a divergence between the requirements and design, introducing inconsistencies between the requirements and the final implementation. While this makes for an exciting integration period and an even more exciting user acceptance test, it is not a recommended method for producing a usable product.

17.4.10 Acceptance/Qualification Reviews

Qualification reviews are used to obtain management approval for the system that has been or is still being developed. These are frequently conducted at the end of the development cycle, prior to deployment of the finished product. These reviews are usually conducted as management reviews, although in some cases that require more formality, an audit may be conducted.

17.4.11 Operational Readiness Reviews

An operational readiness review is usually done prior to deployment to ensure that the operational environment is ready to accept the new or updated product. These reviews often include walkthroughs of operational procedures such as backups and may also include a technical review of security, distributed processing, and other capabilities of the product.

17.5 Review Issues

17.5.1 How Do We Make Our Review Effective?

Now, let's review.   There are six defined phases for a formal review, but these can be followed for any type of review:

- Planning—Understanding the review process, training the reviewers, getting management support.
- Kick-off—Having the initial meetings so that everyone understands what they are supposed to do.
- Individual Preparation—Each individual who will participate must have read the work product to be reviewed and must have prepared their comments. Reviewers who are not prepared will be able to provide only reactive comments.
- Review Meeting—Conducting the actual meeting to the guidelines specified for the type of review that is being conducted. In general, we would expect three possible outcomes from the review meeting: (1) no changes or only minor changes are required, (2) changes are required but further review is not necessary, and (3) major changes are required and further review is necessary.
- Rework—Assuming changes to the work item are required after the review, those changes should be made by the author
- Follow-up—Re-review of changes may be required as indicated earlier. The follow-up phase is also used to look at the efficiency of the review process and to gather suggestions for improvement.

Tool Tip   When we introduce the review process to the organization, we need to be sure that our management supports the effort and understands the costs, benefits, and anticipated implementation issues. We also have to be sure we select the correct review techniques and support those with tools if needed. There are review tracking tools that provide check lists of items to verify as well as a mechanism to track the review results from initiation to implementation and approval.

Reviews have to be conducted in a safe and constructive environment. People should not fear having their work items reviewed; rather they should welcome the input. This requires support from management and a general education process for the project team. Cost savings and time savings benefits should be demonstrated at the inception of the review process and those metrics tracked and updated to show actual return on investment. The metrics include tracking the types of defects found and the cost of fixing the defect in the development phase in which it was found versus fixing it later in the dynamic testing or postdeployment phase. This type of cost information helps everyone to understand the value of finding and fixing the defects as early as possible in the development process.

Clarify the purpose of the review when the process is introduced.

17.5.2 Do We Have the Right People?

What about the people? Do they know how to conduct an effective review? Chances are they know how to conduct a review, but they may not know the most effective ways to conduct reviews. So, we should train them. What if they are resistant? If they resist, we need to convince them by explaining the benefits of the review process, the cost savings, and the efficiencies introduced into the development life cycle.

In any of the previously mentioned review types, key decision makers, project stakeholders, and even customers may be involved. It's important to understand management's role in the review process. Managers are generally not invited to the review session (unless it's a management review) on the assumption that this could inhibit free discussion of defects (no one wants to make their peers look bad). Management is involved in the review process by arranging time in the schedule, by ensuring that reviews are given the proper level of effort and attention, and by looking at process improvement data that comes out of the reviews. It's important to note that defects found in the review process should never be used as performance criteria for the individuals involved in the review. This is the fastest way to kill a good review process.

Review the work product, not the author.

Everyone needs to understand their roles. Managers are responsible for the planning and follow-up activities. They allocate the time in the schedule for the reviews. They control the reward system that will encourage participation in the review process. They also can make the changes that are determined as an outcome of the reviews. Test analysts provide a unique viewpoint. Not only is a test analyst looking at how to test the product that will result from the reviewed work item, he is also thinking about how that item will fulfill the needs of the user. The better the tester's knowledge of the user, the better he will be able to contribute this viewpoint. Test analysts are particularly well suited for reviewing requirements, use cases, mock-ups, and other documents that are oriented toward the delivered product. Technical test analysts are well suited to review the technical documents, specifications, design documents, database design, test automation scripts, and so forth. The technical test analyst is particularly interested in how the software will be implemented and how it will be tested. The test analyst is interested in what the software will be and how the implemented product will be tested.

What about developers? What do they contribute? Developers are looking for feasibility in implementation, conformance and integration with existing products, and adherence to coding standards (in the case of a code review) as well as other technical and implementation concerns.

Experience Report:

What happens when we forget to include our cross-functional friends

I worked in a company where Marketing was considered by Engineering to be out of touch with what the customer wanted. There wasn't any hard evidence of this, just more of a "feeling". As a result, Engineering decided to design a product that they knew would be successful. The engineering specifications were written and duly reviewed, but only by Engineering. Marketing and Sales were not included in the review. What did they know anyway? So, we implemented the product that we, within Engineering, felt was truly superior to anything we had previously produced. It had a snazzy interface, it fit a particular niche in the market, and it complemented our other products. Were we clever or what?

I was the QA manager responsible for testing the product. We tested it, per the specifications. It had some performance issues that were reported and fixed. Life was good. We released the product on schedule (our schedule, of course) and proudly demonstrated it to the Marketing and Sales groups. They were nonplussed. In fact, they were so rude as to ask us who our target market was. When we explained the market niche we were targeting, they explained to us that the market was already flooded with competing products which were, in their opinion, superior.

We spent three months developing and testing this product. It never sold. Not even one license for it. We were very sad.

What did we do wrong? We had the requirements review. Testing and development worked closely together. The product worked. But, no one wanted it. We broke one of the main rules of requirements meetings—we didn't have a cross-functional group. Marketing and/or Sales could have told us the product wouldn't meet the needs of the market. Maybe we could have made a better, more marketable product. Maybe we would have canceled it altogether. Either way, we wouldn't have wasted three months on a product no one wanted. Think what we could have done in those three months! So remember, just having the review isn't good enough. You have to have the right people there too. And, you have to listen to the input.

When we're looking at training that will be needed, we should consider the different roles. Everyone needs to be trained to understand the review process and how they will contribute. They need to understand their areas of responsibility, the expectations for their contribution, and the expected payback for their efforts. Additional training may be needed for those who will serve as moderators or metrics gatherers.

17.5.3 What Should We Do with the Defects?

Fixing them would probably be good! There's not much point in identifying defects in a work item unless we plan to fix them. In some cases, we may decide that a problem requires too much rework and can be deferred to a later time—but that should be the exception. Remember, any defect that is found is likely to cascade into additional defects the longer it remains. Erroneous requirements are easy to fix when they are only requirements. When they become code and then integrated code and then released code, they are much more expensive and difficult to fix.

Fix the requirement's bugs now while they're easy to fix.

In addition to fixing the defects we find, we also want to track metrics that will tell us how much time and money we are saving by finding and fixing the bugs early in the development phases. Tracked metrics often include information about the severity of the problem, the time required to find and fix it, the estimated cost savings, and the root cause. This data is not used to cast blame, but rather to find issues with the processes that led to the problem in the first place.

As with any new process, it's important to track the efficiency of the process and the team at implementing it. There is usually a learning curve when a review process is introduced, and that curve increases with the formality of the review type. Benefits should increase over time as the team becomes more familiar with the process and more effective at identifying defects.

What do we do at the end of the review cycle for a work item? It moves on to the next phase. For example, a reviewed requirements document may advance to become the basis for the detailed design documents. Reviewed code will advance to the dynamic testing phases where we test by executing the code rather than by examining it.

17.5.4 But We Don't Have Time to Do Reviews!

Why doesn't business get smarter?

Have you ever heard this? It goes right along with, "We don't have time to do it right; we'll just fix it later." Annoying isn't it? As a test analyst, you know you can save a lot of testing time if you can get rid of the bugs before they get into the code. Since we are almost always driven by time and budget, why don't we do the one thing that has been proven to be cheap and effective? Sometimes it seems like business has to keep relearning the same facts, over and over.

If you find yourself in an unenlightened organization where folks are still arguing that they don't have time to do reviews, let's look at some numbers. You can tailor these to your organization (I've found that works much better than touting someone else's numbers).

Let's say you just received a requirements document, much like the Marathon requirements document. It gives you a basic idea of what you should do, but it might be lacking a few details (or maybe a lot of details). Honestly though, I have certainly seen less detailed requirements for more complicated systems. There are few standards for requirements in our industry, but that's a topic for another discussion. Let's hone in on just one requirement—sponsor amount.

Here's the requirement: "Sponsoring then [after the runners register] takes place over the next three weeks. Sponsors register via the Internet application and can select any runners they wish to sponsor." You've already started making assumptions, haven't you? You're visualizing the interface. You're seeing yourself as a sponsor, picking those runners. What do you see? As a sponsor, do you have a list of runners from which to pick from based on some selection criteria? Do you enter an individual runner's name? Let's narrow down our analysis even further. How about the amount a sponsor can enter? We know, as good analysts, that we should pin down these requirements right now before the developer starts making assumptions. Let's take two scenarios, one where we have the requirements review and one where we don't.

Scenario 1: No Requirements Review

This is a developer's paradise. They can implement whatever they want within these rather loose requirements. This doesn't mean they are being evil. It means they are being creative!

The developer, assuming that a sponsor would only sponsor one or two runners, implements the interface shown in figure 17-1.

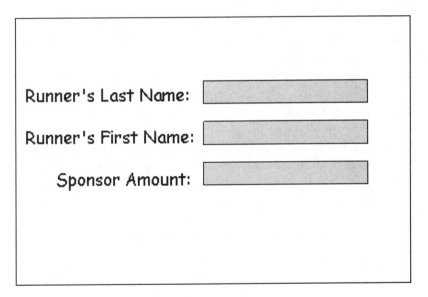

Figure 17–1
The Marathon sponsoring dialog

The test analyst, who was visualizing something completely different, writes a bug and says that this interface doesn't allow the user to enter multiple runners, it requires the sponsor to know the exact name of the runner, and the amount is left completely open—is it even in dollars?

The developer marks the bug as "works as designed". The test analyst double-checks the requirement again and finds that what the developer implemented does meet the requirement, even if it isn't a very good implementation. Let's see what this has cost us so far. Let's assume each person on the team costs the company $100 an hour. This is obviously a nice round number used for the purpose of this example and you would need to put in your own more realistic numbers (probably higher). So, if the developer spent 8 hours implementing this fine application and another 2 hours testing it (hey, we can hope!), then 10 development hours have been spent. If our test analyst spent 2 hours testing it and another 4 hours debating about what it should do and checking and rechecking the requirements, writing and closing bugs, we have spent a total of 16 hours so far on this feature at a cost of $1,600. Despite the test analyst's objections, this implementation is accepted and passed on to UAT. In the meantime, the developer also implements a reporting function that requires a different interface and takes another 10 hours of development time and 2 hours of unit testing time for a total cost of $1,200.

Cold hard cost numbers can help sell the review concept.

The code gets to UAT and the users hate it. They need to be able to enter selection criteria that include runner's name, runner's company, and keywords. They want to see all the entries that meet their criteria. They want to allocate a different amount for each entry. They want to see only whole dollar amounts entered. They want the reporting function to look exactly like the entry screen. Uh-oh. Let's say the test analyst and developer each spent 5 hours working with the UAT people trying to understand what they want. That's another $1,000 spent on this implementation. So, we have now spent $3,800 on a useless implementation. At a minimum, the cost will double when a new implementation is made. This won't look good on our progress report!

Scenario 2: I Know! Let's Do a Requirements Review!

Reviews are undeniably inexpensive, even if we count the donut costs!

Let's look at what it should have cost us if we had a review and the developer and test analyst spent 2 hours preparing. That would have cost $400 and a box of donuts. This is actually an unfair number to assign because in the time they spent, they would have found many issues, not just this one, but that's OK. So we spent $400 up front. Now the developer still takes $1,000 to implement the input screen, but he finds that he can use the same screen for the input and the reporting, so the report implementation takes him 2 hours instead of 10 for implementation and only 30 minutes for unit testing. The total development cost is now $1,250. Testing time is significantly reduced because the requirements are clear, there is no debate, and the code works because it was implemented correctly. Now, instead of the 8 hours of testing required before, the test analyst needs only 2 hours (time is saved testing the reporting function too since it has a similar interface). Testing time costs us only $200. UAT does not require test and development help because this feature isn't a problem. That saves us an additional $1,000. So, instead of costing us $3,800, the implementation costs only $1,850. That's already a considerable cost savings, but that isn't even considering the opportunity cost for both the tester and the developer who can now do other things since they aren't bogged down with this feature. This is the absolute minimum amount of money saved.

Activity	Scenario 1	Scenario 2
Requirements review		$400
Dev implementation—UI	$800	$800
Dev unit test	$200	$200
Tester hours—UI	$600	$200
Dev implementation—report	$1,000	$200
Dev unit test—report	$200	$50
UAT costs	$1,000	
Total	$3,800	$1,850

Table 17–1

Are reviews worth it?

Conclusion: So Should We Skip That Review?

If we can spend $400 and still save $1,950, how can skipping a requirements review ever be justified? It can't. There is always a cost and time savings in having the requirements review. The cost varies depending on the scope of the problems prevented, but a review will always save time and money. It is important for the test team to be sure they are tracking the costs of requirements bugs that get through the system. These should be flagged for follow-up and to help make the case for a better review process. Code reviews, test plan reviews, and design reviews will all show similar returns, but the data has to be tracked in order to convince everyone that there is a cost benefit to conducting reviews.

Tool Tip Because reviews usually occur early in a project, there is a tendency to think they "slow everything down". This is a case where the short-term costs are easily justified by the long-term benefits. But you have to track the data. This is where our bug tracking tools can help us. We can track requirements, specification, design, and other bugs in our tool just as well as code bugs. By classifying these bugs correctly, we can do analysis that will help us determine the costs and benefits of conducting reviews. This will help you determine the level of reviews required in your organization.

17.6 Check List for Success

As the Advanced syllabus states, a successful review process requires planning, participation and follow-up. All of these facets have been discussed, but the following check list helps to monitor the review process and watch for areas for improvement.

- After you have picked the type of review to do, be sure the defined process is followed. This becomes more important as the formality of the review increases.
- Keep good metrics regarding time spent, defects found (classified by severity), costs saved, and efficiency gained.
- Review documents as soon as it is efficient to do so. If the document is partially completed, it may make sense to do a partial review to eliminate problems cascading throughout the document. Be sure to re-review any partially reviewed documents when they are complete to check for consistency.
- Use check lists when conducting the review (or review tools if available) and record metrics while the review is in progress.
- Use different types of reviews on the same work items if needed. Be sure work items are adequately reviewed before they are approved for further progression in the life cycle. The more critical the work item, the more stringent the review should be.
- Focus on the most important problems and don't let the process bog down in unimportant issues like formatting problems.
- Ensure that adequate time is allocated both for conducting the review and for any rework that is required.
- Time and budget allocation should not be based on the number of defects found because some work items will yield fewer defects than others.

- Make sure the right people are reviewing the right work items and that they are trained for the review type being used. Everyone should review items and everyone should have their own work items reviewed.
- The reviews should be conducted in a positive, blame-free, and constructive environment. No one should ever feel attacked.
- Keep a focus on continuous improvement. Share ideas across review teams to encourage the best practices for the organization.

Focus on continuous improvement.

17.7 Let's Be Practical

Reviews and the Marathon Application

We've already taken a look at the Marathon application, but let's not leave this section without considering other reviewable items. We have much more to review in our requirements than the user interface. What about the performance requirements? It is stated that we could have 100,000 runners. Does that mean we need to test for 100,000 runners? Maybe. The problem is that it might be very expensive, so one of the items we need to discuss in the review is where this number came from. Is it realistic? Do we have data that would indicate that we are likely to get this number of runners right now, or is that a number we hope to scale to in three years? That makes a difference in how we will approach performance and load testing. Remember, anything we need to test should be discussed in the review. That means we should be looking for those non-functional requirements that might not be stated. Do we know which browsers we need to test for portability? Do we know what the requirements are for maintainability? How much downtime can we have on this system? When are the races scheduled? Is there a month between or are they back to back, giving us little time to create and test a maintenance release?

Should we have code reviews on the Marathon code? Yes. Database design reviews? Yes. Should we have a review for every work item produced? Maybe. We would need to look at the work items and see if it makes sense to hold a review and what type of review is warranted. We might use peer reviews for the code; we might use inspections for the requirements documents. Marathon offers plenty of review opportunities, as do most projects.

17.8 Learning Check

The following check lists will help you judge the knowledge you have gained from this chapter.

Terms

audit, IEEE 1028, informal review, inspection, inspection leader, management review, moderator, review, reviewer, technical review, walkthrough, qualification

Test Analyst

- Apply a review check list to verify code and architecture.
- Compare review types, identifying strengths, weaknesses, and applicability to various situations.
- Apply a review check list to verify requirements and use cases.

Technical Test Analyst

- Create a review checklist to help find typical defects in code and architecture.
- Compare review types, identifying strengths, weaknesses, and applicability to various situations.

18 Tools Concepts

When we first considered test tools at the Foundation Level, we simply described some of the basic types of tools and discussed how to introduce them. For test analysts and technical test analysts, tools are not just "nice to have". They are an essential part of doing a professional job. In this chapter, we will consider some specific types of tools and consider a number of conceptual issues concerning tool use.

18.1 What Is a Test Tool?

A test tool is some form of software that helps us with our testing tasks. It could be a program, a script, a database, or even a spreadsheet. The purpose of a test tool is to improve the efficiency of the testing and to minimize information loss. A tool that is well suited to the organization will do both. Remember, some forms of testing we have discussed are not possible, or at least not feasible, without the use of tools (dynamic analysis, for example).

The use of a tool is sometimes considered automation of the process. Tools vary in their capability to actually automate the testing process. A static analysis tool that is connected to your defect tracking system would be able to document the defects it finds. There are test case generation tools that will analyze the requirements and create test cases. But tools can deal only with the information they are given. The test case generation tool may generate hundreds of useless test cases that aren't applicable to the users' environment.

A tool is just that—a tool. It must be used by knowledgeable and experienced people in order to provide maximum yield (hence the saying, "A fool with a tool is still a fool!"). Test analysts and technical test analysts use tools every day. We may also be involved in the selection of tools or creating the interfaces between tools. Good knowledge of tools in general and

Watch out for the fools with the tools!

specific tools we can use to assist in testing not only helps with the everyday job, it also helps us to participate effectively in strategic tool decisions.

18.2 Why Would We Use a Tool?

What is the purpose of using a tool? A good tool streamlines the testing process or some aspect of it. It tracks data and makes that data accessible to those who need it. It fits into the overall workflow of the testing process. In short, a good tool helps us get our job done by supporting our process, not dictating it.

Invest time now to save later.   Sometimes using a tool actually requires more effort in some parts of the test process in order to provide benefits for other areas. For example, entering a defect in the defect tracking system might seem like unnecessary overhead. Wouldn't it be faster to just send an e-mail to the developer? Or better, drop by his cubicle and show him the problem? Perhaps give him a sticky note as a reminder? Yes, that would be faster in the short run, but think of the consequences. By not actually recording the defect, we would lose the ability to gather any metrics (and we know defect metrics are rich with information, as we will see in section 19.6, "Metrics and Reporting"), we would not be able to have anyone else work on the defect other than those who discussed it, and, worse, someone might forget about it. The developer might forget to fix it (sticky notes get lost sometimes). The tester might forget to follow up on it and remind the developer. The developer might fix it, but the tester might forget to test it. Everyone might forget to document it in the release notes. The problems just cascade, all because we didn't document the defect. So, while entering the defect into the defect tracking tool requires more effort at the time, it saves considerably later on and provides benefits beyond just accurately tracking an individual defect.

Tools often require effort up front to realize gains later in the process. In some cases, as in test execution automation tools, the development costs for the scripts are much higher than the benefit that is realized the first time the scripts are run. It may take several executions before the return on the investment justifies the cost.

When we're determining if we need a tool, we need to consider the overall costs and the overall benefits (for a complete discussion of costs and benefits, see sections 18.7 and 18.8). It may cost us some money for the defect tracking tool and the training. It may cost some additional effort to enter and track the data. What do we expect to get from it that we don't get from a manual process?

18.3 Types of Tools

Test tools can be divided into several categories as was explained in the Foundation Level syllabus. The individual tools and their applications are discussed in the appropriate sections in this book. In this chapter, we will look at the categories of these tools as follows:

- Test management tools
- Fault seeding and fault injection tools
- Simulation and emulation tools
- Static and dynamic analysis tools
- Performance test tools
- Web tools
- Troubleshooting and debugging tools.

18.3.1 Test Management Tools

Test management tools are those that are used to help manage the testing and the overall project. They include test case management tools, defect tracking tools, requirements management tools, test data management tools, and configuration management tools. They track metrics that are used to manage and control the overall testing project as well as the levels or phases within the project. The following metrics can be tracked:

- Test conditions and environments covered
- Test cases created, pending, executed, passed, failed, blocked
- Time required to execute test cases
- Defects found and classification information

In addition to these metrics, we expect our test management tools to track traceability between the test cases, the requirements, defects found, and risks mitigated.

18.3.2 Fault Seeding and Fault Injection Tools

Fault seeding (sometimes called error seeding) and fault injection tools are used to evaluate the quality of our module tests by actually manipulating the code to create faults or failures. They systematically create limited

Working with mutants can be rewarding.

numbers or types of faults on successful passes of the code. This is some-times done by "mutation operators" that create the code mutants. These act like transformation rules. The mutants generally contain what we would call "easy", or "findable" faults. The goal behind these tools is to create a fault in the code so that the tester can see if the existing test cases catch that fault. For example, if the code has a branch that says

If a > c then

Do some stuff

Else

Do some other stuff

End if;

the fault injector might change the > to < >. The test case should then catch that the wrong stuff is being done. These tools are sometimes called mutation test tools because the fault is considered to be a mutation of the original code and the goal of the tests are to catch the resultant mutants.

In order to make these changes, the tool runs tests against the source code. The resultant code contains the fault, or mutation, which must be detected by the test cases or the test cases need to be improved. Here we have the main purpose of these tools—to evaluate how good our tests are at detecting "make believe" defects and by doing that give us confidence that we will be able to detect real defects. This can be especially useful for safety-critical systems.

When the source code is not available, interfaces may be changed to determine if the failure is detected. For example, rather than changing the source code, we could change values in the database to see if the software detects them. By assessing the code's ability to handle unexpected failures, we are testing the fault tolerance. If an expected value in the database is not present, we would expect the code to handle it gracefully and provide information so the problem can be detected and fixed. If the code just aborts and provides no opportunity to recover, it is not fault tolerant. Fault tolerance is a measure of the ability of the software to respond to faulty data and values. This concept is covered in more depth in chapter 14, "Reliability Testing".

But that could never happen! Fault injection and fault seeding are usually the responsibility of the technical test analyst, although the test analyst could also contribute to data value changes and data stream interruptions. It is very important to discuss this testing approach with development. There may be considerable objections to fixing problems that, in their opinion, can't occur. If the code aborts because an expected value is missing in the database, the developers may respond that the condition is artificial and can never happen. We all know about problems that can "never" happen, but we do have to be realistic in our expectations that problems found with these methods will be fixed by an eager development staff. Code should be fault tolerant, we can all agree on that, but the amount of effort that is expended to make the code tolerant to all faults has to be weighed against the likelihood of occurrence in the real world.

It's important to remember our goal here. We are not trying to create artificial defects for the developers to fix. We may find a situation where the fault tolerance is not acceptable, and that may result in a real defect. But our main goal in this type of testing is to gain confidence in our test cases and our testing approach. If we find a real defect, great, but that's really reliability testing. What we are trying to discover are any weaknesses in our tests that might allow these types of faults to escape detection.

18.3.3 Simulation and Emulation Tools

Simulators are used to simulate the responses of a software or hardware component that interfaces to the software being tested or developed. These tools are typically used during integration and system testing.

Simulators are used when the interfacing software isn't available or isn't working, when the hardware isn't available, or when we need to conduct a test that would result in damage or harm. People building systems of systems frequently use simulators to mimic the interface to another system that is being built elsewhere and isn't yet available.

Simulators are also used to test error conditions or disaster situations that could not be safely tested in real life. For example, an error condition that would result in the escape of a poisonous gas is probably not one you want to test in your lab (not if you have to breathe in there!), so this is a prime case for the use of a simulator. You wouldn't want to test for a failure in the navigation system of an airplane while you're flying the plane (or riding along as a passenger).

Emulators, a type of simulator, are used to mimic all or a subset of the capabilities of hardware. Testers of hardware systems frequently use hardware emulators (written in software) to allow testing of the hardware interfaces without requiring the actual device. The emulators take the

Simulators and emulators replace software or hardware that isn't available for testing.

inputs that would be given to the device and respond with a set of prede-termined responses, some of which may be error responses. Expensive hardware or hardware that is not generally available or not yet developed is often tested in this way. Because emulators are designed to emulate the hardware, they respond to inputs with accurate timing. Although costly to build and maintain, emulators provide the ability to do the time-depend-ant tests that are not possible with simulators. Emulators provide the abil-ity to step through the processing of the hardware to do more extensive tracing and debugging of the functionality. Emulators tend to have high maintenance costs because to provide full value, they must truly emulate all the activities of the hardware. This means that a change to the hardware will necessitate a matching change to the emulator.

Simulators and emulators are used by both test analysts and technical test analysts. The effort that is invested in the creation and maintenance of these tools usually depends on the feasibility of doing all the testing and development on the real systems and hardware. Testing the crash surviva-bility of an airplane is expensive and hard on the humans who might be in the plane. This is clearly a case that justifies the creation and maintenance of a good simulation tools. Testing an out-of-paper condition on a printer probably doesn't warrant creating an emulator, but testing a power spike might.

Since simulators are usually created by the development team, it is important to discuss the needs and uses of these products early in the project—usually during the requirements or design phase. These products take time to create and require time for ongoing maintenance and must be built into the project plan accordingly.

As with all testing tools, simulators must be tested themselves. In the case of safety-critical systems, the simulators have to undergo rigorous testing and may even have to be officially certified for use. In non-safety-critical applications though, it is unfortunately not unusual for software to be tested and approved based on the responses from the simulator only to find that the simulator was not accurately reflecting the behavior of the real software or the real device.

18.3.4 Static and Dynamic Analysis Tools

Static and dynamic analysis tools and performance test tools provide capabilities we don't have without tools.

Static analysis tools are used to test the software without execution, while it's in a static state. They are used to find coding practice violations, secu-rity violations, and other vulnerable or risky implementations. Dynamic analysis tools are used to examine the software while it is executing. These tools find pointer errors, memory use issues, and other manifestations of programming errors. Chapter 8, "Analysis Techniques", discusses tool use for static and dynamic analysis (see the "Tool Tips" margin notes).

18.3.5 Performance Test Tools

Performance tools are used to verify the performance of the software under a specified load. Performance test tools are sometimes considered to be an extension of the test execution automation tools, but performance tools also include the capability to simulate many users (virtual users), monitor server resource usage, and vary the load while measuring the performance experienced by an individual user. For a more complete discussion of using performance tools, see chapter 12 "Efficiency Testing", and in particular section 12.12, "Tools for Efficiency Testing".

18.3.6 Web Tools

There is a class of tools that are specially designed for testing the specifics of websites. These web tools will check for broken or invalid hyperlinks. Some of the tools provide the ability to graph a website to provide the web map (or tree or arborescence of the site), while others track the hits and volume of the website traffic, the number and size of downloads, and the speed experienced by the users. These tools are not just used for testing; they're also frequently used by webmasters (the person responsible for maintaining a website) for monitoring the health and performance of a production website to verify the fulfillment of the service level agreements that may be in place.

More advanced tools exist that will track a user's keystrokes, record think time, and determine abandonment rate (how often people leave the website before completing their transaction). This information is used to improve usability and design navigation paths. While this is not actually a testing tool, it is sometimes used in usability testing to record a user's progress. See section 11.1 for more information about usability testing.

How to find out what our users are really doing

18.3.7 Debugging and Troubleshooting Tools

During testing, it is sometimes helpful to get a more in-depth look at what is really happening in the code. There are various troubleshooting tools that can help us gather more information about a failure and perhaps guide additional testing. For example, we might have a dump analyzer that we use when the system core dumps. This tool is run on the dump and can tell us what failed and what the system was doing at the time of the failure. We can use this information to determine if we have a duplicate of something we have already seen and reported. We can also determine if we need to do additional testing in this area to see if we can repeatedly induce the failure or find similar failures in the same area.

Error logs are a good source of information and can help us figure out what happened. Staring at a failed process is not generally informative, but if we can look at why it failed, it becomes more interesting. For example, if we sent the system a simulated message and it fails when it gets that message, we want to know why. Did our message cause the receiving software to die? Was our message incorrectly formatted, so it was ignored? Having this information can make us better testers by helping us avoid making mistakes when we test. If our message was incorrectly formatted (because we were editing it), then it was our mistake and we need to fix it and rerun the test. If our message was formatted correctly but the receiving system crashed, then we need a developer to look into the failure.

Intelligent troubleshooting saves time for testing and development.

Good use of available debugging and troubleshooting tools can help reduce the number of "defects" that are closed as test errors. They can also help us differentiate between failures. One crash is not necessarily the same as the next, even though it may look the same from the user interface. Usually a trace, a dump, or an error log will tell us the difference. That said, using these tools requires knowledge, and that knowledge is usually in the domain of the technical test analyst, although some test analysts are also adept at using the various tools.

One word of caution here: We are not the developers of the software. There is a fine line between troubleshooting and debugging the problem we have seen versus debugging the code. It is our job to narrow down the problem as much as is justified based on the time available and the seriousness of the failure. When it comes to finding the problem in the code, that is the domain of the developer. The developer uses a debugger to step through the code (line by line), stop or halt the program at a certain point during execution, and manipulate and view the values of variables during execution.

Experience Report: Testing by developing

In one company where I worked, I was the technical test analyst on a project that involved developing our own application language to be used with our product. This meant that to test the language, I had to use it to code programs. While I was coding, I would use the debugger and trace analysis tools that were part of the application language. When I would find a problem, the developers of the language would use their own debugging tools to look at the code in which the language itself was developed. Confusing? A bit. But sometimes your role as a tester crosses into being a developer too when you are actually testing a programming language. By the time we completed the testing on the language, we had written more lines of code in the test scripts that were made with the new language than the developers had used to create the code itself.

18.3.8 How Do I Know It Worked? (Oracles and Comparators)

One of the most difficult aspects of testing can be determining if the software did what it was supposed to do. When doing manual testing, we use oracles (or search for them anyway) to tell us what should have happened. Oracles help us avoid a situation in which we might report a false positive (reporting a defect that doesn't really exist, also sometimes called a false-fail of a test case) or, perhaps worse, assume a false negative (failing to identify a defect that is there, also sometimes called a false-pass of a test case). Oracles are often legacy systems that can run through the same procedures and data and should return the same result as the new software under test. In test execution automation, comparators are used to compare the output results with an expected result. These results could be in the form of a bitmap, a file or even the content of a screen. The expected output has to be carefully defined if it is to work for multiple tests without requiring maintenance. Performance testing is discussed in chapter 12.

It's supposed to do what??

Comparisons can also be done in performance testing when we compare the current results with a benchmark. Depending on how this benchmark is set, we may expect performance to be better (we hope!) or equal to the benchmark. Lower performance is usually not acceptable and is rarely set as a goal.

The goal of having an oracle is to have some way to determine if the software worked as desired. Without knowing the expected or acceptable results, we can end up doing a lot of work that we would like to think is testing and end up unable to draw any conclusions.

18.3.9 Test Execution Tools

Test execution tools are used to run tests and record the results, usually in an automated way. These tools are used to create automation *scripts* that are executed to test certain aspects of the software. Automation scripts are often based on the manual test cases that have been developed for functional testing, but automation is also used for performance and load testing, security testing, and regression testing. Automation tools, when implemented correctly, reduce the costs of repeated executions of the same tests, allow for larger coverage of the software than would be possible with only manual testing, and provide the ability to test facets of the software that would be impossible to test with only manual testing (for example, testing the software's performance, which might require 1,000 concurrent transactions).

Test execution tools utilize scripts that are written in a programming language (sometimes a proprietary language created by the tool producer). When the script is run, it executes its instructions, thus exercising the software under test. For a GUI automation tool, the script will interact with the user interface to simulate a user clicking buttons and filling in fields on the interface. Think time can be programmed in to reflect the time it takes a user to read the prompts on the screen and decide what to do.

Performance test tools bypass the user interface and communicate directly at the protocol level with the web servers (that way we don't need 1,000 clients to simulate a load of 1,000 users). The tools implement scripts running on dedicated servers to generate the necessary load to be simulated (see chapter 12, "Efficiency Testing"). The capability of the tools varies widely, and great care should be used when purchasing a tool to ensure that it will work in your environment. This applies in particular to the communications protocols and operating systems used.

Creating test execution automation is a software development project. Test execution automation tools have become more sophisticated as the nature of our software has evolved. While these tools exhibit more capabilities, they also generally require greater programming ability to design effective automation systems that include the test harness (the driver for the automation), reporting capabilities, and error detection and recovery. A test automation project should be viewed as a software development project requiring architecture and design documents, requirements reviews, programming and testing time, and documentation. To assume that an automation project can be undertaken in the testing team's "spare time" is unrealistic and will lead to significant tool expense without commensurate time and cost savings for the organization.

As the tools become more sophisticated, so does the specialty of automation development. Specific skills are required for a good and effective automator. The automator must have strong design abilities, good programming skills, and a testing orientation. Only with this combination of skills can a successful automation program be implemented. Scrimping on the design time results in code that's difficult, if not impossible, to maintain. Scrimping on the programming time results in code that doesn't work well, is difficult to use, and is fragile. Scrimping on the testing time results in automation code that may cause as many problems as it detects.

18.3.10 Should I Just Use Capture/Playback?

Not if you want to create maintainable automation scripts. Capture/playback can be used to create the initial framework for your automation scripts. Programming is required to make the resultant script maintainable and efficient. Let's look at an example. Figure 18-1 shows the Marathon login window.

Figure 18–1
The Marathon login dialog

We have run a capture/playback tool against the functionality of logging in (enter user name, enter password, and click the OK button). This is the resultant script:

Login.User_Name.Enter("HJones")

Login.Password.Enter("wdft56&st")

Login.OK.Press

That was easy! So what's wrong with this method? It has a number of maintenance issues. The User_Name and Password fields are hard-coded (the text was captured as a string based on the screen input). This means every time we run this script, we will be logging in with the same user name/ password combination. This script is also vulnerable to changes in the GUI. If the OK button is changed to Login, this script may not be able to find it, depending on whether the script identified the button by labeling it as a GUI object or by its position on the screen (less common these days, fortunately).

The script passed, but the system crashed. Now what? Have you detected the biggest flaw with this script? There is no way to verify if it worked. It doesn't check for an error message or for a change of screen or for whatever should happen when the login is performed. We could run this script and the system could crash, and it would still pass.

As you can see, significant work is required to take the "captured" script and turn it into maintainable automation software. Tools that are sold based on ease of use and the concept that the black box testers will be able to generate the automation code themselves are generally unable to deliver on their promises. Good automation code requires good software development work.

18.3.11   Data-Driven Automation

These automation techniques are used to reduce maintenance costs in the automation code and to allow the test analysts to create the actual test scenarios using the test scripts developed by the automator (usually a technical test analyst).

Data-driven automation consists of two main parts, the data and the automation script that will use it. The data is usually maintained in tables or files that the automation script reads. The automation usually cycles through a set of preprogrammed commands and inserts the data from the table to actually conduct the test. The results of the test are then compared to another value in the table to verify correctness. For example, we could have a script for Marathon that tests the ability to enter the sponsor amount for a runner. In this case, we would have a data table that contains the name of the runner, the amount of the sponsorship, and a resultant total sponsor amount. The script would pick up the name of the runner from the table and use that as input to the selection criteria. It would then verify that the correct runner is presented on the sponsor amount input screen. If that runner is present, it would then insert the amount of the sponsorship from the table. If that runner is not present, the script would return an error that would be collected into the report for the overall test run. The script would then skip the remainder of the instructions that were dependent on finding that particular user. It would move down the table, get the next input name, and try again.

When the sponsorship amount is entered, the script would check for any error messages and would check the actual against the expected outcome in the table. For example, if the amount was too large, we would expect to see an error to that effect. Once the amount is entered, the script would check the resultant screen and see if the total sponsor amount matched the value in the input table. If so, the test passes. If not, the test fails.

This is a simplistic example, but it shows how the script can be reused many times to check different conditions (runner not in the database, sponsor amount invalid, sponsor total too high, and so forth). This means that one automation script may be able to replace 100 test cases as it cycles through the table verifying different test conditions. The automator is responsible for building the flexible script that can handle the various input values (remember, input values will also include the expected results verification). The test analyst uses his domain expertise to create the data that will be used by the test script. The test analyst knows what should happen based on the various inputs. The automator doesn't need to know the intricacies of the application, only the aspects that the script needs to know. This provides the best use of the skill sets we have available and maximizes the automation contribution of both the test analyst and the technical test analyst.

Data-driven automation utilizes the skills of the test analyst and the technical test analyst.

Let's look at our previous example with our recorded login script. We already know that one won't provide us with any flexibility and we won't really know if it worked or not. How would it look if we made it data driven? First we create a table (called Login-Data) of the data we want to feed through the script. In this case, we need the values for User_Name, Password and the expected Message. By checking the message, we can verify if the script actually worked or not.

User_Name	Password	Message
HJones	wdft55&st	Password unknown
HJones	wdft56&st	Welcome!
TSmith	Alias3	User unknown
RSmith	Alias3	Welcome!

The script that will use this table is as follows:

DataFile = Openfile("Login-Data")

Read DataFile.LoginRec // read the first "LoginRec" data record in the file

For each LoginRec in DataFile

    Login.User_Name.Enter(LoginRec.User_Name)

    Login.Password.Enter(LoginRec.Password)

    Login.OK.Press

    Verify (MessageBox.Text = LoginRec.Message)

    Read DataFile.Login // read next data record

End loop

This one script lets us cycle through as many entries as we create in the input data file. If someone changes the program so that it displays a pop-up box that welcomes the user rather than just displaying a message, we change it in one place—this script—and all the tests continue to work. In the recorded script, we would have had a separate script for each set of values we wanted to test and would have to change the message to the pop-up box handling in each script. When we get into thousands of sets of data, this becomes a significant effort!

18.3.12 Keyword-Driven Automation

Keyword-driven automation is sometimes called action-word-driven automation.

Keyword-driven automation takes this concept one step further. In the case of keyword-driven, in addition to supplying the data, the input table supplies the action or *keyword* to be used for the test. This keyword is then linked to a script that will be executed by the automation.

For example, an airline check-in system might give the user the ability to change their seat, request on upgrade, or just confirm their check-in. We might see a keyword table similar to the one shown in table 18-2.

Action/Key-word	Confirmation Number	Result	Enter Seat	Enter Credit Card	Result
Change Seat	123456	Display "Found"	18A		Display "Seat Assigned 18A"
Confirm	234567	Display "Found"			Display "Check-in Complete"
Upgrade	345678	Display "Found"		1111-1111-1111-1111	Display "Upgrade Complete"
Upgrade	123aaa	Display "Not Found"			

Table 18-2

Example keyword table for a check-in application

When the automation code sees the action to Change Seat, it knows to call the Change Seat script(s).

Each keyword or action word event must include a way to verify if it worked. In this case, we are depending on the display of the proper message to the user. While this certainly wouldn't be a very safe test, rest assured that it's just being used for a simple example (and to fit on the page). As you can see though, this similar set of information is used for a variety of tests.

Data-driven and keyword-driven automation are sometimes called table-driven automation.

As with data-driven automation, our goal is to maximize our use of the automator's programming skills and our test analyst's domain knowledge. This level of insulation does not require the automator to have in-depth knowledge of the software under test. The resultant automation will be very flexible and easier to maintain. For example, if we change the format of the number from a six- to a seven-digit number, only the table needs to change—the automation script is unchanged.

18.3.13 Benefits of Automation Techniques

Keyword and data-driven automation provide the following benefits:

- The automator concentrates on writing maintainable scripts without concern for test coverage or test data.

- The test analyst provides the knowledge and input data to create the actual test scenarios that provide the required test coverage.
- The script is modular and highly reusable because explicit data values are not embedded into it.
- The automator doesn't require in-depth knowledge of the software under test.
- Additional tests are usually developed by adding more data sets and keyword tables rather than by generating new scripts.

As you can see, designing good keyword and data-driven automation scripts requires a strong architecture of the automation system. The technical test analysts and test analysts need to work together to design a system that will provide independence between the data and the tests, will be maintainable over time, and will provide clear and accurate test results.

18.4 Integrating Tools

What happens when our tools won't talk to each other? We generally have two choices: build our own interface between the tools or fill the gap with manual processes.

For the sake of efficiency, tools need to work together.
Tool integration is a particularly important point for the test analysts and technical test analysts who will be using these tools every day. When the tools don't work together, we have to step in and impose processes that must be followed or we risk losing data.

If we wanted to pick the best-of-breed product for test management, defect tracking, requirements management, configuration management, test data management, and so forth, we might be picking tools from several different tool vendors. While this would give us excellent individual tools, we need to consider the time that would be incurred by trying to glue these disparate tools together and make sure that the effort is justified by the productivity gains we expect to get from the individual superior tools.

Frequently we find tool integration enabled by the use of standards such as common communications protocols, which are generally based on XML. With tool integration, it's typically the test management tool that functions as the *backbone* into which other tools are integrated. Sometimes this integration can be technically quite straightforward, especially where tools have compatibility with the backbone and can be considered as *plug-ins*. The following list includes some typical tool integrations:

■ Integration of defect tracking tool with test management tool. In fact, many test management tools these days come with a defect tracking tool already integrated. The integration here enables test cases to be linked with defects found during execution. We can easily see which test cases need to be repeated when the defect is fixed, and developers can view the test case that was performed when a defect report was raised.

Experience Report: Let's track everything!

I had the opportunity to work with a client who had purchased a high-end tool set and, without adequate research, determined that the defect tracking tool could also be used for requirements tracking and change management. They had completely rolled out the tool, including training, documentation, server purchases, and licenses, when they started getting complaints from their users. Apparently the reporting package that came with this tool was oriented toward tracking defect trends and similar defect-oriented metrics. When they tried to apply these reports to requirements and change management information, the information was almost impossible to interpret. In the end, they had to buy a separate report generation tool to create the types of reports needed, which resulted in a significant effort to create a front end for the report tool that would allow the users easy access to the information they needed. In the six months it took to implement the report producer, the users of the system were forced to continue operating with only minimal access to the information they needed to do their jobs.

■ Integration of requirements management tool with test management tool. The advantage of this integration is to make the task of demonstrating tests case coverage of requirements easier. A bidirectional traceability is established where we can quickly see which test cases cover which requirements and which requirements are covered (or partially covered) by a given test case and, perhaps more important, which requirements are not covered. This can be useful for assessing the impact of a requirements change on testing.

Who needs to talk with whom?

■ Integration of test execution tool with test management tool. The advantage here is to be able to select test cases from the repository within the test management tool and have them automatically executed. Of course, executable test scripts need to be created and then associated with the test cases to make this possible (nothing happens "by magic"). The integration of these tools also provides one base for reporting and one set of metrics for all test case execution, manual and automated.

■ Integration of modeling tool with test management tool. A variety of modeling tools are available to enable test case design to be performed. These tools may be based on a formal specification language or on a modeling language such as UML. Some modeling tools are capable of generating test cases according to particular techniques and can then write them directly into the test management tool's test case repository. With model-based testing, the concept is extended further to include the generation of automatically executable test cases from a model. This is made possible by using standards for the modeling (e.g., UML) and standard languages for test specification (e.g., TTCN-3).

18.5 Other Tool Classification Strategies

In addition to being classified by their use, test tools are sometimes classified by the level of testing in which they are used (component, integration, system, acceptance). For example, there are sets of tools that are grouped together as unit test tools.

Tools are sometimes grouped by the faults they handle—for example, dump analysis tools that are used to investigate the causes of software crashes.

Some tools are designed to work within a specific domain—for example, network analysis tools or traffic simulation and signalling.

Establish tool ownership right from the start.   There are many ways to classify and group tools, so don't be surprised if you find your test management tool being called a system test tool. The classification is considerably less important than the effectiveness of the tool when it is used in your environment. Classification may have some effect on the ownership of the tool, who has the right to configure (or reconfigure) it, and who pays for it. It is always important to know who "owns" the tool and is ultimately responsible for its deployment, usage, and maintenance.

18.6 Should We Automate All Our Testing?

Now we come to the time, money, and capability trade-off. Not everything can be automated. Some types of testing do not lend themselves to automation, particularly those requiring a human assessment as in usability testing. We have to determine the efficiency of automating. It will likely be a waste of time to automate software that is rapidly changing because the maintenance of the automation scripts will be costly and time consuming.

Automation is not the silver bullet to kill the werewolf of spiraling testing efforts.

Automation is not the silver bullet that will solve all testing problems. It is an undertaking that must be carefully considered, and a decision should be made on whether to automate fully, partially, or not at all. The process of deciding what to automate is illustrated in figure 18-2 and shows that a check list can be a useful guide when deciding what to automate.

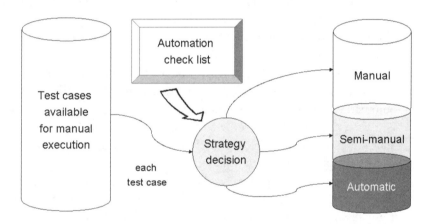

Figure 18–2
Selecting test cases for automation

The automation check list shown in the diagram would typically contain questions like these:

- How often is it likely that we will need to execute the test case? In [Kaner 02], a very important "lesson learned" is described relating to the justifications that are sometimes made in favor of test automation based on the number of test executions performed. Essentially, it's not the number of test executions performed that's important, it's the number you actually need. If you would execute a test manually only three times, don't justify the automation of that test by saying that you're "saving money" by executing it six times.

- Are there procedural aspects that cannot easily be automated? There is a whole range of technical and organizational reasons why full automation will not work or is too costly. There may be manual steps performed within a business process that is only partially supported by your application. There may be aspects of results verification that are more effectively performed by a human. Think of these things before deciding to automate. A partial automation may be the right decision here.

- Do we have the details? Automating a test requires telling a tool precisely what to do and what to expect. Do we have that level of detail? If our test cases are described high level (or maybe not at all), we will first need to establish the fine details of those tests before we can automate. How much effort will be required to specify the test case to a sufficient level of detail such that it can be automated? In my experience, inadequate attention to these details is one of the main reasons test automation runs into trouble.

Use the automation check list before starting the automation effort.

- Do we have an automation concept? Sounds like an obvious question, doesn't it? You'd be surprised, though, at how often those conducting automation projects set off to automate certain types of test and then end up trying to automate others. A classic example here is when we start out automating simple GUI tests and end up tackling the automation of complex end-to-end tests. Do we have a concept for modularizing our automated test cases so that we can chain them together to handle complex business processes? If not, we'd better leave those complex sequences as manual tests, at least for the time being.

- Should we automate the smoke test (sometimes called a build verification test)? This test determines if basic functionality is available and working. It is used frequently and provides a high return because it lets us determine if a new release is testable. This is a relatively quick automation effort and results in a very visible win for the usefulness of automation. It's a good idea to use the successful execution of this script as one of the entry criteria into test.

- What about regression testing? These are usually tests that will remain stable but need to be executed frequently. These are just examples of potential automation concepts. I would strongly advise not to contemplate automation until the automation concept has been formed.

- How much change are we expecting? If requirements are undefined or unstable, we will also need to change automation scripts quickly and efficiently. If this is not possible, we shouldn't take on too much automation right up front. It's probably a good idea to focus automation on the stable parts of the system and leave the rest for manual test execution.

When we're making a decision for automation, we need to answer a fundamental question: Why do we want to do this?

- Do we want to enable a lot of tests to be executed in a short time frame? This might be desirable if we are automating test cases for maintenance testing, where the time available to conduct testing may be severely limited.
- Do we want to support daily build and test cycles?
- Are we trying to reduce costs?
- Do we want to ensure precise test execution of complex sequences?
- Do we need to exactly reproduce a test?
- Are we automating because our test process is chaotic?
- Are there quality characteristics that cannot be tested manually? Performance and load testing frequently fall into this area.

Automating chaos results in faster chaos.

We should proceed with determining the costs and benefits of test automation tools only after we have considered the questions in the automation check list carefully and made a decision in favor of full or partial automation.

18.7 Determining Costs of Test Tools

So now we have established that we want to automate. But just because we want and need tools for automation doesn't mean we will actually get them. We have to justify the costs of the tool by clearly understanding, stating, and being able to realize the benefits of the tool.

So what does a tool cost? Is it just the purchase price? Unfortunately, no. The cost of a tool includes the following:

- Cost of comparing and selecting the proper tool
- Purchase price
- Maintenance fees

- Implementation costs, including customization, configuration, and the creation of any additional software to make it work with other tools ("glueware")
- Maintenance costs for upgrades, changes to the implementation
- Training
- Roll-out

At this point, we're assuming we are going to buy a tool. We'll look at the buy or build discussion in a later section; right now let's assume we're buying a tool. We must first find the right tool for our needs. There may be many out there in the market. We may be able to choose between freeware tools and commercial tools.

Before we jump for the snazziest sales demo (or the company that gives away the best toys at shows), we need to analyze what we want. We should look at the following areas:

- Expected lifetime of the tool
  Will this tool be used for multiple projects and for the foreseeable future? Are we trying to solve an immediate problem or are we looking to change our overall processes and want a tool that will help with these changes?

- Scope of the tool and interfaces with other tools
  What other tools will this tool have to work with? Are we buying a test management tool that has to fit between our existing requirements management tool and our defect tracking system?

Don't underestimate the importance of good reporting capabilities.

- Reporting capabilities
  Does this tool provide the reporting capabilities we need? Can it create clear, well-designed charts? How customizable is the reporting function?

- Required user interaction and capabilities
  What does the user need to do and know in order to effectively use this tool? Are we buying a high-end automation tool that requires good programming and design knowledge? Are we buying a defect tracking tool with an intuitive interface?

- Ease of integration with existing tools and practices
  How hard will it be to integrate this tool with others? Does interface code already exist? If we have to write our own, how hard would that be to do?

■ Life cycle models
   Does this tool require a particular life cycle model to be effective? Are we buying a tool that is oriented toward the agile development model (and we are a waterfall shop)? Is the life cycle suitable to what we do now and what we plan to do in the future?

■ Reputation of the tool vendor
   How reputable is the tool vendor? Will it provide support? Will we get fixes? Does it provide consulting services? (Be careful—this can be a double-edged sword if the vendor has purposely made the product difficult to customize so you have to use its services.)

■ Users of the tool
   Who will be using this tool and will it meet their needs?

■ Start-up costs
   Will there be significant start-up costs for this tool before we begin to realize the benefits (as in test execution tools)?

Many a tool has failed in an organization because it was selected and implemented by an isolated group who did not take into account the needs and requirements from others in the organization. When doing any analysis prior to purchasing (or building) a tool, be sure to get input from all the stakeholders. You don't want the tool to fail because it doesn't provide some piece of functionality that is critical to a group of users. For example, the majority of the tool users could be on-site where the tool is centrally located. They may run the client on their own machines. But, if we also have a remote group that will require the web interface into the tool, we need to be sure the web interface offers the same capabilities and provides reasonable performance.

But, I don't want to use that tool!

18.8 Determining Benefits of Test Tools

Once we have carefully examined our costs and our requirements, we also need to examine the expected benefits. Determining the benefits also serves as a double-check of the requirements. When looking at the expected benefits, we should be investigating the following items:

■ Existing tools
   What existing tools or manual processes are we replacing? Is this tool

compatible with the way we have been doing things? If not, will the requisite changes move us in the right direction?

The long-term benefits of the tool must justify the costs.

■ Cost savings
What cost savings do we expect to gain from this new tool? Will there be an initial period in which the costs of using the new tool are higher than the cost of the previous processes?

■ Data flow
Do we expect to see a more efficient flow of data that will provide information faster and more accurately to the stakeholders?

■ Data security
Will there be a reduced chance of data loss with the new tool?

■ Test status
Will we be able to provide more accurate status information and implement corrective measures more quickly as a result of this tool?

■ Test coverage
Will we be able to do more testing and use our testing resources more effectively as a result of implementing this tool (as in the case of test execution tools)?

■ Portability
Will this tool adapt to different environments that might be used in the future?

■ Life expectancy
Will this tool work for the long run? Will we be able to add to it and improve it as time goes on and we learn more about its optimal implementation? Does it lend itself to maintainability? If we are generating automation scripts, how long will we be able to use them and benefit— this release, next release, maintenance releases for the next five years?

The tool purchase decision is usually made by a test manager, but it is important that the test analysts and technical test analysts help that manager quantify the benefits and costs that may not be visible from the management perspective. We know what we need our tools to do. We also know what happens if they don't work correctly. We need to be able to present that information as part of the tool acquisition process.

18.9 Buy or Build?

Any time we are considering adopting a tool, we need to decide if it would be better to build our own tool, buy a commercially available tool, or implement a freeware tool. There are pros and cons to all approaches. Let's look at some.

When you build your own tool, you can customize it to do what you need it to do. If you are working in a special environment, you may have no choice but to build your own tool because there may not be any others available. One problem with homegrown tools is that they tend to focus on a particular problem in a particular area and are rarely designed as part of an overall tool suite that will solve multiple problems across the organization. Of course, that does not keep us from trying to use the tool everywhere. Many a defect tracking system has found itself doing change management, requirements management, configuration management, purchasing requests…the list goes on and on. The difficulty with this is that the tool probably isn't well suited for its many uses and we end up with a suboptimal tool across many areas.

If we build it, we have to maintain it.

The other main issue with a tool that is developed in-house is that someone has to maintain it. This means that it may actually require a dedicated staff of people to keep it up and running and to implement enhancements. This is a cost that is frequently overlooked when tools are developed in-house.

Buying a commercial tool gives us the benefit of a tool that has been developed for a wide audience. Of course, if it doesn't do what we need it to do, that's not very useful. Commercial tools may be more reliable, but we can all point to cases where commercial tools crash and/or corrupt data. Commercial tool suites usually include components that are very strong and components that don't meet the needs of the organization.

Are commerical tools more reliable than freeware?

Acquiring a freeware tool has the tremendous advantage of being an inexpensive solution. There may be licensing fees involved, but they are generally lower than fees for commercial tools. There may also be an expectation that you will share any code you develop for the tool with the general community. One of the major drawbacks to free tools is the unpredictability of support and the unknown lifetime plan for the tool. But, it's free!!! In some safety-critical or security-critical systems, freeware tools are not allowed because only tools that have been certified can be used. Before you fall in love with a freeware tool, be sure it will meet your requirements and that you will be allowed to use it.

How bad can it be if it's free?

With any tool, we need to carefully research the needs of the users and plan the deployment. Deployment includes training, customization, roll-out and support. If you are the one who will be maintaining the tool, you need to set expectations for service level agreements. You don't want a 2:00 a.m. phone call because someone can't get a defect report to work.

18.10 Care and Feeding of Tools

Test tools have to be managed, just as other aspects of the testing process are managed. Test tools and any "glueware" must be under source control and version tracked. Testing tools that are used as part of the actual testing, such as simulators, must also be tracked as an environment variable that could affect the testing results.

Experience Report: Oh, we needed that source code?

Everyone uses configuration management tools, right? It's something we learn in programming 101—you need to check in your source code so it doesn't get lost. I worked with one organization where the source code had been dutifully checked in when changes were made. A formal CM process was in place with a configuration manager who was responsible for performing the builds and distributing the code to the test systems. Nothing to complain about, right? There didn't appear to be any problems until the build server went down one day. Since the team was all new since the original CM procedures had been established, no one knew where the actual device resided. After tracking it down, we found it under a departed developer's desk. It had experienced a power supply problem and was shut down. When we got the server back up and moved into a controlled lab, we made the further discovery that it had never been backed up. The backup procedures had never been set up for the device. So, while we had been following good CM practices, we had fallen short of investigating the physical location of the server and the backup routines.

When test tools are developed in-house, we should follow good programming practices such as creating reusable components, creating libraries of common code, and creating adequate documentation both within the code and external to the code for the tool users.

Tools must be maintained, and that cost has to be figured into the overall cost of the tool. Many tools have been implemented with great fanfare only to fall into disuse in a couple of years because they are no longer usable with the current environment. Test execution tools must stay current with the code being tested or they will, at best, result in testing a smaller and smaller amount of the software. Test tools that help with test management must adapt to the processes and life cycles that are in use. Flexibility and a view to the future is key to implementing a test tool that will work within the organization for a long time.

Tools have to be flexible to survive.

18.11 Let's Be Practical

Test Tools for the Marathon Project

One of the challenges with the Marathon project is the distributed development aspect. Since we want all defects found during development, regardless of who is doing the development, to be recorded in one database, we will use industry-standard defect tracking tools. Our test management tool is already in use and already interfaces with the defect tracking tool we will require.

Exercise

Given that Marathon has some outsourced development, how would you go about handling the configuration management aspects of the project?

18.12 Learning Check

The following check lists will help you judge the knowledge you have gained from this chapter.

Terms

data-driven, debugging, debugging tool, emulator, error seeding tool, false-fail, false negative, false-pass, false positive, fault seeding, fault seeding tool, keyword-driven, oracle, simulator, test execution tool, test management tool

Test Analyst and Technical Test Analyst

- Summarize test tools into categories based on objective, use, and required skills of the tool user.
- Select the proper tool for a given level or type of testing.

Technical Test Analyst (specific)

- Create keyword or action word tables to be used by a test execution tool.
- Explain how test execution automation can save time with regression testing and when it may not save time.
- Design a performance test using performance test tools. Consider methods for measuring and monitoring the system.

19 Incident Management

In this chapter, we consider incidents. An incident is something unexpected that happens and needs to be investigated. Often, if we are testing in a controlled environment, the incident is identified as a defect after the investigation is complete.

This chapter first looks at the IEEE 1044 guidelines for incident logging and the various life cycles that incidents experience on their way to becoming resolved. We then look at a number of metrics and reporting possibilities relating to incidents.

19.1 Introduction

Both the test analyst and the technical test analyst are interested in accurately recording issues found in their areas. A test analyst will tend to approach the incident from the user's perspective—What would this mean to the user? What would he do when he encounters this situation? The technical test analyst will concentrate more on the technical aspects of the problem—Why did it occur? On what platforms is it visible? Is it affected by environmental factors? This approach to incidents directly corresponds to the quality characteristics the tester is testing. If the problem is a performance issue and likely within the purview of the technical test analyst, investigation of the problem will be different than that conducted by a test analyst for a usability issue.

The defect report originates with the test analyst or the technical test analyst who is performing the testing. We need to understand what a defect is and how defects are documented and handled throughout the life cycle. We also need to understand how the information we enter about the defect is used to create management reports (even though that's a test manager's area of knowledge). Some sample reports are included in this section to help show how the collected defect information is used to determine project status.

19.2 What Is a Defect?

Let's talk a little about terminology. According to IEEE, an *incident* is an unexpected occurrence that requires further investigation. An incident may or may not be a defect—it depends. It could be caused by an invalid configuration. Or it could be caused by a defect in the software. An incident may not need to be fixed. A *defect* requires a fix or a change in order to be resolved. Straightforward so far, right? Don't relax yet—we have a few more terms to go over. An *error* is a mistake that was made somewhere in the software life cycle. Let's take a simple example. Let's say the code is supposed to add the values of the variables A and B and return the sum to variable C. The code should look like this:

$$C = A + B$$

(Please forgive the syntax errors if this is not in your preferred programming language.) Now, let's say the developer is busily eating a jelly donut while he is typing this statement and drops a blob of jelly on his keyboard. While he's cleaning it off, he accidentally overtypes the + with a -. Now the statement reads as follows:

$$C = A - B$$

Incident does not necessarily equal defect.

He has committed an error by typing the wrong sign and that has resulted in a defect in the code. That defect could be detected by static testing—a code review. Alas, the developer does not have a code review (he probably uses the time to run out for more donuts) and releases the code as is to system test. The loyal and dedicated testers run their test cases and find a failure when C does not have the right value. This failure can only be seen by dynamic testing because that's the only time the defect manifests itself into a failure. So, the developer commits the error that results in the defect that is found when it becomes a failure. The moral of this story? Don't eat jelly donuts while typing! Oh, and static testing can eliminate defects before they become potentially costly failures (but we already knew that).

The relationship between the error, defect, and failure is shown in figure 19-1.

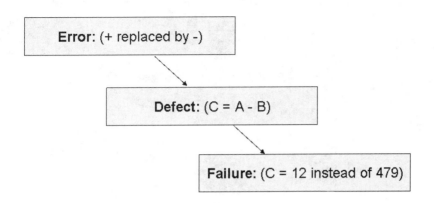

Figure 19–1

Error, defect, and failure

19.3 Defect Classification Process

According to IEEE 1044-1993, "Standard classification for software anomalies", a defect goes through what they call a classification process. This has four steps, each with three common activities. Here are the four steps:

1. Recognition

2. Investigation

3. Action

4. Disposition

Each step contains three activities:

1. Record

2. Classify

3. Identify impact

Figure 19-2 shows the activities and the steps in the IEEE 1044-1993 classification process. Each step is described in the sections that follow.

Step 1: Recognition

Record: The test analyst or technical test analyst identifies a defect. The defect (also called an anomaly in this IEEE spec) is recorded by the person who found it. Information regarding the environment in which the problem occurred is also recorded at this time. Environmental information

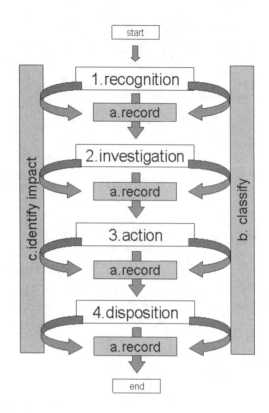

includes hardware, software, database, platform, firmware, and test support software.

Classify: The recognition of the defect is classified based on the observed attributes for the defect as follows:

- Project Activity—What was going on when the defect was found (e.g., analysis, review, audit, testing)?
- Project Phase—During what phase of the life cycle was the defect found (e.g., requirements, design, implementation, test)?
- Suspected Cause—What is the suspected culprit (e.g., product hardware, test system software, platform, third party)?
- Repeatability—How often can the defect be repeated (e.g.. one time, intermittent, reproducible)?
- State of the System—What happens when the problem occurs (e.g., system crash, correct input rejected)

■ Resulting Status of the Product—What is the result of the problem (e.g., unusable, degraded, unaffected)

Identify Impact: Impact analysis occurs at this step and is reverified at all the other steps as well. Impact analysis includes assessing the severity (impact to the system) and the priority (impact to the customer/business) as well as the impact to customer value, mission safety, project schedule, project cost, project risk, project quality/reliability, and society.

In practice, this level of formality is infrequently used.

Step 2: Investigation

Further information is gathered about the defect in this step by the analyst who identified the defect. This is where we look to see if there are any related issues. Solutions may be proposed at this time that may include taking no action at all.

Record: Supporting data items such as date received, investigator, estimated and actual start and end dates of the investigation, hours spent, and documents used in the investigation are all recorded into the defect report.

Classify: Classifying information is added based on information found during the investigation. In addition, any classification information entered in the previous step is reviewed and corrected as needed.

■ Actual Cause—What is really causing the problem (e.g., product hardware, test system software, third-party data)?
■ Source—What is the source of the problem (e.g., specifications, code, database, reports)?
■ Type—What type of a problem is this (e.g., logic problem, computation problem)?

Identify Impact: The impact classification assignments previously made are reviewed and updated as a result of the investigation.

Step 3: Action

This is the step where we determine what to do with the defect. We discuss possible resolution strategies for the defect and any process or policy changes that may be required to prevent the occurrence of similar defects.

Record: At this point, we record the supporting data items, including the item to be fixed, the components within the item, a description of the fix, planned date for action, person assigned to the action, the planned date for the fix to be completed, and any reference documents affected.

Classify: Further mandatory information is added to the defect report as follows:

- Resolution—Does this problem need to be resolved and, if so, how quickly (e.g., immediate, eventual, no fix)?
- Corrective Action—Does something need to change to prevent this from happening again (e.g., department action [implement training, corporate action,] revise process)?

Identify Impact: The impact classification assignments previously made are reviewed and updated as a result of the action steps. Any changes made at this stage may require regression testing and retesting depending on the changes.

Step 4: Disposition

The defect moves to the disposition step at the point it is deemed to be resolved. Resolved could mean fixed, but it could also mean deferred, merged with another defect, moved to another project, addressed by a long-term corrective action, or otherwise put to rest.

Record: The appropriate supporting items are recorded for the defect. These items may include a description of the action that was implemented, the date the report was closed, the date the documentation was completed, the way in which the customer was notified, and the date of the notification and any referenced documents.

Classifying: Defects are completed using one of the following disposition classifications:

- Closed—Resolution implemented, not a problem, not in scope, vendor's problem, or a duplicate
- Deferred to a later release
- Merged with another problem
- Referred to another project

Identify Impact: The impact classification assignments previously made are reviewed and updated as a result of the disposition activities.

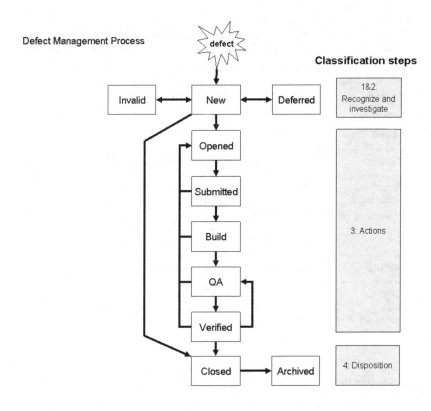

Figure 19–3
Defect life cycle

19.4 Defect Life Cycles

IEEE 1044 defines a standard life cycle as shown in figure 19-3. You can base your own on this if you're just starting up—most people adapt it to their own project needs (more states, less states, etc.). Often a tool captures the states and defines the transitions (who can change the states, e-mail notifications—you know the stuff).

The states are defined in table 19-1 (you probably know some of them already by different names).

Tools are usually used to automate the workflow of the defect process, which includes the life cycle of the defect itself. At any time, many defects are being tracked and are in various stages in their cycle. For Marathon, we can reasonably assume that some number of the defects found during testing will not be fixed before our first release. These defects will likely be found in the deferred state. Some defects may be scheduled for the next release and their fixes may be in progress. We would not want to ship the

Although state names may change, bugs generally go through all these transitions.

Tool Tip

Table 19–1

Typical defect states

State name	Description
New	New defect report has been entered.
Deferred	Investigation deferred (don't forget the date or release/version for renewed consideration).
Invalid	No defect.
Opened	Defect has been assigned and will be worked on.
Submitted	Defect has been submitted for build.
Build	Defect fix has been created.
QA	Fix has been tested by the developer.
Verified	Fix has been confirmed by the tester.
Closed	Defect report has been closed.
Archived	Defect report has been archived.

release with defects in the QA stage because that tells us the code has been released but we have not yet verified the fix (or done any regression testing to see if the fix broke anything else).

Having a good life cycle for defects and tools that support the life cycle helps to ensure effective defect processing. Defects should move through the workflow and not become "stuck" at a stage. Good defect management tools allow us to query on the time a defect spends in any one stage. These tools help us to determine if we are processing bugs efficiently.

19.5 What Should Be in a Defect Report?

The IEEE specs clearly state a set of required and optional fields that are to be included in IEEE standard–compliant defect reports. Depending on the formality of the organization and the need for classificatory information about defects, these lists provide a good set of individual classification information and trend information for reporting metrics. The IEEE 1044.1 specification allows mapping from the IEEE names for fields to any name that makes sense to the organization. This allows considerable customization in bug reporting while still maintaining compliance to the IEEE specifications.

Lesson Learned: Don't just fix one error message!

I worked on a product that was supposed to return error messages for certain conditions. The error messages had not been specified in the requirements documents—the documents just said, "An appropriate error should be displayed." Who determines what is appropriate? I was testing along and entered an invalid value on one of the input screens. I expected to get an error that said something to the effect that the data was invalid. Instead, I got the following message: "An unexpected error has occurred." Not very helpful to the user and therefore a defect.

The defect report opened the discussion that perhaps all the error messages needed to be reviewed, which is what subsequently occurred (even better, we got the technical writers to do the review so they made sure each message made sense and that it was grammatically correct!). In this case, the correct behavior of the software became a judgment call, but the defect report helped to document the issue and drive it to a conclusion, whereas an email would probably have resulted in the specific message being corrected but the global problem of the message review would probably not have occurred.

Most defect tracking tools allow you to add, change, or rename fields. As such, most commercially available tools as well as freeware tools can be made IEEE compliant with a little work to match the fields with the IEEE specifications. A good bug tracking tool should allow this level of customization and should also support the reporting and metrics needs of the organization. Be sure to think about the reports you will need before you invest in a tool to ensure that your tool will be able to present the data as you require.

Tool Tip

Regardless of how many fields you put into a bug report, the end goal is to have the defect be actionable by the project team. This means that there is enough information for the project team to accurately prioritize the fix effort as well as enough information for the developer to determine the cause of the problem and fix the bug. In order to be actionable, bug reports should be complete, concise, accurate, and objective. They should contain all the information about the bug without being verbose. They should clearly and accurately state the problem and the steps required to reproduce the defect. And, perhaps most importantly, they should be an objective statement of fact, not an emotional venting of anger or frustration at the developer. If we stick to these four guidelines, our bugs will be classified correctly and their information can contribute to the risk analysis and process improvement efforts.

Actionable bug reports are complete, concise, accurate, and objective.   As test analysts and technical test analysts, our goal is to be sure our defects are addressed. By taking the time to write good, clear defect reports, we know that our testing time won't be wasted defending badly written or unclear defect reports. Our defects will be actionable and the resulting fixes will improve the quality of the software.

19.6   Metrics and Reporting

In order to be able to manage our defects and create accurate and informative reports, we need to be sure we are tracking the right information. If the test analysts and technical test analysts keep the following areas in mind when designing or upgrading the defect tracking system as well as any time a defect is entered, it will help us to be sure we gather and track the right information.

19.6.1 Test Progress Monitoring

Tool Tip   Ideally, our bug tracking tool is connected to our test management tool. This allows us to track which test cases are passing and failing and which bugs are tied to which test cases. In this way, we can know that one bug is blocking 10 test cases. This type of information helps us to understand our testing progress, our bug yield information, our risk mitigation status, and our relationship between tests run and bugs found.

19.6.2 Defect Density Analysis

Where are the defects gathering (or attempting to hide)? Where we are finding lots of defects, sometimes called defect clusters, we need to concentrate more testing effort because where there are defects, there are likely to be more defects. Defect density analysis allows us to determine the problematic areas of the code so that we can deploy test effort accordingly.

As you can see from figure 19-4, there are some areas of Marathon that look like they may need additional testing. In particular, the runner

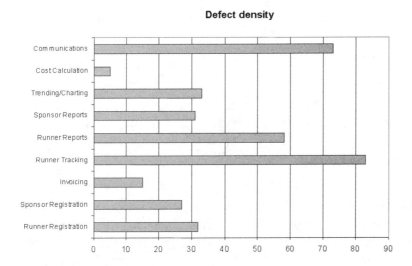

Defect density

Figure 19–4
Defect density diagram

tracking and communications systems are very problematic. Given that we have heavily advertised our ability to track the runners and give up-to-the-minute statistics, this is a very serious issue (or so Marketing tells us). If we cannot track accurately, we cannot bill the sponsors correctly and we may report erroneous data to the runners.

By looking at charts like this, we test analysts and technical test analysts can determine if we need to apply more testing effort to some areas. This information can also be used on the next version of this project. Given the data we see here, we can assume that we will need to put more testing effort into the problem areas and that they have a higher risk (likelihood of failure) than the more stable areas.

19.6.3 Found vs. Fixed Metrics

Found and fixed metrics tell us if we have an efficient bug life cycle. Are bugs being fixed in an efficient manner? Are we seeing the bugs being resolved or are they being rejected? How quickly should we expect development to fix incoming bugs? This information is usually found in a chart that is shown as a pie diagram with two main sections, as shown in figure 19-5.

From this we can see that around 16 percent of our defects are being rejected. That's quite a high rate, so we should look at why they are being rejected. The majority of them are being rejected because the code is doing what the developer thinks it should do (as designed). Now we need to go

Why do bugs get rejected?

Fixed vs. Rejected

Figure 19–5

Fixed vs. rejected diagram

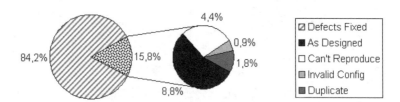

look at those defects. Was the tester incorrect? Is the specification not clear? Is the developer incorrect? This is an opportunity for process improvement in our testing. If the specification isn't clear, we need to spend more time and effort on the specification reviews. If the tester isn't reading the specification correctly, we may need to invest some time in training. If the developer is not following the specification, this may be an opportunity for developer training (or we may need to find out if there is a later version of the specification of which we are not aware).

As you can see, we can gather quite a bit of information about our process just from this one chart. Remember, charts need to present the information that is most applicable to the audience. If our reject rate is relatively low, we probably don't need to show the details to the project team, but we certainly need to look at the details to determine process improvement opportunities within the testing team.

19.6.4 Convergence Metrics

As we are finding bugs, is development fixing them? We should see that as the project progresses we are finding fewer bugs and development is steadily fixing what we have found. If we see that the trajectory on the bug-finding line is continuing upward, we aren't advancing toward more-stable, less-buggy software. If the developers are not fixing bugs at the same rate we are finding them, we are creating a quality gap that indicates we will be shipping new bugs to our customers (they always like that!). The convergence chart is one of the easiest and most effective reports we can create that will clearly indicate the status of the testing and the readiness to release. Let's look at some samples (see figure 19-6):

Does your chart send the right message?   In this first convergence chart, we see that the opened and closed curves are not converging. We are continuing to find new bugs at a fairly

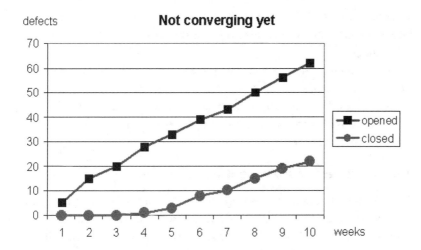

Figure 19–6

Open vs. closed defects: no convergence

constant rate. Development is not fixing bugs as fast as we are finding them and they are falling behind. If we are expecting to ship this release in Week 11, we are in serious trouble!

Let's look at another chart (figure 19-7).

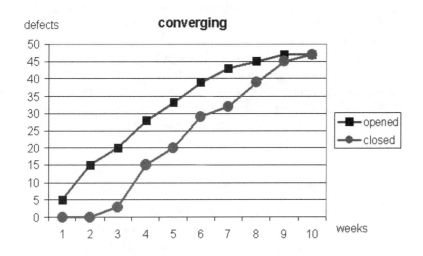

Figure 19–7

Open vs. closed defects: convergence

In this chart we see a much happier view. In this case, the opened line is flattening out, meaning that we have found the majority of the bugs that our test system is capable of finding. We also see the closed line converging to the opened line. This indicates that the developers have fixed the bugs we have found, and if we were to ship now, we are not introducing any new known bugs to the field. If this project is due to ship in Week 11, we are in good shape.

Convergence charts are among the easiest to make and the clearest to present. With a glance we can tell if a project is nearing readiness for release or not. We can also tell if we have a good bug resolution process or if there are issues we need to investigate. Any chart we publish should clearly project our message.

19.6.5 Process Improvement Opportunities

Let's not forget about process improvement information. Our bugs tell us what we have done wrong. Clearly these are areas to look at for possible improvement initiatives. Tracking root causes of bugs and performing root cause analysis tells us exactly where we need to improve processes. If 80 percent of our bugs are due to bad specifications, then clearly we need to

---

Lesson Learned: Tracking more than defects

I often use defect reports to document a decision by the project team. It's not unusual for requirements changes to be discussed in project meetings, but it can be unusual to get them documented beyond the meeting minutes. When you write a defect report to track this change, it will be open for further discussions, scope assessment, time estimates, and scheduling. A change to the requirements usually requires the same type of information as a defect—after all, a change to the requirements is probably due to a defect in the requirements in the first place. Requirements defects are discussed further in chapter 17, Reviews.

---

spend more time writing and reviewing those specifications.

In figure 19-8, we have a sample root cause analysis chart.

One word of caution here: Root cause values vary widely in the industry. There are several sources for root cause definitions. The important thing to remember is to use root causes that make sense for your organization.

Customize root cause lists.   In figure 19-8, we can see that our biggest root cause is wrong requirements. This is clearly an indication of a need for better requirements reviews. Following closely though is interface errors. This is usually a

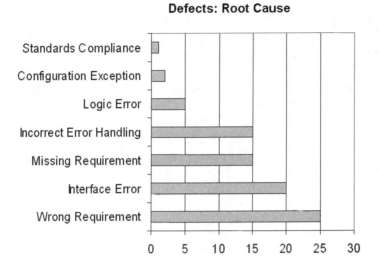

Figure 19–8

Root causes of defects

problem in the detailed design specifications or the overall architecture of the system. Root cause identification and analysis is a rich area for process improvement ideas, and this information can be easily tracked within the bug tracking system.

19.6.6 Phase Containment Information

This is another area that is rich to mine for process improvement ideas. If we see that bugs are escaping from one phase and are being found later in the development process, then this is an area where we can improve. Ideally, a bug should never escape from one phase to another. If the problem is introduced in the requirements, it should be caught in the requirements review meeting. If it is introduced in the code, it should be caught either in code review or in unit testing. These phase containment numbers not only tell us where we can improve the overall process, they can also be used to track cost information that will support additional testing effort and involvement earlier in the software development phases.

Lesson Learned: Use defects to clarify requirements

In another example, a defect led to a redesign. The software was supposed to allow the user to do volume data entry work. While the user could do single data entry, the interface did not help with multiple-record entry (for example, cut and paste was not possible, nor could the user duplicate a record). The stated requirement was that "volume data entry must be facilitated." Again, this is not the clearest of requirements. The above issues were documented as defects and the resultant discussion was recorded within the defect itself as the analyst and developer discussed the best solutions. In the end, we had a redesigned interface and a complete audit trail of what had changed and why. The information was then used to build new test cases and to guide new testers. Lesson learned? Defect reports can be used to clarify the accuracy of the requirements and to document the decisions that are made.

Figure 19-9 contains a sample phase containment chart.

Figure 19–9

Phase containment diagram

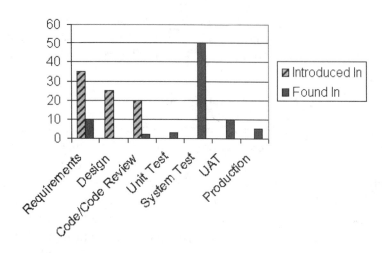

Phase Containment

Perfect phase containment is the goal.

This figure shows us where problems are being introduced and where they are found. Some phase containment charts also track the phase in which the problem was resolved. From this we can see that we are introducing more problems in the requirements and design phases than in the coding phases. This is a clear indication that more static testing is warranted. System testing is catching a large number of the problems that should have been caught in the earlier phases. We also see an uncomfortable number being found in UAT. Ideally, no bugs should be caught in UAT—they should all have been found before. Production problems may be expected depending on the configurations available for testing prior to release. Some production problems are inevitable if the test team cannot completely simulate the production environment and data.

And there's one more obvious area to investigate. If we see trends in the defects that show us concentrations in certain areas, then we can determine that those areas are inherently more risky. This information can feed back to our risk analysis and tell us where we should concentrate testing and preventive efforts in order to reduce overall risk to the project.

The information we can mine from our bug tracking system is invaluable to improving the overall development process, substantiating the need and cost for the testing effort and providing useful project management metrics. Put the time into gathering and tracking the right information and you will have years of valuable information to draw on when you need to make a presentation.

19.6.7 Is Our Defect Information Objective?

In order for our bug information to be useful to the testing team, development, our management, and project management, it must be accurate. It also must be free from accusations. Despite project pressures and late-night testing sessions, we must always strive to make our bug reports objective and accurate, and that includes the information on the bug report as well as the classification information. Many a tester has lost their reputation due to inflating the priority of a bug or, worse, putting a personal accusation in a bug report. Unfortunately, even the best bug tracking systems can't screen for statements that will later be regretted—that comes only from maturity and careful review of the bug report before you hit the submit button.

Lesson Learned: Remember perspectives

Just because we love defects (particularly when we get to find them), it doesn't mean everyone does. Believe it or not, that defect that you are so proud of will not be greeted by the developer with the same level of delight. I was recently testing a report for a developer who had just made significant performance improvements. He sent me a message to please try it out before he officially released it for test. He was very proud of his work and included statistics of the performance improvements I could expect to see. So, I tried it. It failed. I tried it again. Same failure. I sent a message to the developer. This immediately brought him into Instant Message. Here's the dialog:

> Me: "It didn't work."
> Developer: "You're kidding, right?"
> Me: "I wouldn't kid you about a thing like that."
> Developer: "No way."
> Me: "Look at your e-mail, I sent a screen shot."
> Long pause…
> Developer: "☹"
> Me: "Can you reproduce it?"
> Developer: "Yes. How do you do this to my code?"
> Me: "It's a finely honed skill."
> Developer: "Thanks for finding this. I'll have a fix to you in 10 minutes."

I did indeed get the fix in 10 minutes and it worked fine. I had happened to try a date range that he hadn't anticipated (a boundary condition). The dialog is not accusing, but there is a little bit of joking going on. I have to say, while I was happy to have broken it, I was sorry to make him sad. On the other hand, that's my job and he appreciated my efforts. In the world of bugs, that's all we can ask for. We can't expect a developer to be thrilled that we found a problem, but we need to work to the point where the developer appreciates our efforts and shares our goals of releasing the best possible product.

Don't use bug review meetings as a crutch. Bug triage or bug review meetings are sometimes used to help with prioritization of incoming bugs. While this may be an effective means for getting attention focused on the new bugs, don't rely on these meetings to replace an effective bug life cycle that is supported by the bug tracking tools. Meetings tend to bog down and can easily waste the time of many for the benefit of a few. Be sure that bug review meetings are efficient and are used in addition to the facilities provided by the bug tracking system. If your tool isn't meeting your needs, get a new one. Don't resort to manual means to accomplish a goal that is achievable via more automated processes.

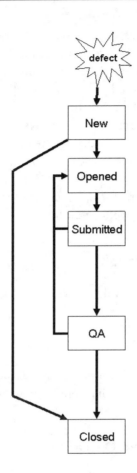

Figure 19–10
Simple defect life cycle for Marathon

19.7 Let's Be Practical

Incident Management in the Marathon Project

For the Marathon project, we have decided to use a common, and simple, defect life cycle (see figure 19-10). When a defect is opened, it receives the status of "new" from our defect tracking system. It is then reviewed by the configuration control board (CCB), who determine if it should be fixed based on the time required and the severity/priority of the issue. When it is assigned to a developer or a vendor by the project manager, the status is changed to "opened". When the developer has fixed the problem, he updates the status to "submitted". When the fix is built and installed on the test system, the status is changed to "QA" by the configuration manager who created and installed the build. When QA verifies the fix, the test analyst changes the status to "closed". That's the normal cycle that we expect to follow at least 90 percent of the time.

In the case where the developer determines a fix is not needed (not a defect, duplicate, can't reproduce), the defect bypasses the Submitted state and is marked as QA with a note from the developer indicating why the defect does not require a fix. If the test analyst agrees, he closes the defect. If the test analyst disagrees, the defect is returned to an Open state and a dialog is opened between the developer, the test analyst, and the project manager.

If the fix does not work, the defect returns to the Open status and goes through the process again with a new fix.

19.8 Learning Check

The following check lists will help you judge the knowledge you have gained from this chapter.

Terms

IEEE 1044-1993, IEEE 1044.1, anomaly, configuration control board, defect, error, failure, incident, incident logging, priority, root cause analysis, severity

Test Analyst and Technical Test Analyst

- Analyze, document and correctly classify defects.

20 Communications Skills

This chapter discusses some of the communications skills we need to do our job properly.

Part of being an effective communicator is understanding your role and position within the testing group and within the overall organization. Testing groups, by necessity, are formed with a merging of various skill sets. We need to understand those skills, who has to have them, and how they work together to understand our role and be able to communicate effectively both within the team and outside the team.

20.1 Knowing Your Place

Test analysts are expected to have a strong understanding of the domain in which the product will operate. This includes understanding the users and their needs as well as the business goals and requirements. The test analyst is expected to be the resource for the team for usability questions, applicability questions, and those nebulous "but would this matter to a user?" questions. The test analyst provides valuable input in the review of the requirements and design specifications because of their knowledge of the real purpose of the software. Test analysts are also well suited to contribute to prioritization and risk assessment discussions. Although performance testing usually falls to the technical test analysts, the test analyst can use his domain expertise to help define reasonable performance scenarios.

The technical test analyst generally brings a more technical approach to the testing process (hence that clever title!). The technical test analyst is expected to have experience in testing practices, development, technical support, and other technical areas. This knowledge of the overall software development process helps the technical test analyst to anticipate where errors are likely to be introduced and can also contribute to implementing preventive practices. Technical test analysts are well suited for attending detailed design walk-throughs, code walk-throughs, and even database design meetings. The technical test analyst is the source within the testing group for technical information regarding the design and implementation of the product.

A strong skill mix is critical to a successful testing team.

The varied experience of the technical test analysts provides the testing team with the skills needed to improve efficiency and depth of testing. Many of the high-end test automation tools require programming experience. Many of the various test management, bug tracking, and requirements tracking tools will work more effectively if they are "glued" together with scripting code that bridges the gaps in the tools. Technical test analysts bring these programming skills to the team and allow the testing team to maintain and effectively use its tools without having to rely on assistance from the development group.

20.2 I Know What I'm Doing. Why Won't Anyone Listen?

We need the skills of both the test analyst and the technical test analyst if we are to have an effective testing group. But technical skills and domain knowledge alone will not make a tester successful. Successful testers must be able to communicate. Interpersonal skills are vital. A tester must be able to give and receive criticism, influence decisions regarding quality, and negotiate. We've all had a defect that we believed to be critical but we didn't get agreement from other members of the project team. A significant part of being a good tester is being able to present your case, listen to the arguments, negotiate as needed, and reach a consensus that is best for the project. Sometimes this means backing down from your position. Sometimes it means escalating the issue to management. The trick is to know when to do what. A lot of that comes from common sense, practical experience, and keeping an honest view of what's best for the project.

20.3 Reading and Writing—Using What You Learned in School

Do you ever feel buried in information?

Should testers be able to read and write? This seems like a stupid question, doesn't it? But, maybe if we modify it to say "read and write effectively" it becomes more interesting. What is the ability to read effectively? That means we have to be able to absorb information quickly, divine the important points from the tons of technical documents we are buried in daily, mow through our e-mails, and still get our job done. People who can't assimilate information quickly are frequently rendered ineffectual just because they can't process the mass of data that is thrown their way.

What is effective writing? Is it being able to type quickly? That's certainly an advantage, particularly in the world of instant messaging, but it's the message that matters. When we write something, does it make sense to the reader? Does it convey the information we intended to convey? Does it contain the proper level of detail for the audience? Have we clearly indicated what response we are expecting? If not, at a minimum we are wasting valuable time, both ours and that of the recipient of our garbled message. At worst, we may have just instructed someone to do the wrong thing. In this information-rich world, everyone is striving to get through the data they receive every day. If some of it is not clear, it may result in our message being ignored or buried. I know I do that. When I get a message that doesn't make sense, if I'm really in a hurry, I leave it to puzzle over later. Sometimes later doesn't come and the e-mail joins the hundreds of others that populate my inbox. (I know, bad habits....)

Communication for testers is not just limited to e-mail and instant messages. We produce test plans, incident reports, metrics reports and charts, and myriad other forms of documentation. We have to ensure that every one of these forms of communication is as clear, accurate, and objective as possible. Oh yes, objective. The more of a hurry you are in, the easier it is to add a comment that might reflect the emotion of the moment but not the objective view that you would like to portray. No matter how hurried you are, read what you are writing before you send it. Are you comfortable if it gets forwarded around the organization? If not, don't send it. There's no such thing as private correspondence.

Assume everything you write will some day become public.

Keeping the communication lines open is vital to the success of a test group. Sometimes that means you have to make the first move. Go visit a developer and ask them how their kids are doing. Its fun to watch their shocked reaction when they realize that you actually aren't there to tell them you broke their software. Communicating shouldn't be limited to just work topics—we need to build relationships as well.

20.4 Is Independence of Testing a Good Thing?

How does test team independence affect communication? The more independent the test team, the more ability the team members have to be quality focused rather than driven by development schedules. But greater independence introduces challenges to effective communication. It's harder to keep the informal aspects of the communication intact as we gain distance. This is particularly important when working with offshore teams as you add time zone and possible language and cultural issues to the mix, which can thwart effective communication. Remember, you are working with people, not machines. Reach out and keep the communication lines open. And not just with the developers. Remember the other stakeholders—business analysts, technical support, documentation, marketing, and whoever else you need to work with. When you need to work on your quality risk analysis, it will be very helpful to know these people and know what is important to them. You'll be more effective in accomplishing your goals, and the end product will have a better chance of meeting everyone's goals, not just those of the development team.

20.5 Talk, Talk, Talk

Look for opportunities to communicate. This doesn't mean you need to be the chairman of the social committee; it means you need to be accessible and part of the team. Testers who become isolated quickly lose access to information and tend to become defensive. Testers who are a part of the overall project team have a better understanding of the business needs, have better empathy with the other team members, and can contribute ideas and suggestions for overall improvements.

20.6 Back to the Real World

I started a job as a test manager in an organization that had been having some difficulties in the relationships between testing and development. One of the reasons I was brought in was to prevent the adoption of the system test group by the development managers. In their opinion, the test team was incompetent and they wanted to own the head count so they could hire their own testers. Not a pretty situation. While I was aware of some of these issues when I accepted the job, I didn't know the extent of the damage that had been done to the relationships between the testers and the developers.

In my first week, I noticed a marked hostility toward me from the individual developers. Since they hadn't known me long enough to develop a healthy hatred, I assumed this had something to do with events that occurred before I arrived. The development managers were cordial but formal (and this was an informal organization). A bad sign, and clearly something that needed to change. So, I wandered into one of the developers' cubicles and asked him about his dog (he had a picture of the dog on his desk). He was visibly surprised and answered my questions with a puzzled tone. After we had talked for about 10 minutes, he asked me the real reason why I was in his office. I told him that I liked dogs. He was even more puzzled. Seizing my opportunity, I said, "Is that so weird?" He looked at me for a moment and then said, "I'm not used to a quality assurance person, much less a manager, coming in here for any reason other than to yell at me or complain." Ah, the light dawned. So apparently the hostility I had been observing had been earned over months of ineffective and, yes hostile, communication.

I called a group meeting to talk to my people about the situation. They said that the developers were always hostile and they only talked to them when they had a problem. What had started as an uncomfortable situation had quickly escalated into open hostilities. The test people didn't understand why the developers were hostile and the developers didn't want anything to do with the testers.

Communication problems can be easy to fix.

The interesting thing about this situation was that it was very easy to fix. When I explained to the testers that the developers thought that all communication with the testers was combative and accusatory, they were horrified. They never intended to have that effect. They agreed to be very careful about that in the future and to stop in once in awhile to say hi without wanting something. For my part, I started meeting with the development managers to understand the issues they had with the testing group and to work with them on how we could fix the problems. In the course of a month, the bad feelings were healed. The testers and developers freely circulated and the testers that had been moved into the development groups were moved back into the testing group.

Communication problems can fester with just one or two bad interactions. As the groups become more withdrawn, the problems get worse. Managers can certainly work to fix these situations, but it's the responsibility of every tester to ensure that they have the most positive relationships

Effective testers are effective communicators.

possible with the various stakeholders in the project. This doesn't mean we hide the bad news—quite the contrary. It does mean that we present the bad news in an objective manner and with the attitude of working together to find viable solutions. Effective testers are effective communicators with all the team members with whom they interact.

20.7 Learning Check

The following check lists will help you judge the knowledge you have gained from this chapter.

Terms

independence of testing

Test Analyst and Technical Test Analyst

- Demonstrate objective and effective communication regarding project information (including risks and opportunities) from a testing perspective.

Appendix A: Glossary

The definitions of most of the following terms are taken from the document "Standard glossary of terms used in Software Testing," Version 2.0, 2007, produced by the Glossary Working Party of the International Software Testing Qualifications Board. You can find the current version of the glossary at [URL: ISTQB]. Please note, we have included all the terms in the ISTQB glossary here but have limited our glossary to terms that we used in this book and felt would benefit from a formal definition. We have also included the terms that are new or changed from those used in the Foundation syllabus that apply to the test analyst and technical test analyst. ISO and IEEE references in a definition indicate the term is further defined in that document.

A

accessibility testing
Testing to determine the ease by which users with disabilities can use a component or system.

accuracy
The capability of the software product to provide the right or agreed-upon results or effects with the needed degree of precision. [ISO 9126] See also *functionality testing*.

adaptability
The capability of the software product to be adapted for different specified environments without applying actions or means other than those provided for this purpose for the software considered. [ISO 9126] See also *portability*.

all-pairs
See *pairwise testing*.

analyzability

The capability of the software product to be diagnosed for deficiencies or causes of failures in the software or for the parts to be modified to be identified. [ISO 9126] See also *maintainability*.

anomaly

Any condition that deviates from expectation based on requirements specifications, design documents, user documents, standards, etc. or from someone's perception or experience. Anomalies may be found during, but not limited to, reviewing, testing, analysis, compilation, or use of software products or applicable documentation. [IEEE 1044]

attack

Directed and focused attempt to evaluate the quality, especially reliability, of a test object by attempting to force specific failures to occur.

audit

An independent evaluation of software products or processes to ascertain compliance to standards, guidelines, specifications, and/or procedures based on objective criteria, including documents that specify

(1) the form or content of the products to be produced,

(2) the process by which the products shall be produced, and

(3)   how compliance to standards or guidelines shall be measured. [IEEE 1028]

B

black-box test design technique

Procedure to derive and/or select test cases based on an analysis of the specification, either functional or non-functional, of a component or system without reference to its internal structure.

boundary value

An input value or output value that is on the edge of an equivalence partition or at the smallest incremental distance on either side of an edge—for example, the minimum or maximum value of a range.

boundary value analysis

A black-box test design technique in which test cases are designed based on boundary values. See also *boundary value*.

branch testing

A white-box test design technique in which test cases are designed to execute branches.

buffer

A device or storage area used to store data temporarily for differences in rates of data flow, time or occurrence of events, or amounts of data that can be handled by the devices or processes involved in the transfer or use of the data.

buffer overflow

A memory access defect caused the attempt by a process to store data beyond the boundaries of a fixed length buffer, resulting in overwriting of adjacent memory areas or the raising of an overflow exception. See also *buffer*.

bug taxonomy

See *defect taxonomy*.

C

cause-effect graph

A graphical representation of inputs and/or stimuli (causes) with their associated outputs (effects), which can be used to design test cases.

cause-effect graphing

A black-box test design technique in which test cases are designed from cause-effect graphs. [BS 7925/2]

changeability

The capability of the software product to enable specified modifications to be implemented. [ISO 9126] See also *maintainability*.

classification tree

A tree showing equivalence partitions hierarchically ordered, which is used to design test cases in the classification tree method. See also *classification tree method*.

classification tree method

A black-box test design technique in which test cases, described by means of a classification tree, are designed to execute combinations of representatives of input and/or output domains.

co-existence

The capability of the software product to co-exist with other independent software in a common environment sharing common resources. [ISO 9126] See also *portability*.

condition determination testing

A white-box test design technique in which test cases are designed to execute single-condition outcomes that independently affect a decision outcome.

condition testing

A white-box test design technique in which test cases are designed to execute condition outcomes.

configuration control board (CCB)

A group of people responsible for evaluating and approving or disapproving proposed changes to configuration items and for ensuring implementation of approved changes.

control flow analysis

A form of static analysis based on a representation of sequences of events (paths) in the execution through a component or system.

D

data-driven testing

A scripting technique that stores test input and expected results in a table or spreadsheet so that a single control script can execute all of the tests in the table. Data-driven testing is often used to support the application of test execution tools such as capture/playback tools. See also *keyword driven testing*.

data flow analysis

A form of static analysis based on the definition and usage of variables.

debugging

The process of finding, analyzing, and removing the causes of failures in software.

debugging tool

A tool used by programmers to reproduce failures, investigate the state of programs, and find the corresponding defect. Debuggers enable programmers to execute programs step by step, to halt a program at any program statement, and to set and examine program variables.

decision table

A table showing combinations of inputs and/or stimuli (causes) with their associated outputs and/or actions (effects), which can be used to design test cases.

decision table testing

A black-box test design technique in which test cases are designed to execute the combinations of inputs and/or stimuli (causes) shown in a decision table. See also *decision table*.

decision testing

A white-box test design technique in which test cases are designed to execute decision outcomes.

defect

A flaw in a component or system that can cause the component or system to fail to perform its required function—e.g., an incorrect statement or data definition. A defect, if encountered during execution, may cause a failure of the component or system.

defect-based technique

See *defect-based test design technique*.

defect-based test design technique

A procedure to derive and/or select test cases targeted at one or more defect categories, with tests being developed from what is known about the specific defect category. See also *defect taxonomy*.

defect taxonomy

A system of (hierarchical) categories designed to be a useful aid for reproducibly classifying defects.

dynamic analysis

The process of evaluating behavior (e.g., memory performance, CPU usage) of a system or component during execution.

dynamic testing

Testing that involves the execution of the software of a component or system.

E

efficiency

The capability of the software product to provide appropriate performance relative to the amount of resources used under stated conditions. [ISO 9126]

efficiency testing

The process of testing to determine the efficiency of a software product.

emulator

A device, computer program, or system that accepts the same inputs and produces the same outputs as a given system. See also *simulator*.

equivalence partitioning

A black-box test design technique in which test cases are designed to execute representatives from equivalence partitions. In principle, test cases are designed to cover each partition at least once.

error

A human action that produces an incorrect result.

error guessing

A test design technique in which the experience of the tester is used to anticipate what defects might be present in the component or system under test as a result of errors made, and to design tests specifically to expose them.

error seeding

See *fault seeding*.

error tolerance

The ability of a system or component to continue normal operation despite the presence of erroneous inputs.

exit criteria

The set of generic and specific conditions, agreed upon with the stakeholders, for permitting a process to be officially completed. The purpose of exit criteria is to prevent a task from being considered completed when there are still outstanding parts of the task that have not been finished. Exit criteria are used to report against and to plan when to stop testing.

experienced-based technique

See *experienced-based test design technique*.

experienced-based test design technique

Procedure to derive and/or select test cases based on the tester's experience, knowledge, and intuition.

exploratory testing

An informal test design technique in which the tester actively controls the design of the tests as those tests are performed and uses information gained while testing to design new and better tests.

F

failover testing

Testing the ability of the system to maintain continuous system operations even in the event of failure.

failure

Deviation of the component or system from its expected delivery, service, or result.

Failure Mode and Effect Analysis (FMEA)

A systematic approach to risk identification and analysis of identifying possible modes of failure and attempting to prevent their occurrence.

false-fail result

A test result in which a defect is reported although no such defect actually exists in the test object.

false-pass result

A test result that fails to identify the presence of a defect that is actually present in the test object.

false-positive result

See *false-fail result.*

false-negative result

See *false-pass result.*

fault attack

See *attack.*

fault seeding

The process of intentionally adding known defects to those already in the component or system for the purpose of monitoring the rate of detection and removal and estimating the number of remaining defects.

fault seeding tool

A tool for seeding (i.e., intentionally inserting) faults in a component or system.

fault tolerance

The capability of the software product to maintain a specified level of performance in cases of software faults (defects) or of infringement of its specified interface. [ISO 9126] See also *reliability, robustness.*

functional testing

Testing based on an analysis of the specification of the functionality of a component or system. See also *black-box test design technique.*

functionality

The capability of the software product to provide functions that meet stated and implied needs when the software is used under specified conditions. [ISO 9126]

functionality testing

The process of testing to determine the functionality of a software product.

G

H

heuristic evaluation

A static usability test technique to determine the compliance of a user interface with recognized usability principles (the so-called heuristics).

hyperlink

A pointer within a web page that leads to other web pages.

hyperlink tool

A tool used to check that no broken hyperlinks are present on a website.

I

incident
Any event occurring that requires investigation.

incident logging
Recording the details of any incident that occurred, e.g., during testing.

independence of testing
Separation of responsibilities, which encourages the accomplishment of objective testing.

informal review
A review not based on a formal (documented) procedure.

inspection
A type of peer review that relies on visual examination of documents to detect defects—e.g., violations of development standards and nonconformance to higher-level documentation. The most formal review technique and therefore always based on a documented procedure. [After IEEE 1028] See also *peer review*.

inspection leader
See *moderator*.

installability
The capability of the software product to be installed in a specified environment [ISO 9126]. See also *portability*.

interoperability testing
The process of testing to determine the interoperability of a software product. See also *functionality testing*.

J

jelly donut
An ill-advised snack food consisting of a donut that has been injected with jelly. It should never be eaten over a keyboard.

K

keyword-driven testing

A scripting technique that uses data files to contain not only test data and expected results but also keywords related to the application being tested. The keywords are interpreted by special supporting scripts that are called by the control script for the test. See also *data-driven testing*.

L

Linear Code Sequence and Jump (LCSAJ)

A Linear Code Sequence And Jump, consisting of the following three items (conventionally identified by line numbers in a source code listing): the start of the linear sequence of executable statements, the end of the linear sequence, and the target line to which control flow is transferred at the end of the linear sequence.

load profile

A specification of the activity that a component or system being tested may experience in production. A load profile consists of a designated number of virtual users who process a defined set of transactions in a specified time period and according to a predefined operational profile. See also *operational profile*.

load testing

A type of performance testing conducted to evaluate the behavior of a component or system with increasing load—e.g., numbers of parallel users and/or numbers of transactions—to determine what load can be handled by the component or system. See also *performance testing*, *stress testing*.

M

maintenance testing

Testing the changes to an operational system or the impact of a changed environment to an operational system.

maintainability

The ease with which a software product can be modified to correct defects, modified to meet new requirements, modified to make future maintenance easier, or adapted to a changed environment. [ISO 9126]

maintainability testing

The process of testing to determine the maintainability of a software product.

management review

A systematic evaluation of software acquisition, supply, development, operation, or maintenance process performed by or on behalf of management that monitors progress, determines the status of plans and schedules, confirms requirements and their system allocation, or evaluates the effectiveness of management approaches to achieve fitness for purpose. [After IEEE 1028]

master test plan

See *test plan*

memory leak

A defect in a program's dynamic store allocation logic that causes it to fail to reclaim memory after it has finished using it, eventually causing the program to fail due to lack of memory.

moderator

The leader and main person responsible for an inspection or other review process.

modified multiple condition testing

See *condition determination testing.*

MTBF

Mean time between observed failures.

MTTF

Mean time to failure. The actual time elapsed (in hours) between observed failures.

MTTR

Mean time to repair. The number of hours needed by a developer to fix a problem.

multiple-condition testing

A white-box test design technique in which test cases are designed to execute combinations of single-condition outcomes (within one statement).

N

N-switch testing

A form of state transition testing in which test cases are designed to execute all valid sequences of N+1 transitions. See also *state transition testing*.

O

operational acceptance testing

Operational testing in the acceptance test phase, typically performed in a simulated real-life operational environment by operator and/or administrator focusing on operational aspects—e.g., recoverability, resource-behavior, installability, and technical compliance. See also *operational testing*.

operational profile

The representation of a distinct set of tasks performed by the component or system, possibly based on user behavior when interacting with the component or system, and their probabilities of occurrence. A task is logical rather than physical and can be executed over several machines or be executed in non-contiguous time segments.

operational testing

Testing conducted to evaluate a component or system in its operational environment.

orthogonal array

A two-dimensional array constructed with special mathematical properties such that choosing any two columns in the array provides every pair combination of each number in the array.

orthogonal array testing

A systematic way of testing all-pair combinations of variables using orthogonal arrays. It significantly reduces the number of all combinations of variables to test all-pair combinations. See also *pairwise testing*.

P

pairwise testing
A black-box test design technique in which test cases are designed to execute all possible discrete combinations of each pair of input parameters. See also *orthogonal array testing*.

path testing
A white-box test design technique in which test cases are designed to execute paths.

peer review
A review of a software work product by colleagues of the producer of the product for the purpose of identifying defects and improvements. Examples are inspection, technical review, and walk-through.

performance profiling
Definition of user profiles in performance, load, and/or stress testing. Profiles should reflect anticipated or actual usage based on an operational profile of a component or system and hence the expected workload. See also *load profile, operational profile*.

performance testing
The process of testing to determine the performance of a software product. See also *efficiency testing*.

pointer
A data item that specifies the location of another data item; for example, a data item that specifies the address of the next employee record to be processed.

portability
The ease with which the software product can be transferred from one hardware or software environment to another. [ISO 9126]

portability testing
The process of testing to determine the portability of a software product.

priority
The level of (business) importance assigned to an item (e.g., defect).

procedure testing

Testing aimed at ensuring that the component or system can operate in conjunction with new or existing users' business procedures or operational procedures.

production acceptance testing

See *operational acceptance testing.*

product risk

A risk directly related to the test object. See also *risk.*

project risk

A risk related to management and control of the (test) project (e.g., lack of staffing, strict deadlines, changing requirements). See also *risk.*

Q

qualification

The process of demonstrating the ability to fulfill specified requirements. Note that the term *qualified* is used to designate the corresponding status.

R

recoverability

The capability of the software product to re-establish a specified level of performance and recover the data directly affected in case of failure. [ISO 9126] See also *reliability.*

recoverability testing

The process of testing to determine the recoverability of a software product. See also *reliability testing.*

redundant systems

A complete copy (or copies) of an existing system that can be used in the event of a failure of the primary system or system component.

release note

A document identifying test items, their configuration, current status, and other delivery information delivered by development to testing, and possibly other stakeholders, at the start of a test execution phase. [After IEEE 829]

reliability
The ability of the software product to perform its required functions under stated conditions for a specified period of time or for a specified number of operations. [ISO 9126]

reliability growth model
A model that shows the growth in reliability over time during continuous testing of a component or system as a result of the removal of defects that result in reliability failures.

reliability testing
The process of testing to determine the reliability of a software product.

replaceability
The capability of the software product to be used in place of another specified software product for the same purpose in the same environment. [ISO 9126] See also *portability*.

requirements-based testing:
An approach to testing in which test cases are designed based on test objectives and test conditions derived from requirements—e.g., tests that exercise specific functions or probe non-functional attributes such as reliability or usability.

resource utilization
The capability of the software product to use appropriate amounts and types of resources—for example, the amounts of main and secondary memory used by the program and the sizes of required temporary or overflow files—when the software performs its function under stated conditions. [After ISO 9126] See also *efficiency*.

retrospective meeting
A meeting at the end of a project during which the project team members evaluate the project and learn lessons that can be applied to the next project.

review
An evaluation of a product or project status to ascertain discrepancies from planned results and to recommend improvements. Examples include management review, informal review, technical review, inspection, and walk-through. [After IEEE 1028]

reviewer

The person involved in a review that identifies and describes anomalies in the product or project under review. Reviewers can be chosen to represent different viewpoints and roles in the review process.

risk

A factor that could result in future negative consequences; usually expressed as impact and likelihood.

risk analysis

The process of assessing identified risks to estimate their impact and probability of occurrence (likelihood).

risk-based testing

An approach to testing to reduce the level of product risks and inform stakeholders on their status, starting in the initial stages of a project. It involves the identification of product risks and their use in guiding the test process.

risk control

The process through which decisions are reached and protective measures are implemented for reducing risks to, or maintaining risks within, specified levels.

risk identification

The process of identifying risks using techniques such as brainstorming, check lists, and failure history.

risk level

The importance of a risk as defined by its characteristics impact and likelihood. The level of risk can be used to determine the intensity of testing to be performed. A risk level can be expressed either qualitatively (e.g., high, medium, low) or quantitatively.

risk management

Systematic application of procedures and practices to the tasks of identifying, analyzing, prioritizing, and controlling risk.

risk mitigation

See *risk control*.

risk type

A specific category of risk related to the type of testing that can mitigate (control) that category. For example, the risk of user interactions being misunderstood can be mitigated by usability testing.

robustness

The degree to which a component or system can function correctly in the presence of invalid inputs or stressful environmental conditions. See also *error tolerance, fault tolerance*.

root cause

A source of a defect such that if it is removed, the occurrence of the defect type is decreased or removed.

root cause analysis

An analysis technique aimed at identifying the root causes of defects. By directing corrective measures at root causes, it is hoped that the likelihood of defect recurrence will be minimized.

S

safety-critical system

A system whose failure or malfunction may result in death or serious injury to people, loss or severe damage to equipment, or environmental harm.

scalability

The capability of the software product to be upgraded to accommodate increased loads.

scalability testing

Testing to determine the scalability of the software product.

security testing

Testing to determine the security of the software product. See also *functionality testing*.

severity

The degree of impact that a defect has on the development or operation of a component or system.

simulator
A device, computer program, or system used during testing that behaves or operates like a given system when provided with a set of controlled inputs. See also *emulator*.

software attack
See *attack*.

software life cycle
The period of time that begins when a software product is conceived and ends when the software is no longer available for use. The software life cycle typically includes a concept phase, requirements phase, design phase, implementation phase, test phase, installation and checkout phase, operation and maintenance phase, and sometimes, retirement phase. Note that these phases may overlap or be performed iteratively.

specification-based technique
See *black-box test design technique*.

stability
The capability of the software product to avoid unexpected effects from modifications in the software. [ISO 9126] See also *maintainability*.

state transition testing
A black-box test design technique in which test cases are designed to execute valid and invalid state transitions. See also *N-switch testing*.

statement testing
A white-box test design technique in which test cases are designed to execute statements.

static analysis
Analysis of software artifacts (e.g., requirements or code) carried out without execution of these software artifacts.

stress testing
A type of performance testing conducted to evaluate a system or component at or beyond the limits of its anticipated or specified work loads, or with reduced availability of resources such as access to memory or servers. [After IEEE 610] See also *performance testing, load testing*.

structure-based technique
See *white-box test design technique*.

suitability
The capability of the software product to provide an appropriate set of functions for specified tasks and user objectives. [ISO 9126] See also *functionality*.

system of systems
Multiple heterogeneous, distributed systems that are embedded in networks at multiple levels and in multiple domains, interconnected, addressing large-scale inter-disciplinary common problems and purposes.

T

technical review
A peer group discussion activity that focuses on achieving consensus on the technical approach to be taken. [IEEE 1028] See also *peer review*.

test basis
All documents from which the requirements of a component or system can be inferred. The documentation on which the test cases are based. If a document can be amended only by way of formal amendment procedure, then the test basis is called a frozen test basis.

test case
A set of input values, execution preconditions, expected results, and execution postconditions developed for a particular objective or test condition, such as to exercise a particular program path or to verify compliance with a specific requirement.

test charter
A statement of test objectives, and possibly test ideas about how to test. Test charters are used in exploratory testing. See also *exploratory testing*.

test closure
During the test closure phase of a test process, data is collected from completed activities to consolidate experience, testware, facts, and numbers. The test closure phase consists of finalizing and archiving the testware and evaluating the test process, including preparation of a test evaluation report. See also *test process*.

test condition

An item or event of a component or system that could be verified by one or more test cases (e.g., a function, transaction, feature, quality attribute, or structural element).

test design

(1) See *test design specification.*
(2) The process of transforming general testing objectives into tangible test conditions and test cases.

test design specification

A document specifying the test conditions (coverage items) for a test item, specifying the detailed test approach, and identifying the associated high-level test cases. [After IEEE 829]

test estimation

The calculated approximation of a result (e.g., effort spent, completion date, costs involved, number of test cases, etc.) that is usable even if input data may be incomplete, uncertain, or noisy.

test execution

The process of running a test on the component or system under test, producing actual result(s).

test execution tool

A type of test tool that is able to execute other software using an automated test script (e.g., capture/playback).

test implementation

The process of developing and prioritizing test procedures, creating test data, and, optionally, preparing test harnesses and writing automated test scripts.

test item transmittal report

See *release note.*

test log

A chronological record of relevant details about the execution of tests. [IEEE 829]

test management tool

A tool that provides support to the test management and control part of a test process. It often has several capabilities, such as testware management, scheduling of tests, the logging of results, progress tracking, incident management, and test reporting.

test plan

Also referred to as a master test plan, a document describing the scope, approach, resources, and schedule of intended test activities. It identifies, among others test items, the features to be tested, the testing tasks, who will do each task, the degree of tester independence, the test environment, the test design techniques, the entry and exit criteria to be used and the rationale for their choice, and any risks requiring contingency planning. It is a record of the test planning process. [After IEEE 829]

test planning

The activity of establishing or updating a test plan.

test procedure

See *test procedure specification*.

test procedure specification

A document specifying a sequence of actions for the execution of a test. Also known as test script or manual test script. [After IEEE 829]

test process

The fundamental test process comprises test planning and control, test analysis and design, test implementation and execution, evaluating exit criteria and reporting, and test closure activities.

test progress report

A document summarizing testing activities and results that is produced at regular intervals to report progress of testing activities against a baseline (such as the original test plan) and to communicate risks and alternatives requiring a decision to management.

test schedule

A list of activities, tasks, or events of the test process identifying their intended start and finish dates and/or times and interdependencies.

test script

Commonly used to refer to a test procedure specification, especially an automated one.

test session

An uninterrupted period of time spent in executing tests. In exploratory testing, each test session is focused on a charter, but testers can also explore new opportunities or issues during a session. The tester creates and executes test cases on the fly and records their progress. See also *exploratory testing*.

test summary report
A document summarizing testing activities and results. It also contains an evaluation of the corresponding test items against exit criteria. [After IEEE 829]

testability
A measure of the effort required to test a software component or system.

U

usability testing
Testing to determine the extent to which the software product is understood, easy to learn, easy to operate, and attractive to the users under specified conditions. [After ISO 9126]

use case
A sequence of transactions in a dialogue between a user and the system with a tangible result.

V

volume testing
Testing where the system is subjected to large volumes of data. See also *resource utilization*.

W

walk-through
A step-by-step presentation by the author of a document in order to gather information and to establish a common understanding of its content. [IEEE 1028] See also *peer review*.

WAMMI
Website Analysis and MeasureMent Inventory. A standardized publicly available usability survey for websites.

white-box test design technique

Procedure to derive and/or select test cases based on an analysis of the internal structure of a component or system.

wild pointer

A pointer that references a location that is out of scope for that pointer or that does not exist. See also *pointer.*

Appendix B: Literature

Books

[Beizer 90] Boris Beizer. 1990. *Software Testing Techniques*. New York: John Wiley & Sons. (ISBN 0-442-20672-0)

[Beizer 95] Boris Beizer. 1995. *Black-Box Testing*. New York: John Wiley & Sons. (ISBN 0-471-12094-4)

[Binder 00] Robert Binder. 2000. *Testing Object-Oriented Systems: Models, Patterns and Tools*. Reading, MA: Addison-Wesley. (ISBN 0-201-74868-1)

[Black 02] Rex Black. 2002. *Managing the Testing Process. 2nd ed.* New York: John Wiley & Sons. (ISBN 0-471-22398-0)

[Black 03] Rex Black. 2003. *Critical Testing Processes*. Reading, MA: Addison-Wesley. (ISBN 0-201-74868-1)

[Black 07] Rex Black. 2007. *Pragmatic Software Testing*. New York: John Wiley & Sons. (ISBN 978-0-470-12790-2)

[Burnstein 03] Ilene Burnstein. 2003. *Practical Software Testing*. New York: Springer. (ISBN 0-387-95131-8)

[Buwalda 01] H. Buwalda, D. Janssen, I. Pinkster, P. Watters. 2001. *Integrated Test Design and Automation*. Reading, MA: Addison-Wesley. (ISBN 0-201-73725-6)

[Copeland 03]: Lee Copeland. 2003. *A Practitioner's Guide to Software Test Design*. Boston: Artech House. (ISBN 1-58053-791-X)

[Craig 02] Rick David Craig, Stefan P. Jaskiel. 2002. *Systematic Software Testing*. Boston: Artech House. (ISBN 1-580-53508-9)

[Evans 04] Isabel Evans. 2004: *Achieving Software Quality through Teamwork*. Boston: Artech House. (ISBN 1-58053-662-X)

[Fewster 99] M. Fewster, D. Graham. 1999. *Software Test Automation* Reading, MA: Addison-Wesley. (ISBN 0-201-33140-3)

[Gerrard 02] Paul Gerrard, Neil Thompson. 2002. *Risk-Based E-business Testing*. Boston: Artech House. (ISBN 1-580-53314-0)

[Gilb 93] Tom Gilb, Dorothy Graham. 1993. *Software Inspection*. Reading, MA: Addison-Wesley. (ISBN 0-201-63181-4)

[Graham 07] Dorothy Graham, Erik van Veenendaal, Isabel Evans, Rex Black. 2007. *Foundations of Software Testing*. Boston: Thomson Learning. (ISBN 978-1-84480-355-2)

[Grindal 07] Mats Grindal. 2007. Handling Combinatorial Explosion in Software Testing. Dissertation 1073, Linköping Studies in Science and Technology. (ISBN 978-91-85715-74-9)

[Grochmann 94] M. Grochmann. 1994. Test Case Design Using Classification Trees. *Proceedings, 3rd International Conference on Software Testing, Analysis, and Review*

[Hambling 06] B. Hambling (ed.), P. Morgan, G. Thompon, A. Samaroo, P. Williams. 2006. *Software Testing: An ISEB Foundation*. London: British Computer Society. (ISBN 1-902505-79-4)

[Jorgensen 02] Paul C. Jorgensen. 2002. *Software Testing, a Craftsman's Approach. 2nd Ed*. Boca Raton, FL: CRC Press. (ISBN 0-8493-0809-7)

[Kaner 93] Cem Kaner, Jack Falk, Hung Quoc Nguyen. 1993. *Testing Computer Software. 2nd Ed*. New York: John Wiley & Sons. (ISBN 0-442-0136-2)

[Kaner 02] Cem Kaner, James Bach, Bret Pettichord. 2002. *Lessons Learned in Software Testing*. New York: John Wiley & Sons. (ISBN: 0-471-08112-4)

[Koomen 99] Tim Koomen, Martin Pol. 1999. *Test Process Improvement*. Reading, MA: Addison-Wesley. (ISBN 0-201-59624-5)

[McKay 07] Judy McKay. *Managing the Test People*. 2007. Santa Barbara, CA: Rocky Nook, Inc. (ISBN 978-1-933952-12-3)

[Myers 79] Glenford J. Myers. 1979. *The Art of Software Testing*. New York: John Wiley & Sons. (ISBN 0-471-46912-2)

[Pol 02] Martin Pol, Ruud Teunissen, Erik van Veenendaal. 2002. *Software Testing: A Guide to the Tmap Approach*. Reading, MA: Addison-Wesley. (ISBN 0-201-74571-2)

[Spillner 07] A. Spillner, T. Linz, H. Schaefer. 2007. *Software Testing Foundations: A Study Guide for the Certified Tester Exam. 2nd ed.* Santa Barbara, CA: Rocky Nook, Inc. (ISBN 1-933-95208-3)

[Splaine 01] Steven Splaine, Stefan P. Jaskiel. 2001. *The Web Testing Handbook*. Orange Park, FL: STQE Publishing. (ISBN 0-970-43630-0)

[Stamatis 95] D.H. Stamatis. 1995. *Failure Mode and Effect Analysis*. Milwaukee, WI: ASQC Quality Press. (ISBN 0-873-89300-X)

[vanVeenendaal 02] Erik van Veenendaal. 2002. *The Testing Practitioner*. Hertogenbosch : UTN Publishing. (ISBN 90-72194-65-9)

[Whittaker 03] James Whittaker. 2003. *How to Break Software*. Reading, MA: Addison-Wesley. (ISBN 0-201-79619-8)

[Whittaker 04] James Whittaker and Herbert Thompson. 2004. *How to Break Software Security*. Boston: Pearson/Addison-Wesley. (ISBN 0-321-19433-0)

ISTQB Publications

The following ISTQB publications are mentioned in this book and may be obtained from the ISTQB website [URL: ISTQB]

[ISTQB-Glossary] ISTQB Glossary of terms used in Software Testing, Version 2.0, 2007

[ISTQB-CTAL] ISTQB Certified Tester Advanced Level Syllabus, Version 2007

[ISTQB-CTFL] ISTQB Certified Tester Foundation Level Syllabus, Version 2007

Standards

[BS-7925-2] BS 7925-2 (1998) Software Component Testing

[IEEE 829] IEEE Std 829™ (1998/2005) IEEE Standard for Software Test Documentation (currently under revision)

[IEEE 1028] IEEE Std 1028™ (1997) IEEE Standard for Software Reviews

[IEEE 1044] IEEE Std 1044™ (1993) IEEE Standard Classification for Software Anomalies

[ISO 9126] ISO/IEC 9126-1:2001, Software Engineering—Software Product Quality

[RTCA DO-178B/ED-12B]: Software Considerations in Airborne systems and Equipment certification, RTCA/EUROCAE ED12B.1992.

WWW Pages

The following references point to information available on the Internet.

Even though these references were checked at the time of publication of this book, the authors cannot be held responsible if the references are no longer available.

Where references refer to tools, please check with the company to ensure the latest tool information.

Reference tag	Short description	Internet address
URL: Aisee	Automatic calculation of customizable graphs	www.aisee.com
URL: ATT	ATT research	http://www.research.att.com/~njas/oadir
URL: CVE	Dictionary of common names (i.e., (CVE® Identifiers) for publicly known information security vulnerabilities	cve.mitre.org CVE is a trademark of The MITRE Corporation.
URL: ECSS	The European Cooperation on Space Standardization (ECSS)	www.ecss.org

Table continues

Reference tag	Short description	Internet address
URL: Fortify	Fortify source code analysis tool	www.fortifysoftware.com
URL: Holodeck	Tool that can be used for simulating error conditions	www.securityinnovation.com
URL: IPL	Structural Coverage Metrics (downloadable study)	www.ipl.com
URL: ISTQB	International Software Testing Qualifications Board (ISTQB)	www.istqb.org
URL: JTest	Java unit testing tool that performs automatic white-box and black-box testing	www.parasoft.com
URL: NIST	National Institute of Standards and Technology	www.nist.gov
URL:OWASP	Open Web Application Security Project	www.owasp.org
URL: Pairwise	Tools for orthogonal arrays and all-pairs	www.pairwise.org
URL: Satisfice	A valuable source of information on subjects like exploratory testing and for all-pairs tools	www.satisfice.com
[URL: Systematic Testing]	Source of freeware tool for classification trees	www.systematic-testing.com
URL: Testing Standards	Group devoted to the development of new software testing standards	www.testingstandards.co.uk
URL: Vijayaraghavan	Giri Vijayaraghavan, Cem Kaner, "Bugs in your shopping cart: a taxonomy" (BISC_Final.pdf)	www.testingeducation.org/articles/BISC_Final.pdf

Appendix C: Mapping to the Advanced Syllabus

The following table shows the mapping of the chapters in this book to the relevant chapters of the ISTQB Advanced syllabus.

Ch.	Title in this Book	Ch.	Title in ISTQB Advanced Syllabus
1	Introduction		
2	Marathon, The Example Application		
3	Management Issues		Many
3.1	Types of Systems	1.3	Specific systems
3.2	Test Process	2	Testing process
4	Specification-Based Testing Techniques	4.2	Specification-based
5	Structure-Based Testing Techniques	4.3	Structure-based
6	Defect-Based Testing Techniques	4.4	Defect and experienced-based
7	Experience-Based Testing Techniques	4.4	Defect and experienced-based
8	Analysis Techniques	4.5 4.6	Static analysis Dynamic analysis
9	Testing Software Characteristics	5	Testing of software characteristics
10	Functional Testing	5.2	Quality attributes for domain testing

Mapping to the ISTQB Advanced syllabus 2007

Table continues

Ch.	Title in this Book	Ch.	Title in ISTQB Advanced Syllabus
11	Usability and Accessibility Testing	5.2.5 5.2.6	Usability Accessibility
12	Efficiency Testing	5.3.3	Efficiency
13	Security Testing	5.3.1	Technical Security
14	Reliability Testing	5.3.2	Reliability
15	Maintainability Testing	5.3.4	Maintainability
16	Portability Testing	5.3.5	Portability
17	Reviews	6	Reviews
18	Tools Concepts	9.2	Tools Concepts
Many		9.3	Tools for the TA
Many		9.3	Tools for the TTA
19	Incident Management	7	Incident Management
20	Communication Skills	10	People Skills

INDEX

Are you already certified?

The International Software Quality Institute (iSQI GmbH), headquartered in Erlangen and Potsdam (Germany), develops internationally accepted certification standards for advanced vocational training in the area of software quality. In order to optimize and safeguard the skills and abilities of software professionals, iSQI was founded in 2004 as a subsidiary of the German non-profit organisation ASQF e.V. and works together with international organizations, e.g. ISO (International Organization for Standardization) or EQN (European Quality Network).

iSQI certifies IT personnel in more than 40 countries. With more than 3000 exams per year in Germany alone, iSQI is one of the most important personnel certifier in the area of software quality.

The advantages of personnel certification are primarily the secured, comparable qualification of professionals across national boundaries and language barriers.

The iSQI certification program includes standards such as

ISTQB® Certified Tester, Foundation Level
ISTQB® Certified Tester, Advanced Level (Test Manager, Functional Tester, Technical Tester)
iSQI® Certified Professional for Project Management
iSAQB® Certified Professional for Software Architecture
IREB® Certified Professional for Requirements Engineering
iNTACS™certified ISO/IEC 15504 Provisional Assessor
iNTACS™certified ISO/IEC 15504 Competent Assessor
TTCN-3® Certificate
Certified EU Innovation Manager
iNTCCM® Certified Professional for Configuration Management
QAMP® Quality Assurance Management Professional
iNTCSM® - International Certified Professional for IT-Security Management
ISSECO® - International Certified Professional for Secure Software Engineering
T.I.S.P.© - TeleTrusT Information Security Professional
V-Modell® XT

In addition, iSQI hosts seminars and organizes different international software conferences, for example the „Conference on Quality Engineering in Software Technology" (CONQUEST) or the „International SPICE Days". The CONQUEST as well as the International SPICE Days provide a platform for experts and practitioners from industry and science to exchange experiences and ideas and to discuss the newest advancements in their special field.

Please visit **www.isqi.org** for further information.